OCEANS OF TIME

Dave Share

STEELE ROBERTS
AOTEAROA NEW ZEALAND

to Bev and our family

National Library of New Zealand Cataloguing-in-Publication Data
Share, Dave, 1940-
Oceans of Time / Share, Dave.
ISBN 1-877338-93-1
1. Title.
NZ821.3—dc 22

Pictures of ships throughout the book kindly supplied by Vic Young;
other photos are from the author's collection. Thanks to Richard Christie,
Colin Bassett and Rachel Woolford for production assistance, and to the
Alexander Turnbull Library (ATL) for photos:
  Cover & title page: the Shaw Savill & Albion Company's *Dominion Monarch*
  leaving the Tyne for her acceptance trials, prior to her maiden voyage,
  February 1939. (ATL EP Transport Ships)
  First page: the *Dominion Monarch* at Queens wharf, Wellington, 1950s.
  (ATL F20505 1/2)

STEELE ROBERTS LTD
BOX 9321, WELLINGTON, AOTEAROA NEW ZEALAND
info@steeleroberts.co.nz — www.steeleroberts.co.nz

contents

A note from the publisher: We deliberated whether to include a glossary of nautical terms, but what's a mystery to one reader is obvious to another, and we would have had to include alternative spellings (soojey, sujee, soogie, soogee — they all mean cleaning) and a guide to Cockney rhyming slang as well (e.g. titfer = tit-for-tat = hat) … where would it end?! We hope most terms are clear in their context or readily definable; if you are in difficulty you are welcome to write or email us for an explanation. Or pop down to the wharves and ask a passing seadog, matlow, jack tar, lascar or ferryman …

foreword

IT HAS ALWAYS SURPRISED ME THAT so little has been written about working seamen from their point of view, and what has been written seems to stop with the advent of the steamship. It is the same internationally, with a few notable exceptions: Dana in *Two Years Before the Mast* and Melville's *Moby Dick* were stories told through the eyes of a working seaman. But most books about the sea seem to be about officers and the loneliness of command. Conrad made an exception with *The Nigger of the Narcissus*, which contains a superb account of the misery of a sailing ship's crew in heavy weather, and the joy of pay-off day. Books by ships' officers give a one-sided story of life at sea, and they are mostly by retired captains who spent a lifetime sailing for one company.

Steamship seamen lived a far more interesting life than the officers. They wandered from ship to ship and company to company, and weren't too particular what flag they sailed under. They often missed their ship or deserted in the strangest of places. When stuck ashore unable to ship out, they were 'on the beach', in their words. They also saw the inside of jails all over the world. Dave Share's recollection of his life at sea is a rare account of life in merchant ships, told through the eyes of a working seaman. He, like many British seamen, jumped ship in New Zealand, and was caught and deported. He sailed on British and New Zealand ships, and this book is an important account of a way of life that has long gone. It was a time when shipping companies all had their own style of shipbuilding, and whilst they were built to carry cargo and make a profit, they were also built with style, and — dare I say it — love. Even the ship's funnel was distinctive. Blue Star Line were inordinately proud of their funnel, and Blue Funnel Line's were their trademark. The ships are long gone, and the men that sailed in them either dead or retired.

Dave ended up sailing on the Kiwi coast, as seamen from all over the world described it. The New Zealand Seamen's Union was a remarkable union, and for many years was at the forefront of the industrial and political struggles of workers, domestically and internationally. The decline of the Seamen's Union marked the general decline in unionism in New Zealand. I am pleased this book has been written, it is long overdue.

Gerry Evans
Michael King Writers' Centre

Oceans of Time

part one

one

BETHNAL GREEN, EAST END OF London, is my place of birth. I only know this because my birth certificate states it. I came into this world on 3 December 1940, when my mother travelled to Bethnal Green hospital on Cambridge Heath Road where I was born. My father was a wholesale fruiterer. Their place of abode was Haverhill in Suffolk.

I was never to meet my parents. Some years later I decided to research the mystery of my past. Birth certificates can be a good source of information. I didn't know why my mother would travel all the way from Haverhill to make sure my birthplace would be the East End. London was being bombed daily. Had they been evacuated? Or was it simply pride that their son should be born a Cockney?

In February 1941 my mother registered me at Bethnal Green. The registrar who signed my birth certificate was a man named Berriff. Oddly, when I requested that certificate 23 years later the registrar was the same Mr Berriff. To give this account of myself meant years of research into my parents, and a sad story of my mother unfolded from it.

My parents were both born in England: my father, Joseph Isaac Share, in 1903 of Polish-Jewish parentage, and my mother Mary Rebecca in 1904. Her grandparents were Russian-Armenian refugees.

I don't know when both families joined the exodus of Jewish families from the eastern Balkans to escape the pogroms and hardships for a life in England. I don't even know if they anglicised their names. Most Jews who immigrated from the Balkans at the turn of the century did so because of persecution in their country of origin. After 1911 it became illegal to change your name except by deed poll, with the change registered with the appropriate authorities. I engaged the help of an 80-year-old woman called Isobel who had seen a letter I sent to the Jewish Society in the UK. Her assistance was invaluable, and her research revealed my parents' marriage certificate, which provided much of my information.

They were married in 1933 and gave Cable Street as their address. I assume they weren't practising Jews as they lived together before they were married.

In many instances the officials got details wrong, as there were many immigrants who could not speak English. Isobel was baffled at the lack of records on my parents, and decided to look up each Share in the London phonebook and find out if there was any connection to my family. Her determination paid off. She wrote and advised me that she might have found a cousin living in Snaresbrook, whose grandfather Alexander was possibly the same Alexander Share as my grandfather. My first contact with my cousin Louis was comical. I sent my father's marriage certificate which recorded our mutual grandfather Alexander and a photo of myself. Louis wrote back that there was no way we were related because his family were Polish and blond. I could understand his doubt, but he soon got over it and accepted my father's marriage certificate and his link to my family.

He and his twin sister Sheila were my cousins, and I met them on my visit to London in 1995. Louis, a London cab driver, was very reserved and could not tell me anything about my mum and dad. His father had died the year before and it was hard for me to believe nothing was ever mentioned of my father Joseph or any legacy my parents may have left. Sheila had the better memory and could recall my father clearly. She described him as a lovely man who used to take her to the market in Goulston Street, just off Petticoat Lane, where he had a barrow selling fruit and vegetables. She didn't remember ever seeing my mother.

My mother was an enigma; no one seemed to know her. It was only by chance that I discovered more about the life of my parents.

During the war the Women's Voluntary League (WVL) took over the evacuation of children from the cities. Many were sent to Australia, Canada and New Zealand, or were farmed out to the countryside. But the League kept no records of the children, so many parents could not locate them after the war. This ineptitude came to light long after World War II. Horrified families wanted answers from the government, but it was not until the early 1990s that the British government admitted there had been a failure. In fact, records were not even kept until 1948. Public demand opened the books to children who were taken from their parents.

In the UK in 1995 there was a two-year waiting list on disclosure. I rang Barnardos, telling them I was from New Zealand and that I came under the category of misplaced children, and that I had only two weeks left before returning to New Zealand. They had sympathy for me, and asked me to come and see them.

At Barnardos my suspicion that all was not well with my parents was confirmed in the next hour. I'd had a sister named Carol; my mother had given birth to a daughter who died within six years. Almost immediately my mother was pregnant again, and Frederick was born in April 1938. My mother's name on the birth certificate had been changed to Shaw, and she was living in Lambeth in the Borough of Battersea. My father's name is omitted and the birth certificate is signed by the resident doctor. This implies that my mother had conceived outside marriage and my father would not agree he was the father. The puzzle continued. Had they separated? Had mum found another life?

In 1940 I was born. My birth certificate bears my mother's married name, and my father put his name to my birth certificate, though further investigations revealed that I too was born out of wedlock.

Barnardos noted that my grandfather Alexander had brought me to the London County Council in early 1941, just a few months after my birth. I was put under the care of Barnardos. During the war every person had to carry an identification card, and on my mother's card was the name Shaw. A report came to Barnardos that Mum had gone to Holloway police station complaining of pains in her head. She was taken to the Holloway Prison hospital. There was no record of any charge against her. It was thought that the police put her in the prison hospital as it was the nearest convenient place. In 1948 my mother died. Barnardos took in Frederick my half-brother when I was born.

I was thankful for the information, but dissatisfied with the scraps of my early life that they offered. I felt strongly they were not telling me everything. It is difficult to access information when you live in New Zealand and the records of your family are in England. Genealogy can be a costly exercise, but I was determined to find out what happened to my half-brother Fred, and so I engaged Barnardos in Wellington.

I told them everything I had gleaned about my family. My research had taught me not to expect much, but genealogy is like searching for the motherlode — sometimes a dig in the dark reveals gold. That's how I felt when a lady at Barnardos in Wellington told me she had received information that could be sensitive. It came in the form of a letter copied from a damaged microfilm, but legible enough to join the missing links and solve the enigma of my parents.

My suspicion that the authorities were keeping information from me proved correct. I can understand their reluctance to impart such unflattering content as was in this letter if I was younger, but I was well into my twenties. And I was over sixty before they thought I was mature enough to assess the information they were holding. The powers-that-be seem to forget that family lineage goes on and on. One day my kids would want to know their roots.

The content of the 1944 letter was not flattering towards my mother. It was a report written by a child welfare officer who had just visited her — but was just one person's view, and written without the expectation that any family member would read it.

My mum had married my dad bigamously in 1933. She had married Harry Levy, alias Domsky, in 1924. I assume the marriage to my father was annulled, and in 1937 she was tried on the charge of bigamy at the Old Bailey and put on probation for three years. Mum and Dad must have had an enduring affection for each other. The report goes on to relate how in 1939 "…she met Share again by 'accident' and cohabited until 1943." What a villainous pair my parents were! My mother had five children. Only Fred and I survived, according to the report.

The report reflected conservative attitudes of the times. Promiscuous behaviour was frowned upon, and the fact that my parents had kids out of wedlock evidently got the author of the report into a lather. But many of the questions surrounding my parents were answered, and no wonder my cousins Louis and Sheila could not recall my mother. My parents must have separated after 1943 and it is believed my mother died young in 1948, but I can find no record of her death. My dad married again to a woman with the same initials as my mother. This foiled my research for years — I assumed she was my mum.

In Stoke Newington there is a cemetery called Abney Park, a peaceful central London reserve open all year round to the public. Many people of all denominations are interred here, such as General Booth, founder of the Salvation Army. Its 31 acres are filled to capacity and new burials are squeezed between existing plots and the centre of some paths.

My father died in 1967. I was told that Abney Park could be where he was buried, and I was directed to a pauper's grave on the side of a path with a single stake to mark the plot. I was appalled at the mention of a paupers' graves. These people had no money for their funeral and are buried in tiers or on top of one another. Though I never knew my father I felt awful that he should end his days in such beautiful surroundings yet pressed on top of other people.

After his death it dawned on me that I had missed an opportunity of seeing my father. The Royal Docks where my voyages began and ended were barely ten miles from where he had worked as a nightwatchman.

Researching my family history was a great undertaking. I may not have found everything but what bits I found were rewarding. My parents' choices leave no stigma with me. Human nature abounds with imperfections, and I still thank Mum and Dad for rocking the conventions in those days, and bringing me into this world to let me sample the joys of life and live it to the full.

two

THROUGH RESEARCH I HAVE FITTED together the puzzle of my pre-adolescent life. The years from 1940 to 1948 were largely blank, but Barnardos and the Surrey County Children's Welfare helped fill in the gaps. Unfortunately Isobel, who had given me so much help, stopped communicating — I found out later that she had died.

My mother sent me to Stoke Newington, where the Share family lived in 1941. My grandfather Alexander Share placed me in care of Barnardos, who in turn passed me on to the Women's Voluntary League. I was put in Jellico nursery in Ware, Hertfordshire. My research into Ware historical archives gave me no information about the nursery. I became a ward of the London County Council. The only event I can recollect is a victory party we were taken to after the end of the war, with men and women in military uniforms and children waving flags.

On 5 July 1948 I came into the care of Surrey County Council and was placed in Hilgarth Orphanage in Hindhead, Surrey. A husband and wife team were in charge, and they had a sick sense of humour — they used to scare the wits out of the children in their care. When it was dark they would don scary masks before going outside and getting our attention by knocking on the playroom windows, like bogeymen. At night they would put on heavy boots and tramp loudly through our sleeping quarters. We would scream in fright and I began to have nightmares and was afraid to go to bed. At this time I was having trouble with my ears and spent time in Farnham Hospital in 1949. A kindly nurse, brought me sweets, but I still had nightmares in hospital. I told the nurse about the 'bogeymen' in the orphanage, and I never saw Hilgarth or its bogeymen again.

In 1950 I was sent to Pinehurst Children's Home in Camberley, also administered by the Surrey Child Welfare Department. On 8 November a resolution was taken by the Surrey County Council to take me under control of the Poor Law; in other words the Council adopted me. I enjoyed my stay at Pinehurst. In charge of the home was another husband and wife team, Uncle Jim and Aunty Robin. They followed the Quaker religion and were very patient with their boisterous charges.

That year I was to meet my half-brother Frederick for the first time, and was very excited about his visit. Frederick is two years older than me, born in 1938. When

Pinehurst, 1953. That's me holding the donkey behind the ears, surrounded by other boisterous lads. Opposite: all the boys from the orphanage.

he visited me in 1950 he was in foster care in High Wycombe in Buckinghamshire. He spent the day with me and I took him into town. In later life as I began to wonder who I was and where I came from Fred became important to me, and I decided to research him. Every avenue I pursued led nowhere. I contacted the Salvation Army missing persons office and the Department of Health and Social Security (DHSS) in the UK.

To get any result from the DHSS I had to write a letter in a sealed envelope and ask them to forward it to Fred. If they had him on their files they would send the letter on but warned that if it caused distress or embarrassment to the recipient, they would not offer the forwarding facility. My letter was forwarded but no reply came. I sent a second letter two years later and the DHSS replied that it was not possible to forward it, and stressed the same reason. Their reply perplexed me. Two years before there was no problem in passing my letter on, so why were the DHSS refusing now? I could only assume that he may have been incarcerated or something of that order. Equally, I wondered if it could be the sensitive nature the authorities had shown in regard to my attempts to find my family.

I was at Pinehurst barely a year before I was moved by Child Welfare to foster parents in East Croydon. I spent the unhappiest eighteen months of my adolescence there, but revealing their name would serve no purpose as those events happened 50 years ago. Mr and Mrs X, an elderly couple whose main motive for taking in kids seemed to be monetary gain, had already taken in twin sisters my age. Their council house was far too small for three foster kids, a son in his twenties and a second at grammar school.

The elder son was called up for the army and sent to Korea. The younger son was a spoilt brat who frequently brought his parents' wrath upon me and delighted to see me get a hiding. Once I took a book of his to school and suffered blows to my face from both him and his father. My bruises could not be hidden from teachers and one had to come home with me because I was scared.

I loved sport and represented the school in cricket, soccer, boxing and athletics. Soccer was my favourite, and one of the few enjoyments I looked forward to was going to Selhurst Park to watch Crystal Palace play on Saturday afternoons whenever they had a home game. I got pocket money for doing dishes and behaving myself, and my school chums and I would go to the Saturday morning cinema. Before the movie began we all had to sing, "We come along on Saturday morning greeting everybody with a smile!" We screamed our lungs out, while others threw popcorn and missiles at those in the front stalls. The manager would stand on the stage and warn us that until the missiles ceased there would be no movies. For sixpence our programme began with a cartoon and was followed by a weekly episode of a serial, always cut off at an exciting part to keep us guessing until next

Saturday. There would also be a full-length movie. Cowboy movies with Hopalong Cassidy or Roy Rogers were my favourites. Old Mother Riley was also a laugh. It was two hours of incredible fun, then a bus to Selhurst Park to watch our team.

I felt happy during those escapes, but at home I retreated into my shell. The girls and I slept in a small bedroom upstairs. The twins slept in one bed and I had my own. There was barely enough room between the beds to move. To use the toilet during the night we had to pass through our foster parents' bedroom, which brought torrid verbal abuse from both of them. The nights were racked by the father's bronchial coughing. I spent tedious school holidays locked in a small back yard and was only allowed freedom on Saturdays. We never went anywhere. As a child you put up with it and enjoyed the times with your chums at school. But even youngsters have feelings. I hated that family and wanted to run away. Stupidly I confided in the twins, who told my foster mother. She caned the hide off me and sent me to bed without tea. It was when my pocket money was confiscated and I couldn't go out on a Saturday that it really hurt.

My escape happened after I had gone to watch Crystal Palace. We were fenced in on the terraces right in front and I wanted to go to the toilet. I tried to force my way through the crowd but knew I would never make it in time. I returned with a big wet patch in the front of my pants. My foster mother was ironing as I walked through the door. Spying the wet patch, she went daft, pulled my arm onto the ironing board and set the hot iron on the back of my hand. I ran out of the house screaming, with her younger son chasing me up the road. My screams attracted neighbours. A policeman looked at my hand, and I refused to go back to the foster home. I was returned to Pinehurst where I felt safe. I missed my

Pinehurst: "I used to live here," I said when I knocked on the door in 1983. "So what?" said the staff member as he shut the door in my face!

Croydon chums but some of the kids who were in the orphanage when I had left 18 months before were still there.

The company of the other children at Pinehurst soon obliterated the unhappy memories of Croydon. During the coronation of Queen Elizabeth in 1953 a fancy dress party was organised by the Camberley Council at a local recreation ground. All the children were decked out as various articles of the crown jewels, and dressed as the crown I won first place. Hundreds of kids sat at tables, stuffing themselves with goodies, and we were all given a commemorative mug.

Surrey Child Welfare chose dedicated people to run their orphanages, none more so than the Quaker couple who gave us such happiness at Pinehurst. Youth gives no thought of appreciation until the maturing years when we can look back and wonder how Jim and Robin put up with us. They gave me my first grounding on the difference between right and wrong. I was wrapped in a cocoon of happiness at Pinehurst, but the Child Welfare had different ideas on what path my youth would take. They were still determined to put me in a family setting.

I was introduced to new foster parents — Roland and Jean Heywood —in Camberley in 1954, when another boy and I were invited to tea at their home. Unknown to us, they were deciding which of us to foster. I enjoyed my visits, which were at weekends. I was quizzed whether I liked the people, and eventually if I would like to stay with them. They had chosen me and I was told I could return to Pinehurst if I was unhappy; their home was not far away. So I was fostered out again. I was 13, and became more aware of the world outside, after the protection that Pinehurst had afforded.

The Heywoods had a son Bryon and daughter Carolyn, both younger than me. Their extensive property seemed to stretch for miles, because of a large wood surrounding the house, an old chapel converted into a home. Apparently the Queen took driving lessons during the war years along the main pathway that ran through their property. My foster mother still lives there today.

My foster father was a Doctor of Philosophy and Science and had a number of titles after his name. He worked at the Structures Department of the Royal Aircraft Establishment in Farnborough. A number of aircraft accidents had occurred, with the loss of all passengers. The aircraft builder, British de Havilland, had built a new model, the Comet, which was going down and causing loss of life. The problem was thought to be sabotage, but metal fatigue was later suspected. This man investigated how different operational loads determined the fatigue life of aircraft components. His work proved that a small fatigue crack in the fuselage could result in a complete failure, and he worked out a test procedure for developing new aircraft structures which was taken up by the aircraft industry worldwide. Through his clever work he made important contributions to the improvement of safety in air travel, and he collaborated on a book titled *Designing Against Fatigue* (1962) which to this day is a valuable source of information for aircraft designers and designers of other structures, machines and components.

My foster mum's interest was acting with the repertory theatre. Her passion was later rewarded when she received a lead part in the 1970s television series *When the Boats Come In*. She had cameo parts in *Coronation Street* and big roles in *All Creatures Great And Small* and numerous other TV productions.

In 1980 my foster mum toured New Zealand with the cast of the stage play *Rose*. Her acting was not confined to the small screen — in 2000 she played the grandmother in the film *Billy Elliot*. Now in her 80s she is still very active, but travelling to the studios in Manchester from her home in Surrey can be demanding.

Family life was very different from the orphanage. I was wary from my previous fostering experiences, but I soon adapted to this happiest part of my growing up. I attended the local school, France Hill House, but other interests outweighed any academic achievements my foster parents might have wished me to pursue.

I joined Camberley Sea Cadets, and though we were far from the sea, the idea of seeing the world in the Royal Navy ignited a strong desire. The cadets met once a week and I looked forward to the activities and skills we learnt. At the National Maritime Museum in Greenwich I was impressed with the array of artefacts from Britain's maritime history. Nelson became my hero and I read everything I could about him. C S Forrester's novels on the exploits of Horatio Hornblower were another favourite. My interest in British 18th and 19th-century maritime history and how those old seadogs spent their daily lives in the Royal Navy has never waned. The cutlass and the broadsides were a way of life — saving for your old age would have had no meaning. I have returned to the maritime museum many times, spending hours drinking up that glorious era.

Part of our education came through a week's trip on the Thames. Three motor launches were hired, each with six sleeping berths. My life had hitherto been closeted and protected by my guardians; now I was with boys far better informed about life than me. I listened to stories of girlfriends and the female anatomy in awe. Girls to me were girls. I knew nothing of sex; a penis was for peeing as far as I knew. I must have seemed very naïve, and was promised that when we arrived back at school they had a girlfriend for me. I was terrified.

I took my first puff on a cigarette — Woodbines became our preference. Each night we tied up at a town wharf such as Kingston upon Thames, Hampton Wick or Thames Ditton and we would go ashore and buy a packet of five fags, telling shopkeepers they were for our parents. Our age didn't come into question — in the '50s smoking was chic and not considered a health hazard.

The object of our week on the Thames was to learn practical seamanship: for instance, learning to steer by compass and to identify the various buoys that marked the waterway. The Thames had locks in its upper reaches to navigate, and we learned the art of mooring a vessel. A week always zooms by when you are enjoying yourself. My stay on the river was a break-out from the cocoon of my youth. Innocence was shed and we learned to make our own decisions, whether right or wrong.

My chums were true to their word. One should never forget one's first girlfriend. Her name was Rosanna, a sporty type like me. She represented the school in athletics and netball; I, in any sport going. It was an innocent relationship of holding hands, going to her home for tea, and going to the movies.

My quest to become a sailor and see the world was well known to Rosanna, who was my only girlfriend at school. She was far more academic than I was. I left school as soon as I could to follow my dream of seeing the world. I returned a couple of years later to see if she was still around, but she and her parents had emigrated to Canada.

There was no pressure in my schooldays to impress employers with academic success — jobs were plentiful. As a lad of fifteen I was in no doubt that the sea and ships were going to be my career, and I went off to pursue that future.

I have much admiration for institutions such as Barnardos and the child welfare councils who care for children like me. Spending my childhood in orphanages has never made me feel inferior: in fact I believe I was more fortunate than some kids who were brought up by their own parents. I had a happy childhood and the grounding I was given has stood me in good stead. Though my stay with my Camberley parents was short, they contributed to my wellbeing, giving me a taste of family life and an emphatic belief in the family unit. Nor do I mind sharing the tribulations that beset my birth parents. They had their problems, and put my brother and me in the best care they thought possible at a time when nations were in conflict and their own future looked uncertain.

Many people coursed through my young life, giving their time to children who sought love and affection. Disclosing information about my parents was a sensitive issue, and I understand the protective line Barnardos took. It is such a hard task to bring up kids that are not your own, with different needs and temperaments, and to put joy into their lives. I deeply appreciate their commitment. I hope my thanks will echo through the ages — they will always have a special place in my heart.

three

ISIGNALLED MY PLANNED CAREER to my foster parents, who informed Child
Welfare of my intentions. The sea training school I went to, TS *Warfleet,* was a
land-based school near Southampton that cost four pounds ten shillings a week,
borne by the Surrey County Child Welfare.

TS *Warfleet* had begun in 1938 at Warfleet Creek near Dartmouth. Vernon
McAndrew, a wealthy shipowner and yachtsman, started an establishment of
'British Boys for British Yachts' in conjunction with the YMCA, to train young men
from distressed areas to serve on merchant ships and private yachts. McAndrew
was lost at sea off Spithead, and his sister Bertha transferred *Warfleet* to Fairthorne
Manor in 1947. Fairthorne became the 'land ship' TS *Warfleet,* until expenses
soared. Its 'Last Post' sounded in 1962, but thanks to the foresight of Vernon
McAndrew and the YMCA I am able to record a career that began at Fairthorne
Manor nearly half a century ago.

Prospective entrants had an interview and an IQ test, so on a bleak December
day in 1955 just after my fifteenth birthday I travelled down to Botley. My foster
father and a representative from Child Welfare accompanied me. At Botley we
were directed to a noticeboard with 'Warfleet Sea Training School' emblazoned
on it. I felt nervous at the thought of the interview as we made our way up the
long drive characteristic of those stately mansions.

My nervousness notched up as a tall flagpole loomed in the distance, seeming
to reach the clouds. We pulled into the expansive driveway in front of Fairthorne
Manor, now TS *Warfleet*. I was mesmerised by the vast structure that I had seen
from the car. The flagpole was in fact a ship's mast embedded in concrete on the
parade ground. A blue flag with the Union Jack in its upper corner flew proudly
on the yard. As every merchant seaman should know, the blue ensign signifies
that the captain of a merchant vessel has served in the Royal Navy or as a Royal
Navy reservist. The red ensign, which is exactly the same (except for the colour),
is a more common sight on merchant vessels, and is known as the 'red duster'.
Captains with no service or affinity with the Royal Navy flew the red duster.

We were shown to the waiting room, and within minutes whisked into the
wardroom dominated by an oval table. We did not have to wait long before a stout
man came into the room, bedecked in a Royal Navy uniform with plenty of gold

braid and rows of war ribbons from his campaigns and service. Accompanying him was a tall man who also sported a row of ribbons.

Captain Southcott had earned a Distinguished Service Order during World War II when he skippered motor torpedo boats (MTBs) as a Lieutenant Commander under the noted ornithologist Commander Peter Scott. Authoritarian in nature, he could not abide idiots and expelled any boy who lacked commitment to the school. The other man was George Vince, whose knowledge of practical seamanship, I was to learn, was second to none. He had a booming voice and an impatient temperament, which flustered those of us who had no knowledge of seamanship.

"Welcome to *Warfleet*, laddie," said Captain Southcott. In his plummy voice he outlined the rules of the school and the hope that today was the beginning of my career as an officer in the merchant navy. But first I was to be tested. Naval history had long been my interest and I was surprised when the captain began to ask me about Lord Nelson and his three famous sea battles. I answered all his questions with gusto and he was stunned. "It's refreshing to hear some lads have taken an interest in our naval history!" he said.

With the oral test over I was left to the written IQ test. As we drove away from Fairthorne Manor my foster father was impressed with my knowledge of naval history. There was now a nervous wait; Christmas came and went and it was well into January 1956 when a letter arrived reporting my entry to TS *Warfleet*. I was to present myself at the start of the new term in March. The dream of seeing the world came a step closer.

At *Warfleet* we were measured for uniforms, shown our dormitories, and lectured on what was expected of us. "You have been selected as future officers in the merchant navy," boomed Mr Vince. If successful we would be apprenticed to the Blue Funnel Shipping Line, whose vessels sailed from Liverpool to the far east. We were to be monitored on our skills and academics every three months.

Very apparent was the old boy-new boy rivalry. I soon became familiar with a place at the back of the manor called 'the lines', where we hung our dhobying and settled disputes by fisticuffs. My adolescent nature was not one of comprehending orders. The head boy was rated chief petty officer and my presence did not ease his temperament. Dispute settlement was done away from the prying eyes of staff. I held my own, but it did not help my ambitions to be an officer.

No shore leave was granted at weekends if you failed the Morse test, a Friday afternoon ritual which Mr Vince delighted in. Attached to the blackboard in the lecture room was a Morse lamp. Curtains were drawn and all eyes were glued to the rapid flicker of the lamp. Each of us was tested on single letters and then a message Mr Vince would tap out. I enjoyed Morse and semaphore but couldn't stand maths, which unfortunately was a major part of an officer's curriculum.

I began to realise that I enjoyed the practical side of things. Sitting in a classroom was boring and this showed in my three-monthly reports. My academics were in trouble, but my practical ability was up there with the best. *Warfleet* had a ketch called *Western Sky*, formerly an onion carrier between France and England. We practised our steering and bearings aboard the *Sky* on the River Hamble, which flowed past Fairthorne down to Lymington and Southampton. I remember the calls of the marks and the deeps as we sounded our way down the river. The lead line was used extensively to avoid sandbanks. Boxing the compass — *"North, North by East, North North-East, North-East by North ..."* — was like learning your times tables. We were expected to sing the compass points by heart and that was another hazard that could ruin your weekend leave if you came up with the wrong sequence.

I enjoyed our trips on *Western Sky* as I did sailing *Kiwi*, a dinghy given to the school by the Queen, a wedding present from the people of New Zealand. We also had two cutters: *Mew*, known as the 'Black boat', and *Mull*. The cutters honed our skills in rowing and sculling. I could never master sculling, and would find myself hitting the bank or missing a stroke and almost falling off the stern.

At the mouth of the Hamble was another officer training school, *Warsash*, with training resources far greater than *Warfleet*'s. At least we could match them in sports. "*Warfleet* expects you to do your duty!" boomed Captain Southcott at the annual cricket match. As a team we were duty-bound to follow the captain's orders, and the captain's orders were to win the game. But the cricket match at *Warsash* was not what the captain had in mind. You would have thought it was the battle of Trafalgar when we lost.

During our training we had an aptitude test, to go as far as we could without using public transport and return to the school in 24 hours. No money was to be carried. We set off from Botley in pairs, and the first step was to get on the motorway. In our No 1 navy uniform we had no bother in thumbing a lift to Basingstoke. We were aiming for my foster home in Camberley and reached it in the afternoon, with three lifts. Upon arrival we had to get proof that we had been there by signature from a resident before returning to *Warfleet*. Would you believe it, no one was home! We were ravenous, but I had no door key, so our plan to raid the fridge failed. We waited an hour, hoping my mum would arrive to satisfy our hunger and give us a note of acknowledgement.

Alas, there was no sign of her. We decided that the police station would give us a signature. We walked the mile into town and presented ourselves at the local cop shop. The policeman at the reception desk called for the sergeant, who took a long look at our uniforms and said, "Hello, hello, what navy barracks are you two youngsters AWOL from?"

He didn't want to listen to our story about an aptitude test, and we were about to be locked up in a cell when my mate thought to produce the school phone number we all had on us in case of the very thing we were faced with. The policeman rang up *Warfleet* to verify our story.

"Aptitude test, never heard of it," he said, but he was most impressed by our tale of reaching Camberley — and asked how we were going to return, suggesting that if we waited there would be a police van going to Winchester Prison to collect prisoners. He bought some fish and chips and coke, since we were penniless. Within the hour we were happily ensconced in the police van on our way to Winchester.

Our travels had been broadcast at *Warfleet*, with the police ringing them up to verify our story. Being transported by a prison van to Winchester would only add to the event. We were dropped off at the Winchester bypass, but if a lift in a prison van was odd, our next lift was even eerier. A van stopped, the driver saying he was going to Shirley, a suburb of Southampton. We couldn't believe our luck. The lift would take us almost back to Botley. In the back of the van was a coffin, but we were assured it was empty and we could sit on it. We explained what we were about and that the use of money was forbidden.

"You must be a hungry pair of matlows!" We agreed, but to our dismay no food was forthcoming and we happily disembarked at Shirley.

Matlows in uniform were a common sight around Southampton, and we had no trouble thumbing a lift on to Botley. We achieved the exercise within the prescribed 24 hours and we were judged the winners. Others had travelled further, but were disqualified for returning outside the 24-hour time slot.

I was getting bored with the idea of being an officer. The academic effort seemed like being back at school, and I was impatient to see the world. At the three-monthly report in September 1956 three people sat at one end of the wardroom: Captain Southcott, Mr Vince and the secretary. I was doubtful of a good report and my fears were confirmed by Southcott, whose opening remarks still echo in my ears: "I do not think you are officer material, laddie." I knew it was true. He suggested that I choose between starting as a deck boy, or giving up the sea. I contained my excitement when in October 1956 I was advised I would be joining the Royal Mail liner, *Alcantara*.

four

Twenty years from now you will be more disappointed by the things you didn't do than by the ones you did do. So throw off the bowlines. Sail away from a safe harbour. Catch the trade winds in your sails. Explore, dream, discover.

— *Mark Twain*

MY FIRST DESTINATION WAS THE Southampton Shipping Federation, known as the Pool, the recruitment centre where seamen could choose a ship and a voyage that took their fancy. Shipping companies needing crew would advertise at the Pool. Every seaman carried a discharge book to record the ships they had sailed on, the date of joining and the completion of the voyage. The master of the vessel determined the most important stamps in the discharge book: the 'ability' and 'conduct' of the employee during the voyage.

If the captain thought your ability and conduct were up to standard you would get two VGs (Very Good) in your discharge book. If your behaviour didn't win the captain's approval a DR (Decline to Report) could be stamped in your book. When going for your next ship a DR could cause difficulty in securing a berth. You would have to hope your explanation was good enough to convince the chief mate that you had turned over a new leaf. A good way to cover up a bad discharge was by getting VGs on your next voyage. Sometimes a shortage of certified seamen would mean the employer took on bad discharges to maintain the required Board of Trade manning levels.

The shipping master directed me to my very first vessel, and with a kitbag over my shoulder that held everything I owned, I trundled off to the docks. The policeman at the gate asked what my business was and what was in my kitbag. "Where can I find the *Alcantara*?" I blurted out that it was my first boat and I was joining as deck boy. It was a spellbound walk as my eyes took in the sight of stately liners along the quay. The *Queen Elizabeth*, the largest liner in the world, was a sight to behold. I would know her sister ship intimately in the future. Further

Discharge book photo for my first ship, 1956.

26

down the quay was a vessel with a long sleek hull and a single yellow funnel. I was soon making my way up the gangway of RMS *Alcantara*.

The *Alcantara* belonged to Royal Mail Line. She was built in 1926 and weighed 22,181 tons. During World War II the Ministry of Transport had commissioned her as a troop carrier. When I joined her she was due to go to dry-dock in Belfast before continuing her passenger and mail run between Europe and South America. My career began as bosun's peggy, which entailed serving the bosun his grub, cleaning his cabin and acting as his messenger boy. The trip to Belfast dry-dock was uneventful, but a milestone for me — the start of a career that was to take me to all around the world sampling other cultures, a girl in every port and the eternal symphony of the ocean's voice.

After my first trip I made my way back via ferry to Liverpool, then by train to London and Southampton. I booked in to the Mission to Seamen, whose lodgings were to become very familiar. The Mission was founded in the early 1870s by Ebenezer Mather, who was working in Gravesend and noticed fishermen who plied the North Sea were arriving home penniless. The distress to families was obvious and Mather learned that Dutch grog vessels got in among the fishing fleets, selling tobacco and liquor. He set up trawlers under the Christian banner to patrol and serve the fishermen and their families around the coast of Britain.

The rules of the Mission to Seamen were formulated in 1881. Missions were to expand internationally and today you can find them in most ports of the world, staffed by volunteers. When I set out on my career there were missions in all

The *'Alky'* in its prime before the war — when I sailed on her she sported only one funnel.
VH Young

the big ports providing not only hospitality but also sleeping accommodation and a restaurant. Its sign was the Flying Angel based on the Book of Revelation. The Angel, affectionately known to seamen as the Flying Tab-Nab (a tab-nab is seamen's slang for a cake) was a refuge for seamen far from their families who needed help. Another prominent institute was the Apostleship to the Sea, run by the Catholic Church.

I reported to the Pool, and on the board were vessels going to various corners of the world. Southampton was mainly a passenger-ship port for companies such as the Cunard and the Union Castle lines. A deck boy allocated to a vessel had to stay on it until he secured his junior ordinary seaman (JOS) rating, which in those days took nine months to complete. Three of the months I had spent at sea training school counted towards my sea time. My allocation meant the *Queen Mary* was going to be my home for the next six months.

The RMS *Queen Mary* and her sister ship *Queen Elizabeth* were two of the most majestic sights of the Southampton waters. For a youngster, these leviathans were impressive. The Queens were the greyhounds of the Atlantic and holders of the Blue Riband award for the fastest crossing. They were easily recognisable, with the *Mary* supporting three funnels and the *Lizzy* two.

I made it my business to record the history of each vessel I sailed in, whether it was a small coastal tanker running out of Fawley, or those that transported film stars and notables across the Atlantic.

In the 1930s the Cunard Line planned to dominate transatlantic passenger trade and provide a weekly service between Southampton and New York. The *Mary's* keel was laid in 1930 at the John Brown shipyard on the Clydebank and her maiden voyage was in 1936. At a massive 81,000 tons and over 1000 feet long she was a sight to behold, with over 2000 portholes adorning her hull. During World War II the government commissioned her as a troop carrier.

Her larger sister, *Queen Elizabeth*, made her first voyage in 1940 as a troop carrier, and between them they transported hundreds of thousands during the war; 15,000 troops were carried at one time. In 1947 the *Queen Mary* was spruced up with her pre-war livery and she resumed weekly passenger service between Southampton and New York.

I strolled aboard through the lower gunport door reserved for crew and other such common folk who had business aboard the vessel. Stepping aboard this ship was mind-boggling. The *Alcantara* seemed like a rowing boat.

Reporting to the bosun was the first ordeal. "Could you tell me where I can find the bosun?" I must have sounded like a parrot asking directions as I lugged my case up many stairwells on my way to the petty officers' quarters. Finally I stood before a small rotund man bedecked in a uniform that would have done justice to the Royal Navy. The air was blue with smoke as he got up steam lighting his pipe. "So you've been on the Alky, eh?" He was referring to the *Alcantara*, not asking if I had been on the bottle. "Who was the bosun on there?" I must have sounded like an old sea dog as I described the trip I had made to the Belfast dry-dock.

I settled in as one of three bridge boys, or 'brass monkeys'. There were four of us deckboys to a cabin. I don't know how we ever put up with such cramped conditions. I soon began to find my way around and the path to the bridge where I would spend a lot of my time on the next three trips. I was put on the shift starting at midnight and finishing at four in the morning. I then had eight hours off, starting again at noon and finishing at four in the afternoon.

"Where are you, boy?" came the voice out of the darkened bridge. "Take this to the sparkie." Who was the sparkie and where was he? Such was the confusion on my first night on the bridge.

The *Mary's* bridge must have been worth a fortune in brass. It was everywhere and looked grand when polished. Unfortunately it was the deck boy's job to ensure it was kept up to its polished state. In charge of each deck boy on the bridge was a quartermaster (QM) who gave us our jobs. Each of us had an area of brass to polish daily and a section to soojey — to clean the bulkheads (walls) with detergent.

Trips to New York and back to Southampton lasted ten days. Turnarounds were amazing, when you considered the disembarkation of one or two thousand passengers and the cleaning of the ship in a few hours. The record was about seventeen hours for a full turnaround.

There was no seamanship for us on this vessel — it was all spit and polish for us deck boys. Not only did we maintain the bridge and act as bottle washers and cleaners for one and all, we were expected to keep our own appearance up to standard. Bridge boys were to present themselves on the bridge with clothes dhobied. This became second nature as we matured. Life at sea teaches you to be independent and keep up appearances as there is no one to mollycoddle you.

The *Queen Mary* gave me an insight into life at sea and was special to me, so

The *Queen Mary* was nearly a quarter-mile long, and I never did manage to get to the after end.
VH Young

I took an interest in her future. The upstairs/downstairs attitudes that abounded on the *Mary* are laughable in today's world at sea. Officers had still to come out of the 19th century and their lofty attitudes would nowadays not be tolerated. Don't get me wrong — skippers are in charge of their vessels and are generally respected by the crew, but barriers have been broken down during my time at sea. First names are used rather than the surname. "The name's 'Mr' if you want to address me by my surname!" was a popular retort from seamen to smarmy officers. Separate messrooms for officers and ratings have been abolished and communal messrooms are now preferred. The most enduring barrier was the 'us and them' attitude which officers and ratings alike fuelled. The ship-owner required a competent crew to get his goods from A to B. The best way to achieve that was teamwork and a happy crew who respected each other. I'm glad to report that the Nelson-era 'us and them' has well and truly been dispatched to the garbage bin, and respect for each other is standard practice on vessels today.

In 1967 the *Mary* completed her 1000th crossing of the Atlantic, and her last. Cunard sold her to the city council of Long Beach, California for use for a hotel and maritime museum. Today she still rests at Long Beach, as a permanent reminder to those who were lucky to have sailed on her.

Her sister ship the *Queen Elizabeth* met an ignominious end. In 1970 she was laid up, and was idle for two years. Sold to a Hong Kong shipowner and renamed the *Seawise University*, she caught fire in Hong Kong in 1972. Every effort was made to save her failed. One of Cunard's greatest ships keeled over and the waters of the harbour ended her agony.

Shore leave in New York was limited by time and depended on the watch you were on. Four-to-eight watches could have the day off until four in the afternoon. Deck boys were not permitted ashore without a stewardess to chaperone us. I don't think this was a company directive, but more to do with American authorities being protective of youngsters who included no end of bell boys as well as deck boys. New York was my first foreign soil. Everything seemed gigantic with skyscrapers soaring around us. I didn't care whether we had one or a hundred chaperones, being ashore in another country was exciting.

My six months on board the *Mary* flew by. I was looking forward to my higher rating of junior ordinary seaman and a rise in pay. The *Queen Mary* was the second entry in my discharge book. On signing off in March 1957 I was glad to see it in mint condition and my discipline record intact.

I felt very affluent collecting my wages. Deck boys were paid about £12 a month. At the end of the table was an official of the National Union of Seamen (NUS). Every youngster who went to sea had to become a member; there were no ifs or buts, and refusing to join would spell the end of your career. Unions and politics held no interest for a lad of sixteen and I paid the six month's union fees I owed while on the *Mary*. My sense of affluence was reduced after the union had got their whack.

The value of money had no meaning for me. Going home to Camberley to see my wonderful foster parents after six months of independence seemed boring, and I guiltily decided to enjoy the delights of Southampton with another deck boy who had followed my lead and paid off. It was an irresponsible decision, but such was life for me at that time. We were in and out of Southampton on the *Mary* and there had been few opportunities to venture into the city. Booking a room each for a week in the Seamen's Mission, we dumped our cases and with crisp pound notes in our sweaty hands we set off into town.

My night out left my head pounding the next morning. We had made our way to the Bargate pub, later to become a favourite with seamen as the Juniper Berry. Its attraction was the opposite sex, not that we could remember after a couple of pints of scrumpy. My bleary eyes focused on the small change on the table. In a panic I searched through the pockets of my jeans hoping to find the rest of my money. I located a couple of quid, but that was it. I had a bed for a week, but very little money. You would be amazed how much our pound could buy in the 1950s. A night out on ten bob was a good night out, but a couple of quid was not going to keep me in clover for long. I could go to a café and buy a mixed grill for two and sixpence once a day and I could take in a movie for one shilling and threepence.

I told my equally stupid mate I would have to get a ship because I had almost blown my money.

"What about those birds we picked up?"

"What birds?" I wondered what sort of fool I had made of myself in front of them. Any thought of getting a job disappeared from my mind, and I got him to relate the events of the previous night. He was as bad as me but remembered we were supposed to meet them in the pub at six. We had apparently made a date to take them to the movies.

The young ladies were met at the appropriate time, and mine, Jane, was very pleasing to look at. I was a novice in the art of dating. Her blonde hair in a ponytail was the style of the bobbysoxers I had seen in New York. It was the era of skiffle and rock'n'roll, and if going to see *The Battle of the River Plate* was for the boys, it was made plain that we would be watching the movie without them.

Beer was not my favourite drink, but juveniles have to show off in front of the ladies. Jane lived in Shirley, not far from the city. As the movie was out, we made

A DESCRIPTIVE SOUVENIR LAVISHLY-ILLUSTRATED, OF THE WORLD'S GREATEST SHIP

our way to the nearest dance hall. I immediately took to rock and roll, making a complete hash of it, to Jane's amusement. But what took my eye was the dress of the young generation and I was determined to be part of it. Teddy boys — with their long jackets and velvet collars, drainpipe trousers and bright coloured socks, topped off with slim jim ties — attracted the girls. Hairstyles were swept back with plenty of Brylcreem and duck-tail finishes at the back, and long sideburns. We two Cunard cowboys in our denims looked out of fashion and were both eventually abandoned as the girls had an eye for the local teddy boys. We departed feeling duped, after paying their entry into the dance, and returned to the pub to drown our sorrows.

The teddy boys' predecessors were from turn-of-the-century East End gangs called 'cosh boys'. The fashion had last been seen in the Edwardian era, and signified a change not only in individuals, but in Britain as a whole. There was a feeling of liberation and a new expression, and the winds of change in Britain began blowing. Bill Haley and his Comets led the new era of expression with hits such as *Rock Around the Clock*. Elvis Presley, Tommy Steele, Cliff Richard, and the incomparable Little Richard swept away the 1940s and made us forget about the war. Oh yes, there was outrage at first as customs and ideas were dented when rock and roll — in which young ladies dresses were lifted, exposing their panties! — and teddy boys appeared. Just as the Roaring Twenties had rejected the dull Victorian era with fashion and music, so the 1950s signalled another collective change of expression, once again set in motion by fashion and music. You don't find it, you go along with it, and there was no going back to the old ways no matter how hard they tried to turn the tide back. I was lucky to have experienced this new era, and a few years later we were to witness another change with the advent of pop groups such as the Beatles.

I embraced the era with gusto, but my money was fast running out after only two days ashore. The girls had dumped us and our best option was to seek a job at the Pool. We were both junior ordinary seaman and we waited with bated breath after handing our discharge books to the shipping master.

The blackboard showed three jobs, but only one JOS was needed on each vessel. It meant the parting of the ways for us, but a friendship I was to renew some three years later. My chum chose to stay with the Cunard Line and signed on the *Mauretania* bound for the USA. I selected the Union Castle liner *Carnarvon Castle*. This choice was to bring a new dimension into my life, and change my perception that the world was one happy family. I was bound for South Africa.

five

The Union Castle liners with their lavender-grey hulls and black-topped red funnels made weekly departures, and were a common sight at Southampton. The company was a century old when I stepped aboard the *Carnarvon Castle* one spring morning in 1957.

The Pool doctor passed me fit and all I had to do was confirm my employment with the chief officer. The 20,000-tonner was a baby compared to my previous vessel, the *Queen Mary*. Built in 1926, she was still in immaculate condition after 30 years on the briny. The chief officer's cabin was behind the bridge and I felt like an old hand locating it. My credentials were accepted, but I couldn't help but notice his interest in my features.

"Have you been to South Africa, Share?"

"Not yet, sir."

Nodding his head thoughtfully, he told me to report to the bosun. I walked out of his cabin wondering if he knew something I didn't.

The encounter was soon forgotten as I introduced myself to the bosun, who must have been 100 years old. A deck boy directed me to the ordinary seamen's cabin, which berthed four of us. I was to be a watch-keeper with the able seamen (ABs). He told me to be back on board for signing articles at 9am the next day. I felt elated as I walked down the gangway. I had secured the job, and had another day ashore to enjoy myself. Though I had not signed articles, I was at liberty to sleep aboard. I could add to my worldly worth if I signed out of the mission and slept on the vessel. With this masterstroke in my mind I set off to collect my bag and my rebate.

The four-berth cabin for the JOSs was cramped, with two sets of iron bunks. Another JOS was sleeping aboard in a bottom bunk, so I grabbed the other lower bunk. My new cabin-mate, Peter, seemed a know-all at first, but he was glad to have someone to talk to. He had served his time as deck boy on the *Carnarvon* and it was to be his first trip as a JOS. He knew the vessel inside out and I was glad to have him around.

That afternoon I went ashore to see if my remaining money could buy a pair of drainpipe trousers and a jacket, in the style of the day. The price of clothing in the '50s meant a choice between spending all my money on a teddy boy outfit or having a good time that night. I forfeited my night ashore and became a teddy boy.

The following morning the ship came alive. Hundreds of crew members mingled around the decks waiting for the arrival of representatives from the Board of Trade, headed by the shipping master and company representatives. At 9am we all lined up ready to sign on the ship's articles, a ritual that has its roots way back in the 17th century.

The ship's articles, a contract with the shipowner, record each crew member's name, age, and next of kin, their rating for that trip and monthly wage. Sections stating the entitlement of food for each crew member and warning of punishments the master could inflict should we step out of line were displayed in the crew's quarters. In an age of plentiful food, you'd think the allocation of food came from the 17th century.

There were two sets of articles. Foreign-going ship's articles were signed on the *Carnarvon Castle* since the vessel was trading internationally. We called them 'deep sea articles'. Then there were the 'home trade articles' for vessels plying around Britain and the continent. I was to sign those articles many times doing run jobs to the continent for extra pocket money.

The historical value of the ship's articles is immense. At the Office of Public Records in the UK we can view or buy copies of the records of our ancestors from the 17th century through to our own sea-going records up to the present day. In New Zealand, the signing of articles was discontinued in 1994.

The manning on deck was extensive. The bosun was in charge of the seamen and answerable to the chief officer. There were three bosun's mates, one for each watch, answerable to the bosun, who set out the daily chores deck ratings would carry out.

On the day of sailing I was to take part in a boat drill. My role of bridge messenger boy on the *Mary* never brought me into contact with lifeboats during boat drills. It is a mandatory rule set down by the Board of Trade that fire and life-boat emergency drill take place before sailing, and today it is a global safety standard, so that each crew member knows their allotted job in the case of fire and their lifeboat station in an emergency. Fire and boat muster rosters were placed in the crew accommodation stating each crew member's task, so there was no excuse for anyone not knowing their role. I was soon to learn the mechanisms of the davits that held the lifeboats and to experience the operation of a lifeboat as it was lowered to the water, a reminder of my training school days. The seamen were issued with a Union Castle jersey and the common Royal Navy hats, which we youngsters stamped on to make pliable for shaping a bow wave into the front of the hat. The chief mate was not amused to see the trend worked into company property.

I found myself on the four to eight watch. As a bridge boy on the *Mary* I was well acquainted with the four-hour watch system. Deck manning was far greater in those days than when I finally swallowed the anchor 48 years later. Our watch was stationed aft as we let go the mooring ropes. Ordinary seamen coiled up the ropes as the massive windlass heaved them in. The wharf thronged with people and streamers farewelling their loved ones, who were returning to South Africa or seeking a new life there.

The *Carnarvon Castle* glided down the Southampton waters and out to the Solent. My cabin-mates were from various parts of Britain and we settled in well. Three of us were on watches and the other on day work. It wasn't a good situation, as we had to put up with our sleep being interrupted when the light was turned on as one of us was called to our watch, but we adapted to the inconveniences. My watch seemed to be filled with endless hours of barbarising the decks with the holystone, a soft sandstone block attached to a long handle and pushed to and fro to scour the decks. They did a superb job of bringing a wooden deck up gleaming white. Holystones were used in Nelson's navy, although those hardy seafarers knelt and operated the stone by hand. Today the holystone is a relic; machines bring decks up to shipshape. The 'bear' — a heavy wooden block with hard bristles — was another means of cleansing the deck, reserved for JOSs.

The four of us lived a cramped existence. When one of us could not contain bodily functions, this cleared the cabin in no time, much to the mirth of the perpetrator. The smell of rotten feet added to the mix, and unwashed socks got a passage through the port-hole. There were, unfortunately, seafarers who liked to live 'chatty, but happy'. Cleanliness was not a priority for some.

Throughout my sea career, most seafarers observed the conventions of having to live together aboard ships for long periods. We did not have the luxury of leaving the office at 5pm and forgetting about those who got up your nose. We had to learn to live together. Seamen are a unique brand in their need to keep themselves presentable, and mindful that each of us needed our space and privacy. Our situation on the *Carnarvon* offered no privacy, and the luxury of a single-berth cabin was some years away.

Lifestyles and habits on ships in the 1950s were very different from those of today. Dietitians would have been horrified that the majority of meals were cooked in the frying pan. The anti-smoking lobbyists would have been in shock had they encountered the JOS cabin, thick with the smoke of Woodbines, John Players and Weights cigarettes in that confined space. Health and the evils of smoking were not issues in those days, and that was probably the reason for our tolerance.

Arguments arose between the four of us, mainly over utensils, cups and stores. On joining the ship each crew member was given a knife, fork and spoon, which we kept in our respective drawers in the cabin. There was tea, sugar and a tin of sweetened condensed milk or 'conny onny', the substitute for milk. The stores were issued to cabins every week, and we had to manage our rations so they lasted. The Union Castle Line is the only company I sailed on that had this archaic system of victual rationing. If someone found his utensils ('fighting irons') missing, accusations would come thick and fast. Nor did any of us have the foresight to think about bad weather crossing the Bay of Biscay, and stowing our precious stores safely so they didn't end up on the cabin deck in a congealed mess. The conny onny was always used well before the week was up because it was just as delicious on bread as in a cuppa. We finally learned to preserve our rations after the unsympathetic storekeeper decided we were a pack of teddy boys who needed to be taught a lesson. We adapted; cadging our way out through the week, we ironically ended up with more tea and sugar than we started with.

Not far from our first port, Las Palmas, in the Canary Islands I had my first encounter with one of the ship's coppers. To youngsters, the master-at-arms (MA) was the enemy. They kept a special eye out on the ordinary seamen.

Just before arrival at Las Palmas I was given the task of wiping the salt off the varnished taffrails on the upper salon deck. One could not ignore the young females around the deck, and I proceeded to do what any young lad would do, which was to chat them up. I was getting on famously until a booming voice behind me dampened my high spirits.

"What are you doing on this deck, sonny?" The girls fled at the sight of this overweight entity, hands behind his back, swinging to and fro on his highly polished shoes as though all his birthdays had come at once. Cockily, I asked him if he was blind and carried on wiping the taffrails. It didn't pay to get smart with the masters-at-arms because they carried far more authority than most on board. They were usually ex-military personnel, displaying lines of campaign ribbons across their smartly-pressed uniforms, topped off with peaked hats. Their job was policing the vessel, much like policemen ashore. They seemed to be everywhere on the *Mary* but usually I gave no reason to attract their attention. To my surprise he ignored my cockiness and began to lecture me on the rules laid down by the company, and stated that his job was to enforce those rules. Passengers were out of bounds for crew, unless your job interfaced with them.

My rebelliousness simmered as he reasoned with me. I tested Charlie's patience to the limit until reluctantly I took on board his warnings. First impressions are not always what they seem, and this old war veteran was to become a good friend of mine. He looked out for me on board and was the first to suggest that my swarthiness might have implications when we arrived in South Africa. Charlie held out a hand to a rebellious youngster and treated me like a son. I was to enjoy my home leave with his wife and family in Shirley, just outside Southampton. I cannot say the same for any other MA with whom I came into contact.

The Islas Canarias or Canary Islands are a 400-kilometre chain of seven islands off north-west Africa. They are administered as part of Spain, divided into two provinces, Santa Cruz de Tenerife, and Las Palmas. The principal islands, Tenerife and Gran Canaria are in the middle of the chain. The islands have a colourful history and were known in antiquity as the 'Fortunate Isles'. Nelson lost his arm in the assault on Santa Cruz de Tenerife in 1797. The dictator Miguel Primo de

The *Carnarvon Castle*, my first ship to South Africa.
VH Young

Rivera banished political opponents to the islands, and in 1936, General Franco used them as bases for his nationalist uprising against the Republic.

Las Palmas city, on Gran Canaria, developed into an important oil bunkering port in the Atlantic because of its strategic position. All Union Castle liners stopped here on their way to the Cape. An idyllic scene of red-roofed, white-walled dwellings dotted the hillsides as our vessel manoeuvred along a wharf that seemed to stretch for miles. While I was mooring I noticed a vast number of taxis from another era, which rushed past on their way to the end of the wharf, returning to park alongside the ship in anticipation of customers. My interest in cars has never risen above the fact that they have four wheels, but I recognise character, and these classic cars from the 1920s and '30s were a joy to behold. It seemed an innovative idea and a great tourist attraction. On the wharf were Spanish singers and flamenco dancers in traditional dress to greet the ship. There was a hustle and bustle as passengers streamed down the gangway to spend a few hours on the ventures on offer.

We arrived in the morning and departed in the evening. I was skint so there was little point in me exploring the town. I did have cartons of cigarettes, which were good for bargaining with the vendors who displayed artistic goods and sold Spanish plonk. We youngsters pooled our fags together and purchased a couple of bottles of local brew, against our better judgement.

Also on sale were the Las Palmas dolls. Unique in their Spanish lace, they were to become prized by collectors all over the world, but in my day two cartons of fags was a fair swap. I later saw one auctioned in New Zealand for $800.

My sampling of the local brew did not endear me to the bosun's mate or those in my watch, because I spewed the contents of a bottle on the deck. I promised myself if I spent another day in Las Palmas I would steer clear of that Spanish rotgut called 'vino calypso' by the old seadogs. Future trips to South America made my promise a futile jest.

The Atlantic gave me my first taste of tropical weather, and was also my first crossing of the equator. I wanted to know when we would cross the equator and my watch mates seemed serious when they told me there was a signpost with a monkey perched on it pointing to the equatorial line. I took this all on board and spent hours searching for a signpost with the monkey.

"Have you seen the signpost yet?" The ribbing went on until I finally caught on that it was a joke.

The traditional crossing the equator ceremony was a huge attraction for passengers, presided over by one of the crew dressed as King Neptune, god of the sea, in a tunic, crown, with long rope hair and a beard. The passengers' initiation was tame compared to what crew novices had to endure. The crew gathered on the well-deck, while those of us who were about to experience the full force of King Neptune were led out onto the deck. Every gash-bin in the crew's mess and the galleys was brought up on deck, and the foul contents emptied over our heads. King Neptune uttered wise words and the deck hose was turned on to capacity to drown his new subjects. It was all good fun, and I was to participate as a member of Neptune's court in many crossing ceremonies later on.

I'm sure I wasn't the only youngster who fell for the dupes the seadogs played on us. I went to the fog locker for a pail of fog, and to the paint locker to get some striped paint — where I was told by the storekeeper that if I asked one of the ABs where the locker for a 'long wait' was, I would find what I was looking for. I could sympathise with the youngsters who I was later to send on fruitless journeys to those fictional lockers.

It was a thirteen-day passage from Southampton to Cape Town. In 1938, after a major refit, the *Carnarvon Castle* recorded the fastest passage to the Cape in twelve days and thirteen hours, and held the record for sixteen years. Records for passage times were a matter of prestige for the major shipping lines. Those grand old vessels raced across the oceans, bringing the world closer together, but in the second half of the century prestige was not so important as the conservation of fuel. Union Castle Line required a reduction of passage time to the Cape for their mail service. This led to the construction of seven fast cargo liners in 1965, cutting the passage to eleven days.

Excitement grew as we neared the Cape. We were scheduled to unload passengers, mail and cargo at Cape Town, East London, Port Elizabeth and Durban. The homeward journey began in Durban, and returned us along the coast to the ports we had unloaded at, for cargo, mail and passengers to the UK. I had heard stories from my shipmates about a system that operated in South Africa called apartheid. It certainly did not concern me, and the prospect of stepping on African soil was to me another measure of achievement.

six

The brave man is not he who does not feel afraid,
but he who conquers that fear.

— *Nelson Mandela*

EARLY ONE MORNING MY EYES focused on the distant landmark of Table Mountain, a sight that has greeted mariners since the 17th century, when the Dutch East India Company began to use the Cape of Good Hope as a victualling station. Spread out below the mountain is Cape Town, the Dutch settlement founded by Jan van Riebeeck in 1652.

We repaired to the after-mooring deck at 6am to tie the vessel up. The quay was crowded, but well away from the throng I noticed a bunch of shabbily dressed African men looking on at the arrival of the mail ship.

Customs were aboard soon after we had moored, and passengers disembarked down one gangway as dockers streamed aboard another. I was aghast at the procession winding their way up the gangway, dressed in motley rags. Some were smoking long-stemmed pipes, which I was told later contained things that were a bit stronger than tobacco. They seemed to be chanting a song, and looked untroubled with their appearance. I stood there staring at the dockers as though they had arrived from another planet, then went below to the messroom for breakfast and witnessed our gash bin being raided by Bantus. There seemed to be an air of sympathy among some of the seamen, who offered cigarettes and leftovers to the locals.

But there was also an outcry. "Get the fuck out of our messroom, you black bastards!" I lost my cool and dumped my breakfast over the head of the seaman who said it. My reaction was instinctive. He then directed his scorn at me, damning my black skin. I was offended and took matters into my own hands.

Reports of my fight went round the ship in no time. I got plenty of support, as my aggressor was known as a loudmouth who thought he could lord it over his fellow crew members. In the coming years I was to find there was no shortage of guys who wanted to dominate a crowd. I am not aggressive and I am not a fighter, but I would not put up with his bullshit.

I was still shaking from the encounter when a QM stuck his head round the messroom door. "Dave, the captain wants to see you in his office."

Blimey, the news of the fight got back to him quick. I followed the QM up the mountains of stairs, arriving at the skipper's office. His subdued tenor and the presence of a man in a white collar told me my brawl was not the cause of my summons. Also present was the chief officer, who looked ahead with solemnity. The QM was dismissed and I was introduced to the padre who ran the Mission to Seamen in Cape Town.

I was confused. What did I want with a padre?

"Now then, Share, I don't know if you are familiar with the law in South Africa."

"No, captain," I said tentatively.

"I have asked the port padre to inform you how you must conduct yourself ashore. Please do not take this personally."

The padre told me that I may experience difficulty in having access to buildings, transport and seats marked 'Europeans Only'. My dark features, from my mother's Armenian roots, did not fit what they would class as European. I learned that blacks, coloureds and Asians had separate facilities, which were marked 'Non-Europeans'. Racial segregation was present in every aspect of South African life.

His voice got on my nerves. So what if I had a bit of tar brush in me? I didn't want to listen to any more of this crap, so I walked out — a bad idea. The chief officer told me that the laws were strict and he did not want to see me getting into trouble. Does a sixteen-year-old take that sort of advice? I decided as I walked out of the captain's office that no one was going to stop me going anywhere I wanted. I brushed the advice off as a joke and returned to the messroom, where I related what the padre had told me. My mates thought I would be okay if I was with them. Others said I would be classed as a 'coloured' and we could all go to the shebeens in District Six, a part of Cape Town notorious for murders and every other conceivable vice.

The messroom has always been the venue for advice and tall stories.

"Do I look as though I've got tar brush in me?" I asked.

I should never have asked. The golliwog label on Robinson's Jam had nothing on me, according to my audience. "If they chuck you out then we all get chucked out!" Encouraging sentiments echoed around the messroom. The warnings from on high seemed ludicrous and the camaraderie buoyed me up.

After work there was a scramble for the showers in our eagerness to sample what was ashore. I dressed in my drainpipes and long jacket. None of us youngsters paid attention to the hot weather. We preened ourselves and dreamed of the birds ashore waiting for us. The sight of teddy boys was something new to the South Africans and as we walked to the city people gawked as though we had just arrived from another planet. The wonderful sounds of Bantu chanting caught our ears as we passed a building complex which housed the wharf labour. Blacks came from all parts of the country to find work, and these huge dormitories housed the single men.

I couldn't help but notice the seats on the sidewalk, stencilled 'Europeans Only'. They became more frequent as we arrived in the heart of the city. Bus stops, buildings and transport all proclaimed which race could enjoy what facilities. Your age didn't matter, as long as you could read.

It could be very intimidating to someone who was not Boer or European. I knew that my colour might cause me grief, but I chose not to let it worry me. I was with the crew and they would look after me.

There seemed to be no age limit for drinking and we made our way to Cape Town's favourite watering hole for seamen, Delmonico's, packed with young ladies looking for sailors. Many of the girls had regular boyfriends who sailed the Castle boats that pulled into port.

I noticed the 'Europeans Only' sign and passed through the entrance. I forgot all about the colour bar as we seated ourselves at a table and took in the array of crumpet. Our teddy boy apparel was of interest to the fair sex. We ordered drinks and soon we were all mouth and trousers, urging the girls to our table. We had no idea how much booze we could consume before we'd had enough. Our young instincts got the better of us, and we were all unceremoniously thrown out of Delmonico's and told not to come back.

We were given the same reception at the next pub. A taxi back to the ship was the best decision we made that night. Other crew members saw our performance and at breakfast the four of us were given a detailed account of our conduct.

We all thought it a big joke, except my antagonist from the previous day who wondered aloud how a 'wooden spoon' (slang for coon), was allowed into a European Only facility. The banter died away and before I could react, a host of voices sang out telling me not to take any notice of him. I wanted to retaliate, but wiser heads restrained me and I felt the boys were on my side. He was to continue his vendetta in more ways than one, to achieve what he could not achieve physically.

Having unloaded our cargo, we set sail for Port Elizabeth, taking on passengers to various destinations around the South African coast. There was no discrimination among the travellers, and I often wondered how white South Africans coped with having a black family in the same quarters and sitting at the same table in the passenger salon. The Union Castle Line had no-segregation policy, and when anyone stepped aboard their vessels they would have to leave their politics behind. This is not to say all white South Africans agreed with apartheid. In fact, on future sojourns to that unhappy nation, it occurred to me that some of the most fervent supporters of the regime were ex-pat Britons.

Port Elizabeth was famous for the surfer's paradise, Kings Beach, but notices all along the beach and on the seats proclaimed it 'Whites Only'. It was about the only attraction in Port Elizabeth, and I committed the illegal act of taking a dip in the surf. No one seemed particularly interested in this dark person swimming in the rip-curls, and I still came out the same colour. We were only there a day and left that evening for East London.

There was nothing to compare the East London where I was born with the African port on the East Cape between Port Elizabeth and Durban. East London is the only river port in South Africa, at the mouth of the Buffalo River. Its beaches stretched for miles.

Durban was a major port on the Indian Ocean. The Portuguese explorer Vasco da Gama dropped anchor there in 1497, and the Zulu tribe inhabited this eastern province of South Africa. The Boers conquered these fearless warriors, led by the great King Shaka, in the battle of Blood River in 1838 and founded the first Boer Republic, renaming it Natal. Their hold lasted until 1842 when the British took over.

When we made headway into the harbour my knowledge of its history was zilch. It was just another place, and hopefully better than the last two. We were about to spend a few days in Durban unloading the last of our cargo and loading South African products such as canned fruit and gold bars, which were stowed in the strongroom in one of the holds.

Once again my attention was drawn to the dockworkers making their way up the gangway. I was not aware at the time they belonged to the same tribe whose warriors fought the Boers. Here they were in rags, but they seemed happy enough. My interest in how people and other cultures lived was nurtured by my visit to Durban. A visit to South Africa in 1957 would be enough to outrage any budding activist who witnessed what I saw, and what the world condoned.

Tradesmen came aboard to do repairs, and I came into conflict with one on the first day. Outside our messroom was an old black guy. I asked him what he wanted and he pointed his finger at the mess. Sitting in our mess with a cuppa was a guy who I assumed was a non-crew member.

I asked, "Is that your mate outside?" He replied he was his 'boy', and I was surprised to hear a South African with a Scouse accent. I told him his 'boy' was old enough to be his father. Then I really put his nose out of joint in signalling his 'boy' to come and have a cup of tea. All hell broke loose — he let go at his 'boy' to keep out. You would have thought that Scouse owned the messroom. I told the man to take no notice as there was no colour bar in our mess, but he was obviously frightened of his boss. I was seething and asked what an English guy was doing treating a human being like that.

He told me they were not allowed in the same room, let alone to sit at the same table. A seaman butted in that the law ashore did not apply on this vessel and to fuck off out of our mess. I was dazed by the slanging match that ensued. Scouse told us that immigrating to South Africa was the best move he ever made: "Out here you can hire servants to do your cooking and washing." What was left of his cup of tea ended up over his head and he was thrown out the messroom door. But he was only one of many British immigrants whose lowly status in the mother country was elevated (they believed) by cheap black labour.

I got up to mischief the next day when Scouse and his 60-year old boy were doing a job down the alleyway from our cabin. Picking up a John Player 50 cigarette pack from my drawer, I handed it to his 'boy'. His eyes lit up and the packet was accepted with many thanks. I said to the old fellow, "Tell me if he takes them off you," pointing at Scouse provocatively. Scouse had decided that he could gain no support for his lifestyle ashore.

My first venture ashore in Durban was a lesson in how far people would go to humiliate their own countrymen. I knew right from wrong, and by the time the ship had reached Durban I was aware that something was desperately wrong with South Africa. When the pigment of your skin prevents you from having a normal life, then you will have something to say.

The watering hole that seamen frequented in Durban was the Harbour Lights. As we walked in the pub I noticed the seaman I had fought in Cape Town sitting with a pretty girl. Above the din, and loud enough for everyone to hear, he shouted, "Coloureds are not allowed in this bar!" He was standing up and pointing wildly at me. He was drunk but his words had brought attention to me. We sat down at a table and a JOS went to the bar to get the first round. He came back to say they wouldn't serve us until the 'coloured guy' left. We were all taken aback and, adopting the musketeers' "One for all and all for one," began to exit. But the madness of the moment got to my companions and we all made a beeline for the seaman's table.

Two burly Boers threw me out, cracked my ribs, and advised that the kaffirs' drinking place was next door. Two of my cabin-mates were hauled off to the police cells for adding more battle wounds to the stroppy seaman's face. We slunk back to the ship before the evening had started.

My ribs were giving me pain in the morning and I lined up outside the ship's surgery. My injury excused me from work for a couple of days.

The messroom was abuzz with the events of the previous night, and my antagonist was conspicuous by his absence. No one knew where he was and there was consensus that his profanity against me was appalling. The night's events went further than the messroom. The chief officer called me to his cabin to ask what had happened ashore and why he was missing two ordinary seamen. The latter question was solved when the bosun appeared at the door to say that my friends had just arrived back after a night in the cells, but fortunately no charges had been laid against them. After I had related the events ashore, the chief officer was amazed and sympathetic, but suggested I should have taken the advice I was given in Cape Town.

My answer was given in no uncertain terms — I did not accept the rules ashore, or his, or any other rules. Unfortunately, in that small cabin in 1957 I was fighting against a system that few countries cared about and most western nations ignored.

I was angry that a crew member had sought revenge by using my colour. If I made a political statement in my answer to the mate, it was not a mature statement. I just knew the situation was wrong.

It did not end there. A report went to the captain who, after interviewing other crew, decided the villain was the AB. He gave notice that he was not going to tolerate any crew member causing dissent aboard his vessel and recommended that the AB be transferred to a Union Castle vessel due to leave Cape Town for Southampton within the next few days. The trouble was, he had not returned to the vessel for turn-to the following morning and his transfer never took place. He had jumped ship and disappeared into some veldt ashore.

Seamen cannot break their contract with a company and vanish into thin air when and where they like in foreign lands. We sign articles at the beginning of each voyage, which only terminate at the end of the voyage when you sign off. The company would have been notified and so would the police and immigration authorities, but I never heard if he was apprehended. He was an unpleasant man to all he came in contact with, and there was an air of relief in the messroom when he was gone.

You could set your clock by the Union Castle Line itinerary. Having reached Durban at 6am on the Monday, the vessel unloaded the last of her cargo and began loading tinned fruit for the UK. On Wednesday afternoon the vessel left Durban to begin the homeward journey, arriving in East London on Thursday and Port Elizabeth Friday, where we stayed overnight. We spent one day at sea before arriving in Cape Town Monday at 6am.

Thursday afternoon was the day of departure. Leaving Cape Town was like leaving Southampton: the wharf was thronged with people farewelling family and friends. Our mooring lines were let go, and the parting of colourful streamers ended the final contact with those we were leaving behind. We were homeward-bound and as my eyes focused on the receding Table Mountain I was dismayed. Its treatment of indigenous peoples had been a shock to me. At that moment I was sure I would never set foot on that country again.

The homeward journey on any voyage is always an interesting time in the crew mess. Everyone had yarns to relate about their adventures in port. My status among the seamen was lifted, as I was the one who got rid of the standover man. The friendly air was a marked difference from the surly outward-bound atmosphere.

A mountain peak rising out of the Atlantic made a striking view as we neared the Portuguese island of Madeira. The archipelago was discovered 500km off the Moroccan coast in 1419 by João Gonçalves Zarco and Tristão Vaz Teixeira. Madeira is the only habitable island, and its location astride the Atlantic shipping routes was a welcome break for passengers. Vessels such as the *Carnarvon* had to anchor in Funchal Bay since shallow waters in the dock could not accommodate large liners. Sitting on the mooring bitts, I soaked up the warm climate and took in the scenery of the volcanic island while passengers boarded tenders to go ashore. The usual hawkers were aboard selling their wares — embroidery, lace napkins and tablecloths — and refreshments from the vineyards made their way aboard. The label 'Fundador' comes to mind — it could have been aptly named 'Chundador'. I have quaffed many potent firewaters all over the world, but the Madeira strain would always be the benchmark. We pulled up anchor eight hours later and set sail on the last leg of the journey.

The weather grew decidedly colder as we made our way through the Bay of Biscay and into the English Channel. Most seamen are familiar with 'channel night', the night before the return of deep-sea voyagers to English waters. Usually it was heralded with a visit to the crew's bar, the Pig & Whistle or, for some, a cabin full of booze. We celebrated the end of another trip and said goodbye to shipmates we might not sail with again. It was rather like shooting yourself in the foot, since you needed all your faculties to read payslips and make travel arrangements next morning, but nobody worried about the consequences of a tradition of the sea-going fraternity whenever we hit the English Channel.

The bosun popped his head round our cabin door, noting his ordinary seamen were celebrating channel night. He was an old fart, we reckoned, but he had never bothered us during the trip. He left the running of us youngsters to the bosun's mates, so we were surprised to see him grace our cabin, hanging off his beloved pipe that appeared to be a permanent appendage to his face.

"Now which of you kids are coming back next trip?"

The dumb looks on our faces must have exasperated him.

"I haven't all night, are you coming back or not?"

Why I said yes, after vowing never to set foot on the Cape again, must have been due to drink and the shock of being offered the chance to sign on for another trip. After all, hadn't I made myself visible for all the wrong reasons on the South African coast? And endless hours of pushing a bloody holystone were not part of my future plans. I had planned to rejoin the *Mary* or the *Lizzy*, so I surprised myself by putting my name down with my cabin-mates to retain our berths. We had our little tiffs, but in our small domain friendships were forged and we felt safe in each other's company. The incentive of working on the vessel and earning extra cash while the *Carnarvon* spent the next two weeks in Southampton was another impetus for us to forego any leave.

We arrived in Southampton at 6am Friday, having left this port six weeks before. The ship bustled with passengers, and the crew scurried about in their 'whistle and flutes', the alleyways dotted with sea-bags and cases at the ready in anticipation of signing off and pay. Waiting for the shipping master and company representatives to arrive with the money always tested the crew's patience. They had not seen their families or girlfriends for six weeks and hanging around at the pleasure of the company seemed unfair. A few years later I complained to the National Union of Seamen about shipping companies prolonging the contract by keeping their crews until it suited them to send their paymasters aboard, and learned that the Board of Trade (BoT) were the villains — they presided over all things relating to shipping and seamen, including the signing of articles. Our frustrations were the fault of a government department whose civil servants began work at 9am and not a minute before. How dare we arrive at a time which would disrupt the bowler hat and brolly brigade's daily timetable.

Wages for seamen were paid monthly. During the voyage you could draw cash advances against your entitlement for expenses ashore, and from the bond locker you could buy cigarettes, tobacco, toiletries and other creature comforts on tick. Married seamen, of course, had commitments to their families. An allotment note was forwarded with the designated amount on a weekly, fortnightly or monthly basis to the seaman's spouse.

My rating as a JOS in 1957 attracted the princely sum of £17/2/6 a month — but the paltry wages related to the cost of living at that time. A pound was worth a pound in the 1950s, and would buy far more fun than it does today. A pocketful of money was just an added bonus to the thrill of travelling the world free. What more could you want, with free food thrown in?

I should have gone to Camberley to see my foster parents and let them know how my career was progressing; I had not seen them since I began training at *Warfleet*. This irresponsibility carried on for many years, and brought an increasing sense of guilt as time went by. It took eighteen years, and a simple sentence from the missus, "Why don't you contact them?" before I finally resurfaced, much to their delight, and their shock to find I was living in New Zealand. But plenty of water was to flow under me before that happy event took place.

The Union Castle Line operated a mail run with precision, and a strict timetable was in place during the two-week respite in Southampton. For me, leave was an interruption and I was looking forward to sailing day. Sustaining myself financially for such a long period in port was always going to be difficult. Flush with my pay-off, my first few days of leave were spent at venues where the girls were. Feeding myself was another cost. Transport cafés were the cheapest feed in town, and I would grace one each day, as the mixed grills were only two and sixpence. After a few days of strutting the town like I was a Rockefeller, my cash reserves became precarious, forcing me to adjust my lifestyle. The movies at one and threepence offered a cheap evening's entertainment. My happy-go-lucky attitude towards money was to stay with me for years — spend it and jump on the next ship was my motto. I was certainly not alone among seamen in this way of thinking.

Excitement heightened on the day of signing on, always the Tuesday before the day of sailing. Three days were set aside for crew engagement, and there were old and new faces as activity aboard the ship increased. That meant a reunion with my old friend, the holystone. Those decks had to be up to scratch for the hundreds of passengers who were about to board. We left our berth dead on the appointed time of 4pm.

Again, our first port of call was Las Palmas for bunkers. I kept away from the local brew and as I was not on watch, and managed a couple of hours ashore, not so much to see the sights but to feast eyes on the local señoritas. Spanish ladies had no interest in the antics and wolf-whistles of jack tars and we were confined to just looking, no touching, but it was always good to stretch the legs on *terra firma* when the chance presented itself.

We crossed the equator eight days after departing Southampton, and a few more passengers met King Neptune and his court at the ceremony. I could sympathise with the first-trip deck boys who like me had been put on watch for the equatorial signpost. The warm weather of the South Atlantic became stifling in our cramped quarters below. Passing one of the company's homeward-bound vessels would break the monotony for passengers and crew — horns blew and life-saving rockets were set off. It was all company hype to us youngsters, but it was put on for the passengers and part of the joy of sea travel for them.

I shall not dwell on the South African coastal run. I was much wiser from my experiences of the previous trip, and my cockiness in sticking two fingers up at the racial laws was moderated. We were told about District Six, a notorious township in Cape Town where the Cape Coloureds lived. Feeling bulletproof, a band of four of us waltzed into the township to sample the local hospitality. Famous were the shanty pubs, known as shebeens. South African law prevented the coloured folk from socialising with the white folk; that was why shebeens sprang up in the townships. They were places for illegal gatherings and the sale of firewater.

Drinking was not the only attraction. African music was like no other music I had heard before. I noticed there were many whites in the shebeens and it was certainly a different world from the restricted city. The many times I visited District Six during my sojourns to the Cape, I can honestly say I saw none of the notorious sights that the District was famed for.

The same odour permeated each shebeen as I had smelt coming from the holds of the ship. Some of the black community smoked *dhaka,* marijuana. One could not help inhaling the smoke that escaped from the long-stemmed pipes of the locals, so the four of us decided to sample it. A bag of *dhaka* and a pipe cost three rand, and that was the end of our night ashore in District Six.

I was later to try marijuana in South America, and came to the conclusion that it was an anti-social drug. It caused no hangover, but I couldn't see the point in sitting there like a dummy in my own little world. I liked to socialise and pot didn't do that for me — I had no trouble rejecting what others thought was the elixir to wipe away all their troubles.

"Get up, you lazy bastards! Turn-to!"

The ship's itinerary did not take employees' hangovers into consideration. There were many mornings when I thought the phrase 'turn-to' should have been wiped from the English language.

On this coastal run I entered places closed to me and sometimes got away with it, and at others I was asked to leave. No one at that time could combat the Boers and their colour bar. District Six and its shebeens were a refuge where the colour of your skin was not the focus. Afrikaaner governments tried to shut the shebeens down, since they flouted apartheid. They were in people's homes, opened up to the public for drinking, gambling and other vices. The shutting of one led to the opening of another, until in 1987 the government admitted they were impossible to police and opted to ignore them.

Anyone who has braved a rickshaw ride in Durban would agree it is one of the most interesting forms of transport. Zulu rickshaw men are ferocious characters, and they run the rickshaws dressed in their tribal costumes. I was thankful after I was conveyed through the streets of Durban by a Zulu that I was not around at the time of the Battle of Rorke's Drift in 1879, when a British force defended themselves against thousands of these warriors. I could never understand why a tribe with such a rich history as the Zulus would accept penury under the Boers.

Our homeward trip included a stopover at a British outpost, the island of

St Helena, Napoleon's last place in exile. The Union Castle Line plied the sea route near these islands, which included Ascension Island and the loneliest island in the world, Tristan da Cunha. Essential supplies had to be maintained, thus we made a deviation to St Helena's only port, Jamestown, where we dropped anchor for the day and passengers went ashore to take in the sights. Madeira and her picturesque port of Funchal hove into view a few days later.

We ploughed through the Bay of Biscay and turned right into the English Channel. Once again channel night was upon us. The bosun showed up at the most inconvenient times, taking names of those who wanted to sign on for another trip. Channel night celebrations were not the time to get straight answers, and I had to enquire the next morning as to what I had told the bosun. Apparently I had followed the trend and given notice I was on for another trip. I knew after leaving the South African coast that I'd had enough of the Yarpies and their apartheid laws. I had gained a lot of good shipmates, but I was desperate to seek other destinations in the world. It is unique to seamen, living as a family in close quarters for months or years on end, that lifelong friendships should spring up.

I signed off the *Carnarvon Castle* in Southampton.

My British seaman's identity photo.

seven

I SET OFF DOWN THE *Carnarvon Castle* gangway. Once again I dismissed the idea of going home to Camberley and booked in to my familiar digs at the Flying Angel. I was on my own with no shipmates to lark about with and the idea of finding a ship appealed to me. A youngster who wanted to keep up with the teddy boy fashion of the day did not always spend money wisely. I dumped my newly purchased suit in my room, took one look at my remaining money and sauntered off down to the Pool barely 24 hours after signing off the *Carnarvon*.

The only vessel on offer was a Union Castle liner, and I was not going to suffer another trip down to the Cape. The shipping master told me to come back in the morning as there was a JOS position on an in-bound coastal tanker due to dock at the Fawley oil terminal that same evening. I had seen huge tankers moored in Fawley when we went out on *Western Sky* in training school. The smell of oil was an incentive to steer clear of tankers, but when the dough gets low there is no choice. After all, I still had to eat, so why not let the shipowner keep my tummy full?

Next day I was outside the shipping federation early, and was given a docket to say I had been sent from the Pool to fill the JOS position aboard a tanker called the *Pass of Leny*. I was expecting to see a huge tanker when I arrived at the terminal, but I couldn't see any tanker called the *Pass of Leny* and decided to report back to the Pool. I was about to exit the main gate when I was pulled over by a copper wanting to know my business on the docks. I showed him my docket and he directed me to the vessel.

No wonder I couldn't find it. The hull of the vessel was below the wharf, and the only fact to signal there was a ship tied up was a woodbine funnel visible above the wharf. When you had just completed voyages on slick vessels, it was a shock to be confronted by a derelict from the 1920s. The gangway looked precarious, slanting steeply from the wharf down to the deck. An Irish brogue greeted me from the bridge window asking if I was the ordinary seaman from the Pool. The skipper wore a cloth cap and looked like a dock-worker. He signed me on and then asked where my gear was. It was still in the Flying Tab-Nab.

The shipping master had forgotten to tell me the vessel was sailing that evening for Holland, but there was plenty of time to gather my gear. The skipper was griping about the crew who were supposed to be on board but had not returned from the pub.

The tide rose while I was away collecting my effects, which made boarding the vessel much safer, but not for one AB who staggered aboard in a drunken haze and attempted to negotiate the gangplank. He was carted off to the nearest hospital with broken bones and a hangover to deal with when he came to.

A tanker has nothing in common with a passenger liner. It was a new experience for me, but I was not going to be versed in the intricacies of operations that evening. Three of the deck ratings were drunk and one went to hospital, leaving one AB and myself fit for work. I noted the crew were Irish, which suited the name of the vessel. The skipper cursed "those drunken bastards" and he and the mate were on deck helping to clew up the vessel for sailing to Schiedam.

The *Pass of Leny w*as one of seven small coastal oil tankers owned by the Bulk Oil Shipping Company. Built in 1928, she was diminutive compared to my previous ships, grossing a mere 796 tons. The names of the vessels all began with 'Pass of', with three of them built in the 1920s and four in the '40s. None grossed more than 903 tons.

There was no fanfare leaving the wharf such as I had witnessed before, and the informality seemed odd. "See you next week!" called the linesmen from the wharf as we faded into the night and made our way down the channel.

The remaining sober AB told me he was going to relieve the skipper at the wheel and once we were clear of harbour waters I was to take over steering. He noticed my panic and explained that the other ABs who were supposed to be on watch were flaked out in their bunks, so it was up to me and him to take turns at the wheel through the night. I did have a steering certificate, gained on the *Mary* under the Board of Trade certificate qualification that required a minimum of ten hours steering a ship. (Not all at once, of course.)

I sat in the small messroom on tenterhooks, drinking coffee like it was going out of fashion. The wheelhouse was a cubby-hole compared to that of the *Mary*. Nervously I relieved the AB at the wheel and put into action all I had practised on the *Mary*. The mate was the only officer on the bridge and I told him I had only steered a ship when I took my steering ticket. His laid-back manner gave me confidence and he stood beside me, making sure I was on course.

There was an awful din each time I turned the wheel. Seamen who have experienced rod-and-chain steering will echo my sentiments. As we steamed into the North Sea the high waters were merciless and the rocking and rolling went to the very pit of my being — I turned green and felt like dying. Seasickness is a curse that hits one and all until they get their sea legs, and become acclimatised to the roll of the oceans. There is nothing shameful in being seasick. I know a skipper who gave up going to sea because he could never rid himself of the affliction. For a while it affected my ability to keep the ship on course. Once I was relieved of further duties, I spent the rest of the night retching and waiting for the undertaker.

Calm waters carried me back to the real world. We were making our way up a river to Schiedam. Those who were drunk on leaving Fawley were nursing their heads in the messroom. The sight of me brought grins to their faces. I was ribbed mercilessly and told we had greasy pork chops for tea.

The ABs looked like granddads to me, but they were a good bunch of seamen. Our cabin slept four and was even more restricted for space than my cabin on the *Carnarvon*. We reached Schiedam that evening. The ABs seemed to have been there before and I joined them, leaving an AB aboard to manage the unloading operations. The skipper and his men were all pals and they argued and called each other choice names when they were liquored up, but the camaraderie among them was unforgettable. I came back aboard early to make up the sleep I had lost the night before. With four in the cabin and three of them arriving back in the early hours of the morning drunk, sleep became impossible. I needed sleep and the last thing my tired body wanted was drink. Their drinking sprees came to an end as I turned to for work, and they turned in. Lucky for them there were engine troubles and we were delayed for over a day.

Our next port of call was Truro, in Cornwall, and I was dreading the trip across the tempestuous North Sea. It was calm on our return journey, but that did nothing to alleviate the motion of the small vessel and I had another day or two in hell. I saw nothing of Truro as our berth was further down the River Fal, well away from the city, as is usual with oil berths. Then we returned to Fawley where I had begun this nightmare trip, and no amount of pleading by the skipper could reverse my decision to pay off the vessel when we pulled in. To the amusement of my Irish crew-mates, the passage from Truro to Fawley gave one last heave to add to my discomfort and I vowed that I would never enter another transport café for a greasy mixed grill. Fortunately, I was never to suffer the wretched pangs of seasickness again.

"The Flying Angel, please," I said as my taxi manoeuvred along the quay.

"Good trip?" asked the cab driver.

"Oh yer, great," I replied with the conviction of an old seadog. I took a last look at that woodbine funnel with its purple band, the focus of my misery as it swayed across the North Sea. Bulk Oil could stick their ships — I never wanted to see the *Pass of Leny* again.

By this time my face had become a familiar sight to those who managed the reception desk at the Flying Tab-Nab. My latest escapade had lasted no more than ten days and I was not about to ruin my reputation as a seaman by revealing I had spent the last week or so sick as a dog. My assignment on the *Pass of Leny* generated barely enough money for me to hang around Southampton, let alone pay the foster parents a visit. I would be at the Pool next morning.

Dumping my gear, I headed off to the Juniper Berry down near the Bargate. I spied a familiar face, a deck boy from the *Mary* and gave him a rundown on the mad crew I had just sailed with on the *Leny*, omitting the seasickness. He caught my interest when he told me about a non-Pool job on a yacht owned by Lord and Lady Docker. "Who the hell are Lord and Lady Docker?" I asked. I had seen plenty of dockers around the wharves but never one of the noble kind. He didn't have a clue who they were, but said they were going to the south of France somewhere in the Mediterranean. That was good enough for me and I would make a point of visiting the shipping federation offices as soon as they opened. He was staying at the Flying Tab-Nab so we both downed our drinks and arrived at the greasiest food outlet in town, the fish and chip shop. So much for the vow I made on the *Pass of Leny.*

At the Pool early next morning I was not the first in line. When the doors opened all eyes went to the board and to the jobs on offer. I saw my old favourite, the *Mary,* and a JOS for the *Leny*. I had forgotten to ask my friend the name of this yacht, and there were a number of vessels listed on the board. The guy in front of me was offered a vessel called the *Shemara.* The shipping clerk was trying to impress on him that the vessel was desperate for an AB as it was sailing that night. I couldn't help but hear the able seaman's outburst, telling him to stick the *Shemara* where the monkeys stick their nuts. He was quite adamant that he wanted no truck with the effing *Shemara*. I noted a JOS was required and when it was my turn I asked where the *Shemara* was going, what was meant by a non-Pool job, and why it was listed. He explained, but it went right over my head. There would be no record stamped in your discharge book.

"What is she, a tanker or cargo ship?" I asked.

"No, a yacht. Ever heard of Lord Docker?"

I had not, apart from the night before, but I was about to learn a lot about this extravagant couple. I accepted the JOS berth, but I was interested to know why the AB wanted no part of the *Shemara*, and asked him, saying I was about to join it. "You'll regret it. The skipper's a bastard and so is that bloody Lady Docker." Expletives came thick and fast as though I had reminded him of some bad dream. He didn't make much sense to me and I left him still effing and blinding.

The *Shemara* was a luxurious floating palace that graced such destinations as Monte Carlo and Cannes. She was a steel vessel, weighing 860 tons, and a product of the famous boat builders, Thornycroft. The crew numbered about 30. Everyone seemed to be dressed like Lord and Lady Muck; you couldn't distinguish crew from guests. The sailors were decked out in uniforms and there were 'no-go' areas all around the vessel. My sojourn aboard this floating palace was to last barely ten days. Even today I chuckle over the ridiculous foibles of 1950s high society, and their minions who brown-nosed and hung on every pompous word uttered.

So who were Lord and Lady Docker? Bernard Docker was chairman of Daimler and on the board of a number of companies. He was knighted for his services to charity in 1939. Way back in 1936 he gave his first wife the *Shemara* as a wedding present. The marriage obviously failed and he married his second wife Nora Collins some time in the 1940s. She was said to be a dancer in the famous Café de Paris.

Their fame was based on their extravagance: gold-plated cars, mink coats and champagne. It was an eye-opener for me, though my young mind had no set views on the upper class as it would later. Lady Docker was known to be a friend of the worker. There was a story that she asked a group of miners on board the *Shemara* for a drink. About 40 miners took up her offer, and as the story goes, they were not impressed with the glass of pink champagne they were given.

My stay on the *Shemara* was brief, but memorable for its insight into how high society conducts itself, though I hesitate to say the Dockers' style was a benchmark for all aristocracy. It was also memorable for the indiscretion I committed during our passage to Ville Franc, not far from the playground of the rich and famous, Cannes.

Apparently we were about to spend a week or so swinging on the hook while her ladyship wined and dined ashore. Lord Docker was not aboard on this trip and Lady Docker ruled the roost. The *Leny* was a much bigger vessel than the *Shemara* and crossing the turbulent Bay of Biscay in this tub was a nightmare.

I was on the wheel just before our arrival in Lisbon, and was to be relieved by the quartermaster who would take her into the port. Lady Docker and all her cronies were in the wheelhouse, talking in their hoity-toity voices on the delights of Lisbon.

The workings of one's anatomy do not discriminate, even in the company of the aristocracy. Unthinkingly, I let my body do its natural thing. Silent, but deadly to my employers, the odour wafted around the array of noble noses, then all hell broke lose. My innocent look won me no sympathy with the ladies of high society. Bejewelled hands were frantically waving in front of crinkled noses and all eyes were on me as though only the working class could cause such a stink. I was immediately ordered from the bridge as windows were wound down and one of the officers took the wheel.

My crime was to accuse one of them for the atrocity. I could not contain myself, and made things worse by laughing my head off at the reaction of those elegant ladies. The captain was not amused at my behaviour and advised me I would be paid off on reaching Ville Franc. That suited me fine, as this floating champagne palace was not my cuppa tea. Even today as I pen this small cameo, I am full of mirth, seeing those poor ladies who were in the wheelhouse at the time.

Being given my marching orders because I farted on the bridge sounds ridiculous today, but some minds in the '50s were still in a Victorian hangover. My trip through France was a boring affair as I could not speak French and no one spoke English. Reaching Dover, I had to dig into my own pocket for a train fare to London plus a connection to Southampton. Cash-strapped as usual in Southampton, I booked in to the Flying Tab-Nab, and the next morning made my way to the Pool.

And Lord and Lady Docker: the last I heard some years later, they were hocking all their fancy cars to sustain their extravagant lifestyle, and eventually the *Shemara* was sold in 1968. The Dockers, it was rumoured, became tax exiles on Jersey in the Channel Islands.

The Royal Mail Line's *Alcantara* had been my first introduction to the merchant navy. As I scanned the ships on the board at the Pool, my eye caught the name of the Royal Mail Line's most celebrated vessel, the *Andes*. A JOS was required and I hoped the job would not be taken before my turn in the queue came. The same clerk, who ten days before had pointed me to the *Shemara,* perused my discharge book.

"Had a good leave?" he asked.

"Wonderful," I replied. They see so many seamen in their capacity they can't remember everyone. "Does the *Andes* go to South America?"

"Yes, she does the mail run down there." I accepted the position and he advised me that if the chief officer accepted me I was to see the Pool doctor. It was a requirement for all seamen joining vessels that they be deemed fit by a BoT appointed doctor before joining any vessel.

The Royal Mail Line flagship was a sight to behold after my adventures on the two previous tubs. The *Andes* was painted in her Royal Mail livery, a black hull, white superstructure, and a buff funnel. I had no problem in passing the mate's scrutiny, and signing on would begin the next day.

eight

THE ROYAL MAIL LINE was one of Britain's premier shipping companies, with a pedigree rivalling the Shaw Savill and Union Castle lines. The company traded between Britain and South America, its main cargo being chilled beef and the Royal mail. As I humped my battered suitcase up the *Andes* gangway and through the gunport door, the familiar odour of food and tobacco hit my nostrils. Unlike the *Leny*, which reeked of oil, passenger vessels smelled of the various culinary delights cooked in the galleys for the passengers. Those of us who savoured the various ships would agree, the smells were a unique part of the golden era.

The *Andes* was the second vessel of that name. She began her maiden voyage at the outbreak of World War II, carrying over 4000 troops, and continued in that capacity until the war ended. After a major refit for commercial service she rejoined the Royal Mail Line in 1947 and began life as a passenger and mail runner to the east coast of South America.

Built in the Harland & Wolff shipyards, Belfast, the *Andes* weighed 26,860 tons gross with a service speed of 21 knots. She had a capacity for about 500 passengers divided into first and cabin class. She was famous for having made the fastest round-the-world trip to date in 1940 from Liverpool to Panama, Wellington, Karachi and the Suez, returning to Liverpool in 72 days.

The *Andes*, Royal Mail's flagship. I paid off her with appendicitis in Las Palmas and rejoined her on another voyage.
VH Young

"Drop your jeans … cough," said the doctor as he assessed whether I could stand another voyage. I couldn't understand what part my cobblers had to do with being fit and gave the doctor a second look as I exited his room. I never mentioned that I was experiencing abdominal pains rather like the stitch.

I signed on and once again the ordinary seamen shared four-berth cabins. Our six-week voyage was to take us to the French port of Cherbourg; Vigo, a fishing port on the Spanish coast; Lisbon, which held memories from a previous trip; and Las Palmas for bunkers, before setting off across the Atlantic to Rio de Janeiro and another Brazilian port, Santos. Then we would head up the River Plate to Montevideo. Just across the Plate is Buenos Aires, our last outward-bound port. We would return home along the coast and to Southampton. It was to be the *Andes'* last mail run before she went cruising.

The *Andes'* departure was subdued compared to Union Castle departures, where the quay was chocker with people seeing their folk off.

I was appointed the salon deckman's assistant. It was the first time I had struck a day job, and meant I could have the night in my bunk instead of getting up or turning in at all different hours.

It was also a job where I mixed with passengers. My main tasks were to put games such as deck quoits and shuffle-board out every morning, to make sure the decks were spotless, and to empty the gash bins around the passenger decks. I became a dogsbody but didn't mind. Old Nobby, the salon deck man, had been on the *Andes* since its major refit and had an armchair in the locker that he was rooted to, and only arose when a smoko or meal break interrupted his leisure. But he seemed to know when the chief mate was about the decks and would be showing off his industrious self by the time the mate found him.

Every day at 3pm afternoon tea and tab-nabs were served to passengers around the decks by the stewards. Nobby and I would arrive at the deck pantry for our tab-nabs and a cuppa. The pain in my stomach had not gone away, so I went to the ship's doctor after departure from Lisbon and he told me it was something I had consumed. The night before arrival in Las Palmas I keeled over and was put in the infirmary. This time the doctor was not so keen to blame my malady on food. He diagnosed me with appendicitis, and told me I would have to go to hospital on arrival. My condition worsened, and the doctor feared I had peritonitis, a serious complication. He advised that all speed was being made to Las Palmas.

On berthing a crane hoisted my stretcher over the ship's side to an ambulance on the wharf. I was surprised how many of the crew wished me well. Nobby and I had become good mates, and I said I would be back for my old job next trip.

After the operation I awoke in the fetal position in an anaesthetic haze. Gradually my eyes grew accustomed to the surroundings, but I felt like a hand had wrenched my insides out. Soup was fed to me and goat's milk, which I hated. Each morning a team of Spanish students would accompany the doctor's visit. They would peer at the surgeon's handiwork, crowding around my bed and babbling in Spanish. Such was my discomfort I wondered if the students had performed the operation.

I learned that I was in the International Hospital and sharing a ward with other seamen from foreign nations. As one seaman was discharged another would take his bed. I had sympathy for each guy dumped there after an operation. It seemed a never-ending meat market. Complications kept me in that hospital for four weeks — they never told me what the complications were.

Appendectomies today leave a very thin scar, but mine was huge and very visible. I struck up a friendship with a Swiss nurse, who told me that medical students were always present during operations and performed under supervision.

One day a shipping agent for the Royal Mail Line visited to say I was to be discharged and repatriated on the *Highland Princess* under the status of DBS (distressed British seaman). He duly took me to the ship and made sure that I was a confirmed DBS. I was going home as a third class passenger in a dormitory cabin with twelve bunks. There were six more DBSs who had been picked up on the passage from South America. Distressed British seamen were paid one shilling a day, a piffling token recognition that the company had kept its part of the contract. The shipowners were out of touch, as a shilling would hardly sustain a daily living allowance. Food, bed and medical access were all they needed to provide in those days.

Steerage or third class was a product of the turn-of-the-century immigration of passengers to new lands. Transport of passengers by sea had changed remarkably by the '50s and '60s, when they started offering first or tourist class. It was rare that a shipping line would still be operating steerage. The *Highland Princess* was one of four vessels that included the *Brigade*, the *Monarch* and the *Chieftain*, carrying immigrants from Spain and Portugal to Brazil, Uruguay and Argentina. The vessels were built in 1928 and 1929 for the then Nelson Line, each around 14,000 tons. A later addition, the *Highland Patriot*, made her maiden voyage in 1932. Unfortunately she was torpedoed in 1940 with the loss of three lives.

Third class accommodation was down aft. A luggage hold separated the male cabins on the portside from the female cabins starboard. Cabins for married couples and family were also available. It was easy to envisage the cramped lifestyle of immigrants long ago. Third class passengers were attended by Spanish and Portuguese stewards, which made sense as most of the passengers travelling were from those countries.

There were two sittings for mealtimes and DBSs were assigned to the second by order of the third class chief steward — which meant the menu for the first sitting had usually run out. This had become an item of disagreement between the DBSs and the chief steward. The names he was called did not help matters, but it was resolved when the vessel emptied its Iberian passengers, cutting mealtimes to a single sitting. But I didn't really care about the grub, as I could always go to the seamen's mess if I was hungry.

I did not know the London crew, as I had been shipping out of Southampton, but as a Cockney in distress I was welcomed in their mess.

"Why are you shipping out of Southampton? There's more ships sailing from London."

"Bleeding Castle boats, they're full of Mooshes [seamen from Southampton]!"

And so the banter went on. I was not completely deaf to the advice, even if it was in jest. I was attracted to the choice of vessels and destinations London might offer. Southampton had plenty of passenger boats and tankers, but what about a tramp ship? I kept that in mind and promised I would join the *Highland Princess* on the next trip. I felt at ease among the seamen on the *Princess*. Cockneys are natural comics and I enjoyed their company.

Christmas 1957 passed as we made routine calls at Lisbon and Vigo, and the dawning of the New Year 1958 greeted our arrival in London. I said goodbye to friends in the seamen's mess as I pocketed seven days' wages from the *Andes* and the measly DBS stipend. At least I was given a train ticket to Southampton, generous of the company since they were only obliged to set me back on English soil.

Joining the *Highland Princess* went on hold as all my records were in Southampton and I had to wait until they were transferred to the London Pool. I could not afford to hang around London, so I caught the train out. It was the middle of winter and I was 'schooner rigged' as far as owning warm clothing was concerned. I was freezing my cobblers off — my suit was of a thin cloth, no match for a UK winter, so I bought a duffle coat from a second-hand shop for ten and sixpence. This lowered my funds considerably and I had some serious thinking to do, but my purchase became my companion for years after that. Its warmth paid me back in full while on lookout for icebergs around Newfoundland and in the numbing winters of Canada. It is not often one offers a eulogy to second-hand clothing, but I count it as one of my most astute acquisitions.

DBS status prevented me from shipping out until the Pool doctor passed me fit. My appendix scar would not help my chances and I presumed I would be put on convalescence — but there was no way my money would cover a long stay ashore. I decided I would either have to go home to Camberley, or go over to Shirley and ask Charlie, the master-at-arms on the *Mary*, if he could put me up. I hoped he would be home, as he had told me I was welcome to stay any time. It sounded presumptuous on my part, but dire times demand bold remedies.

I trotted off to the shipping federation next morning. Ships on offer included the *Andes*, which had completed a mail run during my time away and needed ordinary seamen. I fronted up to the clerk and made sure he knew I was interested. My discharge book showed that I had paid off sick from my last vessel and my fears proved correct when he said, "You need a medical clearance before we can accept you for employment, but I will pencil you in for the *Andes* if you are passed fit."

The good thing about the Pool doctor was that he was always available during shipping office hours. My records of hospitalisation were open to him and when he saw the scar the operation had left a stream of words such as "Good grief!" lowered my hopes of shipping out.

"How do you feel now?" he asked.

"Fit as a fiddle," I lied.

He wanted to test my fitness. Touching my toes was torture, as were the other exercises I had to do to satisfy his concerns. My impressive physical show must have swayed him, as he passed me fit for duty. The occasion may seem trivial, but for me at the time it was crucial. Small events in our lives can change our course, and I often wondered what I would have done if I had been declared unfit. As it was I walked out of his office clutching a certificate saying I was fit for work.

It was January 1958 as the *Andes* began her South Atlantic cruise. Her livery was still the black hull and white superstructure she had on her mail runs to South America. When she began full-time cruising in 1959 her hull was painted white and port and starboard lifeboats would be installed on the forward well-deck. Her cruise took her to Cape Town and Rio de Janeiro. She became a one-class vessel and the number of passengers who signed on implied it was a popular pastime for those who could afford it.

I was reunited with my old mate Nobby and retained my previous position as assistant salon deck man. I regaled my fellow crew members about my time in hospital and the butchers who operated on me, showing my wound to all and sundry. The crew were full of expletives for our Spanish friends, which would have put a smile on the face of Sir Francis Drake.

There was no discharge of cargo on this trip. We seemed to be in and out of ports, anchoring here and tying up there. It was a new experience for all of us. One of our destinations was Tristan da Cunha, part of the Ascension Islands in the Roaring Forties, the name given by sailors to the latitudes between 40° and 50° South, which are marked by heavy winds. (Interestingly Wellington is the only capital in the Roaring Forties.) Tristan was reputedly the most remote island to be inhabited. It was discovered by the Portuguese navigator Tristão da Cunha in 1506. In 1816, the British imprisoned Napoleon on nearby St Helena and at the same time annexed Tristan da Cunha, establishing a small garrison ashore. After vacating the garrison a soldier named Glass chose to stay with his family on this remote outpost. The ensuing years saw not only the mingling of the blood of Nelson's navy, but also of many shipwrecked survivors of different nationalities.

The population had obviously grown by the time the *Andes* anchored off Edinburgh (Tristan's seat of governance, named after a visit by the Duke of Edinburgh in the 1860s). A party had been planned for local children and they clambered up the gangway in high spirits. Activities were scheduled including sack races, tug-of-war and other games that would need the expert attention of the keepers of the salon deck.

Nobby and I were run off our feet keeping up with these excited kids, but it was even more interesting to hear them talk. It certainly made us think, "Where on earth did you get an accent like that?" We could have been transported back 200 years, listening to the locals chatting away in 18th-century Georgian dialect. So this was the sound of Nelson's sailors conversing! It was quaint and charming to this modern-day sailor.

With happy faces and armfuls of goodies, the children disembarked onto the longboats, back to their isolated existence. The ship's whistle farewelled the islanders and as we got under way I took a last look at Tristan da Cunha. The island was volcanic, rising out of the depths of the ocean. In 1961, just three years later, there was an eruption near the settlement, causing the whole population of 264 to be evacuated to Britain. After two years it was considered safe to return to their homeland and only a few of the original Tristans elected to stay in the UK. Our few hours' visit to this outpost of the empire was the highlight of this cruise for me. My short visit to this island left me with fond memories, and of course, the lilt of the voices of King George III's subjects.

I was later to visit another isolated British outpost in the Pacific Ocean, colonised by the Empire's favourite sons, the mutineers from the *Bounty*. These were the inhabitants of Pitcairn Island, whose refuge on that island was depicted in the movie *Mutiny on the Bounty*, starring Marlon Brando. A few years later I was to see first-hand where they sought refuge from harsh British justice.

We sailed into Rio de Janeiro in February and the famous Mardi Gras carnival was fully into stride. Rio de Janeiro is a port that sailors never forget. The women are beautiful and the seasides where I had ventured as a child seemed like backwaters compared to the golden sands of the Copacabana. We 'buckos' (ordinary seamen) rushed ashore after work to experience the beat of the carnival. Our eyes had never seen such grandeur. Everyone looked drunk to me, but it was the beat of the samba that caused the mass to sway. The beautiful ladies who zeroed in on us with swinging hips and come-hither looks easily impressed us three seventeen-year-olds. Blimey, the females were not so free and easy in the Juniper Berry as they were here! The provocative movement of her body against mine was a promise of things to come. I couldn't understand a word she was saying but who needed to talk when body language said all?

My dreams were shattered by my shipmate's screech of "She's got a fucking cock!" He was pointing his finger at the dusky 'lady'. She looked like a lady to me! Giggles spread on the faces of 'her' mates. It took a while for the penny to drop. We had been picked up by bloody drag queens! At least they looked more like women than the variety we had aboard the ship.

The moral to this story is, don't be keen to stick your hand in a cookie jar since you might not get the variety of cookie you expected. I wondered if this meant I would have to ask each lady to cough before going into a passionate embrace.

It was disappointing, since we thought we were in for a night of passion, and it was an adventure that would haunt the three of us for the rest of the trip, since nothing is secret on a ship. The story grew, as each and every would-be comedian had a different version of the event, and we were not allowed to forget it. Even old Nobby's interest was stirred when I related the events, much to his amusement.

Drag queens were a common sight aboard many vessels. They were usually to be found in the catering section as first class stewards (or 'wingers'). In the 1950s and '60s the world was intolerant of the gay community. Discrimination against minorities was just as it was in the era of Oscar Wilde. Seamen, I believe, were far more modern thinking, and we took these things in our stride. Crews lived together for weeks or months at a time, and we had no choice of who we would be stuck with during a voyage.

Most seamen had no problem with gays, though a few showed their bigotry by saying that the moral fabric of the world would be torn asunder. They would prescribe all manner of purgatory that queers should suffer, including being thrown over the ship's side.

As the saying goes, it takes two to tango, and that was okay if that was your preference. I had no desire to 'tango' myself, but I found them very witty, and if we took the piss we'd get a ribald retort back. You could always share a good laugh with them. On occasion, as on my trip on the *Andes*, there were talented and creative 'ladies' who could break the monotony of days at sea, putting on a cabaret show for the crew in the Pig & Whistle. In most countries today discrimination against minorities is not tolerated, but like the seamen before us, we who plied the oceans of the world 50 years ago saw no impediment to the operation of the vessel or breakdown of crew morals because we had a few queers in our midst. Who was I to judge others anyway? I have mixed with people of many different cultures, creeds and persuasions aboard vessels around the world, and my happy-go-lucky disposition gave me an open mind.

The *Andes* cruise lasted just under two months, visiting Cape Town and Las Palmas before sighting the harbour waters of Southampton in March 1958. I said goodbye to old Nobby and thought about rejoining the *Andes* for the next voyage, but my adventurous mind held sway and I decided to go to London to check out the advice my mates on the *Highland Princess* had given me. I made a point of spouting out that I had finished with Moosh land and was off to the big smoke.

Flush with my pay stuffed in my back pocket and my worldly possessions in my battered old suitcase, I rushed down the gangway with every intention of catching the next train to London. Taxis were a luxury but a seaman could indulge on pay-off day, and I shared a cab with an AB of the same mind. To change our port of engagement we needed to get a clearance from Southampton, a bit of nonsense that could have been solved by a phone call or letter instead of physically fronting up. But that was life in the 1950s. Jumping out of the cab and asking it to wait, we made our way to the counter. I casually eyed the board showing vessels and ratings needed. It was the same old fare: Castle boats, Cunarders, and the *Andes*, my home for the last two months.

"Ah, just the man we need for the *Golfito*," said the voice behind the counter.

"No, I want a clearance certificate to transfer to London. We've got a taxi waiting outside," I said impatiently.

"You almost have your time in as a JOS. We are prepared to sign you on as a senior ordinary seaman," he replied.

A SOS was five quid better off a month than my present rating and this was not to be dismissed. Required to make a quick decision, with a taxi outside, and not forgetting the confusion of my main mission, the clink of more money won the day. I told my fellow traveller who was now waiting in the cab that I had been offered a promotion if I signed on the *Golfito*.

"Elder bloody Fyffes, go for it!" he crowed. "It's a banana boat, five week trip to the West Indies. Give me love to Big Mamma in the New York Bar in Kingston."

I wasn't exactly worried about Big Mamma, but my mind was made up. Snatching my case and paying part of the cab fare, I told him I would see him in London after this trip.

Once again, unforeseen events had kept me in Southampton but this time my decision was good. Going home to Camberley would have to wait, since the *Golfito* was to sail within two days. The effects of my operation had almost disappeared during the two-month sojourn on the *Andes*, though my appendix scar still had the Pool doctor concerned. The signing of the articles had finished by the time I made my way to the chief officer's cabin. A young-looking mate with a Yorky accent perused my discharge book as I dumped my case outside.

"You went to *Warfleet*?"

I nodded. The name of your sea school was stamped in every discharge book.

"The shipping master will be on board tomorrow morning with the articles," he said.

Within four hours of paying off the *Andes*, I was aboard the *Golfito*, ready for my next trip. There was no need to book in at the Flying Tab-Nab as accommodation was available aboard. This was the first vessel I had joined without being skint.

Cocky with my sudden promotion, I lorded my senior rating over my two cabin-mates, lowly junior ordinary seamen. I grabbed the single bunk while they argued who would sleep top or bottom on the double.

Tim the bosun was a Londoner, and recognising my Cockney accent, thought it great another Londoner was aboard. I learnt more seamanship from him than any other bosun I encountered. Tim was what we termed a 'super sailor'. He would make fancy knots that had us mesmerised.

"You kids wanna learn what I'm showing you," he would say. In the foc's'le head we would follow every instruction, from the most basic of hitches such as the bowline and reef knots to more exotic artworks such as monkey fists and Turks heads. I learnt the value of the fid, an ingenious wooden tool from the 17th century, which came in various sizes depending on the gauge of the rope to be spliced. Wire splicing was more difficult, with an iron marlin spike used to separate the wire strands to make a tuck. I was to learn the Liverpool wire splice, which was the most common.

The *Golfito* was an 8700-ton fruit-carrying passenger vessel owned by Elder Fyffes, a subsidiary of the Elder Dempster Line of Liverpool. Built in 1949 in Scotland for the fruit trade between the UK and West Indies, she had a service speed of 17 knots and could carry over a hundred passengers. Her tall funnel, three-quarters buff with black topping, seemed too large and looked oddly out of balance with the lines of the vessel. Maybe it was because I found myself for the first time swinging on a bosun's chair soojeying the funnel.

Bananas and sugar were the main commodities exported from Jamaica to world markets. Kingston was like any other port for seamen. In this case, a sample of the lethal local cane rum and the women helped to empty our pockets as we staggered from one girly bar to another. I later learnt the history and the brand name behind a bottle of Captain Morgan rum.

Captain Sir Henry Morgan was a 17th-century privateer who was the scourge of Spanish and French shipping and who later became Governor of Jamaica. Britain chose to ignore his piracy since he brought wealth to the royal coffers by raiding shipping and sacking towns around the Caribbean. His most audacious feat was the sacking of Panama. However romantic the adventurous life of piracy sounded, his crews were said to be cruel and vicious and some buccaneers may not have lived long enough to enjoy their plunder. The pirate's legacy is visible in the form of forts, which are dotted throughout the Caribbean.

The *Golfito* had a set timetable from Southampton to Kingston. With two weeks at sea each way and five days in port, I idled away time in the tropics improving my seamanship. My first trip to the West Indies was a feast to the eyes and ears. Like the kids of today, music played a big part in our lives. Rock and roll and skiffle groups topped the music world, and then there was calypso, made famous by Harry Belafonte. His huge hits, the 'Banana boat song' and 'Island in the Sun' put Jamaica on the world stage. Black men ashore with dreadlocks had me gaping; I would never have guessed that in a few years long hair would not be the exclusive domain of women, but men also. The dreadlocked men were Rastafarians, who were to become prominent through the pop idol, Bob Marley.

Britain's advertising boards were flooded with Elder Fyffes' adverts. "Unzip a banana!" was one; there was also the more famous, "Have you had your Fyffes today?" On the bulk head in the crew's mess was yet another advert — "Men are like bananas, the older they get, the less firm they are." But the *Golfito* stood firm, plying her trade until going to the breakers in 1971.

England's spring felt like the North Pole after the West Indian weather we'd had for the last few weeks. I was back in Southampton in April after my first trip as

The *Golfito* — a banana boat, with hairy-legged stowaways.
VH Young

senior ordinary seaman. Another trip was tempting, as there was a lot of overtime we could work, boosting our wages substantially. Subs drawn against wages in Kingston had depleted the nest-egg I had accumulated on my way out. I worked every bit of overtime offered on the homeward journey and amazed myself by reaping the largest pay-off I had earned thus far. I turned the offer of another trip down so I could do what I meant to do when I paid off the *Andes* — get clearance from Southampton to ship out from London.

Procrastination was a state my happy-go-lucky youth seemed afflicted with. I never managed to get to the Pool, let alone the railway to London. In a taxi into Southampton with two other seamen, intending to be dropped off at the Pool, we decided first to have a drink in the Juniper Berry. It was around midday and the archaic pub hours that Britain kept meant we had only a couple of hours before closing time. I reasoned I could go to the Pool and get my clearance, then jump on the train to London. As all well-versed seadogs know, nothing ever goes to plan on pay-off day, especially if a watering hole is involved. As I quaffed my lager my reasoning began to waver. I could have a night in the Flying Tab-Nab and make good my plans in the morning. On closing time we all agreed to meeting at the Juniper when it re-opened again that evening.

Booked in at the Seamen's Mission, I decided to change my teddy boy image and buy a pair of wrangler jeans and a denim jacket. I had noted that most of my fellow shipmates couldn't give two hoots about keeping up with the latest fashions and denim was the only outfit they knew. Discarding my teddy boy gear, I presented myself at the appointed time at the Juniper wearing my latest acquisition. We all knew that chatting up birds became easier after slurping a few ales. Shy youngsters, normally tongue-tied in the presence of the fair sex, begin

The *Cape Town Castle*, I must have been a glutton for punishment, off to the Cape again.
VH Young

spouting lines to impress the ladies. I had come a long way in eighteen months and had tales to tell of far-off lands.

Trying to sneak a woman into the Flying Tab-Nab was doomed to fail, but when you're two parts to the wind you don't take that into consideration. The nightwatchman on the door, probably a retired seaman, was not impressed with this randy youngster. The altercation was solved by the lady herself deciding we could go to her abode, which required a taxi.

I never did get the name of the suburb where my night of frolicking ended. I came back to reality after having the life shaken out of me. She was holding my clothes and I gathered that this panic-stricken woman wanted me out of her house pronto. My brain not yet in full working capacity, I uttered the unforgivable, "Are you her mum?" Well, if looks could kill! My clothes were thrown at me, and I assumed I was no longer welcome. Her old man must have been on night shift.

How many times have we seadogs found truth in the adage, beauty is in the eye of the beholder, until the next morning, when a bleary eye focuses on the lady that was the object of our desire? You would always tell our shipmates in the mess the next day about the gorgeous bird you spent the night with, even if you had seen a better head on a pint of beer. But then none of us were exactly oil paintings ourselves.

Public transport was running and I found the middle of the city in no time. It was still early morning and my first stop would be the Pool for a clearance. Trains run to London all the time, I figured, so I had it all worked out when I arrived back in my room at the Flying Tab-Nab. Waiting outside the Pool that morning was a cabin-mate of mine from the *Carnarvon Castle*. He was still a JOS and I told him the story of my promotion to SOS. He said the *Cape Town Castle* was signing on and he hoped for a job on it. I wish I had not met him, because my plans yet again went haywire and I found myself signing the articles for another six-week trip to the Cape and back.

Bob was a fellow Cockney and said it was going to be his last trip from Southampton, so why didn't we both do this trip and then piss off to the big smoke? It was a lame excuse for yet again delaying my transfer to London, but Bobby's plan sounded great and we sailed a couple of days later.

Once again I was on a watch and Finlay, the bosun's mate in charge of the watch was a Scotch git I could not get along with. He hailed from Barra, one of the Outer Hebrides off the northern Scottish coast. They were hard taskmasters, but very good seamen. The Western Islanders loved a drop of Johnny Ski, causing them to burst out in Gaelic shanties that only they could understand — the rest of us in cabins nearby would plug our ears. It was certainly not top of the pops material. I had the pleasure of sailing with many of the Western Isles clan during my time in the merchant navy, but there were one or two whose sense of humour was non-existent.

The same archaic system of weekly rations, unique to Union Castle Line, of conny onny, sugar, tea and eating utensils existed on the *Cape Town Castle*; I'm sure no other shipping company required employees to keep victuals in their cabins. As the senior seaman in the cabin of four I suggested that I look after the rations and draw them each week. This was agreed to after Bob and I related the troubles we had on the *Carnarvon*. I made sure that the victuals were stowed away so they couldn't roll off the table in bad weather. The fighting irons were up to each of us to keep in our own drawers and you were not to nick anyone else's if you mislaid or forgot to take them with you after meals.

The *Cape Town Castle* weighed in at 27,000 tons, with the sleek elegant lines of her sister ships. Built by Harland & Wolff, she had her maiden voyage in 1938 and could carry 250 first class and 550 tourist class passengers. During the war she was commissioned a troop ship and refitted in 1946 to resume commercial service.

The voyage of six weeks was to travel to the same ports as the *Carnarvon Castle*. If I had any self-esteem I should have asked myself why I would bother to expose myself again to the humiliation of racial discrimination, but seventeen-year-olds are rarely discerning and the freedom to jump on a ship and venture anywhere in the world was exhilarating.

It was probably the first time I began to show a sense of responsibility. I found that I was the one the bosun would target if any of my cabin-mates got into mischief. "You tell that cabin-mate of yours to turn-to on time or else!"

As usual, our first port for bunkers was Las Palmas. The scar on my stomach would always be a reminder of this Iberian outpost. Then on to Cape Town, where I once again tried to ignore the colour bar. We were happily seated in Delmonico's, when the waiter came back with only two beers instead of the three we had ordered. It was a subtle way of telling me I was not welcome. Seamen always stick up for each other, and it was no different in this case. Bob passed his beer to me and told the waiter that we had asked for three beers. No sooner had the glass got to my lips than a huge Afrikaaner bouncer appeared at my table. You don't argue with the likes of these guys. They have been brought up with the myth that their white skins are superior to someone with a different tint. Had I been older, I might have felt embarrassed at the eyes watching me as I was escorted out. Instead it was a game to me and I walked into the next watering hole and was served with no hint of discrimination. Bob came out in sympathy with me as I got the heave-ho from Delmonico's. On getting our second round the barman asked me if I was European.

I said, "Yes, I was born in Europe, where were you born?"

He said he was born in South Africa.

I said, "That makes you the non-European and me the European."

That was my last drink in that bar! On the South African coast, my dusky hue got up the noses of those who thought they were the superior race.

It beats me why I ever bothered to jump on any vessel going to the Cape after my first experience. I did not need to suffer under the laws that sad country inflicted on those who could not blush. I remember walking out of that bar with Bob calling the Yarpies choice names and me berating my stupidness in putting myself in the position to be humiliated again. There were plenty more places in the world to go to than this hole. He made the point that sailing from Southampton, nine out of ten ships would be going down the Cape.

The following day I made it my business to annoy the white shore tradesmen, giving their black labour grub out of the mess at meal times. I was reported by one of these shore workers to the bosun, who ordered me to stop. I told him to get fucked, as this was British territory and there was no colour bar here. The rebel in me had awakened and the look on the bosun's dial was one of shock at my retort. He promised to report me to the mate, but he had no answer to my statement.

Some crew members who ran to the Cape permanently had been brainwashed by apartheid and seemed to forget that the vessel was not a part of the regime ashore. When I was reported I took this reasoning to the mate. But he was one of the crew members I have just described, and was married to a South African. I got no change there. He insisted that I was interfering with the running of the vessel while in port. Giving coloured folk a cup of tea and a sandwich was going to bring the cargo operations to a halt.

When questions become difficult, pulling rank is an easier way to solve the dilemma. And that is what he did, warning me that if he heard another peep out of me I would be heading for a bad discharge. Ideals have their place, and the warning was enough to simmer down the rebel within me. Fuck Southampton and their poxy Castle boats, I sounded out in the safety of our cabin.

I kept my counsel as we made our way round the coast, which was amazing even to me. It had consolidated my intention to move to London as soon as I got off the tub. Channel night arrived and the bosun informed me my services were not required next trip. I gladly replied he could stick his ship and Union Castle up his arse.

To my surprise, my discharge book still showed two VGs. I happily walked off that vessel. There was no procrastination on this occasion and as I jumped into the cab with Bobby the thought of finally going home to see my foster parents after two years of non-contact struck me again.

We stopped at the Pool to get that all-important clearance. We were given a commentary by the official behind the desk, of a trip to paradise in the West Indies on a banana boat looking for a couple of ordinary seamen.

I quickly retorted, "Why, have you been there?"

That stopped him in his tracks. Clutching our clearances, we took a taxi to the railway station and my last view of Southampton was the tall liner funnels towering above the cargo sheds. It was the end of a nautical era. I had no idea, gazing out of the taxi window, that I was witnessing the last chapter to these fine vessels that had graced the Atlantic, carrying rich and famous and penniless mortals alike for the previous 80 years. In a short time these elegant ladies of the sea were to be replaced by aeroplanes. The economic realities of sea travel were to spell the end for the sea-going fraternity and the ships we took pride in. No one can take the memories from those of us who experienced the privilege of living and working aboard these grand ladies. Only when they were consigned to history did we realise we were part of a nautical dream.

The *Cape Town Castle* became news in 1960 when a compressor in the engineroom exploded, killing seven people, and hit the headlines again in 1965 when there was a report of gold ingots to the value of $100,000 missing from the bullion room. They were found cemented in one of the holds on the following trip and two crew members were subsequently jailed for theft. In 1967 she arrived in La Spezia for breaking up.

nine

A s the train pulled out of Southampton I reflected on my two years of sea life. Passenger liners were the main employer for seamen shipping out of Southampton. They went to a lot of trouble to impress their passengers — too much for this free spirit. If I had wanted to be regimented I could have joined the military. So it was that this happy-go-lucky soul set off to London on a new adventure.

Bob's parents lived in a council house in Bow, and his mother cried as she welcomed her son home. I felt guilty as she hugged him. What was I doing here when I should be making my own way home to Camberley, only a train ride away? A bed was made up on the couch for me in the front room and, like all caring sons, Bob took his mum and dad down the local for a night of knees-up.

Next morning we hopped on the tube to Plaistow and caught the No. 69 double-decker to Custom House. Our destination was the shipping federation in the King George V Dock (known as KG5 Pool). KG5 was one of two shipping federations in London where seamen could go for work; the other was in Aldgate East. Turn right as you come out the tube station and walk to the bottom of Leman Street, turn left at the horse trough and you were on Dock Street. This pool (later renamed Prescott Street Pool) offered what I used to call 'mystery trips'. You could bet your life that signing on a vessel from Dock Street was a ticket to unknown destinations on a tramp ship that brought you home to Blighty two years later.

But wasn't that the fun of going to sea? It suited me, as I had no family ties, nor was I married. In the messrooms of the great passenger liners we had listened to yarns from seamen who had sailed out of KG5 on the Shaw Savill plying the Australia and New Zealand route, and the Royal Mail shipping lines that went to the west coast of the States, and the famous Blue Star Line which covered the South American trade, with a huge blue star funnel logo that anyone could spot away on the horizon.

My first introduction to Custom House was the throng of dockers in their cheese-cutter caps going about their business. The cacophony of ships' horns and cargo cranes told us we had arrived at the Royal Docks.

This area of London is known today as Docklands, but was Custom House to all who sailed from there. After all, many of us seadogs spent what would seem

The Custom House Mission to Seamen, also known as Stornaway Castle and the Flying Tab-Nab.

a lifetime running around the Royal Docks, joining vessels and negotiating the various locks. And who of us KG5 mariners could forget the Steps and the Roundhouse and Kent Arms, to name a few of the pubs. We can thank our lucky stars that walls cannot talk. These watering holes were household names to the sea-going fraternity and all have stories to tell. I decided I would spend some time researching the history of the port of London on my 1995 visit to the UK. It was this haven, as only seamen could appreciate, that gave so many of us the memories we hold today.

The port goes back to the Roman era of around 50 AD, but it really got started during the Tudor reign when London became the centre of trade and commerce. Elizabeth I set up twenty 'Legal Quays' between London Bridge and the Tower of London where goods could be landed and governed by appointed customs men. Between the 15th and 18th centuries, ships went from a mere 50 tons to hundreds of tons, and international trade grew proportionately. The 600 mooring piers were not enough for the 1400 vessels that waited to deposit their cargoes. City merchants answered the shortfall by building the West India Docks in 1806, and the East India Dock followed in 1828. St Katharine Docks were commissioned and had cost £2 million by their opening in 1830.

The first of the Royal Docks was the Victoria Dock opened in 1855, followed by the Albert Dock, opened in 1880. In 1921 the King George V Dock was completed with all three docks connecting. A lock was built because the entrance from the Thames into the Victoria Dock was 14 metres below London Bridge and about 40 metres above the pilot station at Gravesend. The Royal Docks estate covered 450 hectares. Road access, rail connections, ships' berths, warehouses and dock offices were all duly added. A dry-dock was built in the George V Dock. During World War II the Germans meted out special attention to areas of commerce on their bombing raids and dockyards around the British coast came under nightly attack.

Post-war, the golden era of shipping began. The port of London became an international hub, rivalling Rotterdam and Antwerp.

It was into this melting-pot of trade and tradesmen that Bob and I alighted from the bus on Freemasons Road. Bob knew his way around and as we turned the corner onto Victoria Dock Road I noted Custom House station on the opposite side of the road and the eye-catching brick building that dominated the skyline ahead. The Flying Angel in Custom House offered bed and victualling, but there were no licensed facilities on the premises. She was dubbed 'Stornaway Castle' after the many mariners from the Western Isles who patronised the place.

Most patrons who graced the Castle would remember the overseer nicknamed the 'Iron Lady'. Mrs Harvey was a strict administrator, and of course she had to be. Woe betide any seadog sneaking alcohol or a woman up the stairs to their room. She was a relic from the Victorian era, very prim. I often wondered why she ever took on the task of administrating an unruly bunch of seamen. What would we have done without these level-headed people such as Mrs Harvey, who saw to our comforts after a long voyage?

Mrs Harvey's stern eyes followed Bob and me going into the café for a cuppa before we made our way to the Pool. She probably knew we were not booked in. The Mission café offered a cooked breakfast at reasonable price and it was the venue for meeting with others who were going to the Pool.

The Steps, next door to the Mission to Seamen in Custom House.
Fall out of your bunk in the Mission and step in for a livener!

Leaving our bags at the Flying Tab-Nab, we set off to the KG5 Pool. It was a walk with distinctive features that are not there today. We tagged along with a few other lads looking for a job. On one side of the road was the railway line to North Woolwich. Halfway down the Vic Road we came to a landmark on the corner of the Victoria Dock Road and Prince Regent Lane: Gregory's Army & Navy Store, which became one of my favourite shops. I must have laid out hundreds of quid buying up denim suits and heavy weather gear. Mr Gregory was a kind old gentleman, but he had the gift of the gab and you would often find yourself forking out another few quid for an article. I got to know him well and he was always interested in what ship I was on and where it was going. Unfortunately, this harmless old man was later robbed, and the villains, not satisfied with ransacking his shop, murdered him.

The Royal Albert Seamen's Hospital was just around the corner. Though I had no reason to visit its facilities, some seamen did after a 'red light' fling. There was a ditty that went like this: 'He squeezed and he squozed until a bubble arose, the size of a regulation football.' Off to the doctors the unlucky Romeo would trot. Venereal disease was a common malady among sailors, given the many attractions around the globe.

The Thames wasn't your ideal waterway for a swim. All manner of nasties clogged this river. If you fell in the Thames in the '60s you would be whizzed off to the Royal Albert for a stomach pump.

Carrying on to the end of the Victoria Dock road, we turned right onto Connaught, a main entrance to the Royal Docks. On our left was the entrance to the Royal Albert Dock. New Zealand Shipping Company vessels docked here, and also had a crew office run by the officious Mr Moxley.

Just across the railway lines was the Connaught Arms. It was a monument then, and I was happy to learn in 1995 that it had been deemed an historic building and was preserved, although the Edwardian brick toilet in front of the pub was not saved. Next to the Connaught was a dockers' canteen decked out with long tables and benches. The aroma wafting from this place was a strong inducement for a hungry sailor on his way to the Pool. I found it difficult to go past the canteen without wolfing down a bun filled with a greasy sausage and onions and a mug of hot sweet tea. The calorie intake would have given health conscious folk a heart attack.

A National Union of Seamen branch office was next to the canteen. I was to be a frequent visitor to the NUS and I have some cynical memories of those who were elected as our advocates to safeguard our wages and conditions from aggressive shipowners. When I transferred to KG5 Pool after a couple of years' sea service I began questioning why union fees were being deducted from my wages after each voyage. Who were these faceless union bosses we were keeping in clover, whom most of the rank-and-file never saw? There are seamen who went through their careers happily paying their fees, but without any interest or input to their union. That was their prerogative.

Further along Connaught Road we came to the swing bridge that separated Victoria Dock from the Albert and King George. Just past the bridge was the KG5 dock gate manned by a copper. The object of our trek lay just inside the gates. KG5 Pool could have been any of the brick buildings that were dotted around, were it not for the throng of denim-clothed seamen who congregated outside.

There were a number of ships listed on the board and among them was the *Highland Monarch,* a sister ship to the *Highland Princess* I was sent home on from the Canary Islands. Unfortunately it was calling for two JOSs and as I scanned the list further I noted SOSs wanted on the *Gothic,* the Shaw Savill liner famed for carrying the Queen and Duke of Edinburgh down-under in 1953.

Another passenger ship? No thanks. I didn't fancy the Australian or New Zealand run because I was told it was no different from our own country. Why go halfway around the world just to experience a copy of our own land? Bob pointed out two jobs on the *Beaverburn,* sailing the following day. Our papers were in order and the delight of the shipping clerk in filling his quota was evident. After passing the medical we were each given a Pool chit that showed the mate our presence aboard was authorised by the shipping federation.

I had no idea what type of vessel we were joining, let alone the company. The *Beaverburn* was docked in Victoria Dock, and the easiest way there was the railway bridge spanning Custom House Station. I was glad that I was with someone who knew his way around. Apparently we were on our way to Canada, compliments of Canadian Pacific Railways (CPR). The *Beaverburn* was clearly identifiable with its red and white chequered house flag emblazoned on the tall yellow funnel, but

The *Beaverburn.* What a work-up on deck this vessel was — thirty-two derricks!
VH Young

it was the forest of derricks that caught my eyes. I was looking at my first cargo vessel and some real seamanship. The mate seemed relieved that the pool had found two OSs, making us sign on immediately lest we change our minds. We were told to be aboard and ready for turn-to at 8am next day. It gave me a chance to visit Gregory's Army & Navy Store to buy a denim jeans and jacket suit, and a belt with a large removable buckle with a horse welded on it. I still have the buckle, but it's becoming a fossil like its owner — it is 46 years old. They made things to last in them days.

The 9800-ton *Beaverburn* rolled down the stocks in 1944. She was immediately commissioned for war duties by the government and named the *Empire Captain*. After decommissioning in 1946 she rejoined CPR as the *Beaverburn*. In 1960 she was sold to the Ben Line and renamed the *Bennachie*.

The crowd was a mix of Cockneys and Scouses. *Beaver* boats were heavy on deck, with some vessels featuring 32 derricks and a couple of jumbo derricks for good measure. My first attempt at stowing the gear was mind-boggling. I had topped and lowered the few derricks on the *Golfito*, but she was a six-hatch ship with eighteen derricks. It was certainly a baptism in the art of preparing a ship for sea. By the time I walked off the *Beaverburn* a few weeks later Bob and I were experts on every part of a derrick, its heel and head blocks and the running parts. We could well afford to take the piss out of those passenger boat men. I don't think there would be a seafarer who can say he felt confident on first hearing the bosun's call of "Clew up number three hatch!"

Our destination was Quebec and Montreal with general cargo, and a return to Liverpool with huge rolls of paper. The western Atlantic is wild in any season, and we had to batten down on the ten-day crossing to the St Lawrence. On this particular trip the western, in the spirit of summer time, showed its gentler side. My old duffel coat came in handy at night on lookout — icebergs were the danger as we neared Canada.

The St Lawrence is the only tidal river that freezes up during the winter, putting its three main ports — Trois-Rivières, Quebec and Montreal — out of operation. Canadian Pacific rerouted their vessels to St Johns, New Brunswick, but this state of affairs had to change if Canada was to compete in modern global trade. The use of ice-breakers and the opening of the St Lawrence Seaway in 1959 gave access through the Welland canal to the Great Lakes and the American market.

My first impression of Quebec was its old buildings and its roofs green with age. This was a bi-cultural society with two languages, French and English. Wasn't this the land of the famous Iroquois Indians and General Wolfe who defeated the Marquis de Montcalm just down the way at Abraham's Height in the 18th century? It seemed that over 200 years later the French were still peeved at Wolfe's audacity.

There was an arrogance in the French Canadians. If you spoke English to them you were noticeably ignored. However, they seemed to have an affinity with the English brand names of cigarettes such as State Express and Senior Service, which the dockworkers preferred to the smelly old Gaulois fags.

Bob and I got a real knock-back when we showed our youthful faces in a bar. Underage drinking was taken seriously and if you didn't look 100 years old you were refused service. One of the ABs was also refused and had to show his ID to prove he was well into his twenties. That was fine with us since we found a milkbar full of bobbysoxers of high school age and far better looking than the old fogies in the pubs.

Little Richard's hit 'Good Golly Miss Molly' was blaring out and his beat was enough to get you going even on a milkshake. Jukeboxes were like the pokie machines of today, you kept putting money in, but at least you were certain of music.

We never had any luck enticing any of the local beauties, even after our mammoth effort trying to impress with a huge dollop of bravado. Next night we fronted up again to the milkbar, hoping to score. One girl took a shine to me, but Bob was rather unkind about her, and I had second thoughts myself. The only way I could get rid of her was to refuse buying her a milkshake. That was the old Cockney Jew coming out in me, but it worked.

At Montreal, about 240km upstream, I fell in love — the state of the heart where you are captivated by the girl of your dreams, logical thinking is replaced by daydreaming and sensible decisions are scorned.

Bob and I set off ashore, our mission to buy the best denim jeans in the world, Cowboy Kings, which had thicker denim and were far superior to Wranglers and Levi's. I asked the stunning shop girl where her favourite milkbar was in this dump. Taking offence at my description of Montreal as a dump she gave me a right old earbashing in support of her city. Boy, she was a mouth and trousers, and we cleared off pronto.

Expecting to be turfed out of the noted seamen's pub, Joe Beef's, we were surprised to find that there was no such order. I was amused at the Canadian custom of flavouring their beer with salt! Bob and I felt chuffed to beat the age barrier and we sampled the Molson lager like two kids with a treat.

"When you've drunk that, you kids go and find a milkbar."

It seemed we had not fooled anyone. With heavy hearts and a burp of Molson's we took heed of the barman's command, to the amusement of fellow shipmates. We quit the pub and set off to find the milkbar described to us by the shop girl.

Bob and I soon forgot the humiliation of the pub. The milkbar was crowded and there were plenty of girls to please our eyes. As we settled into our mint juleps, an arm snaked its way round mine and a voice asked what I thought of the dump. It was the girl from the shop. No one could have been more surprised than me, but I was to learn this was part of her personality. I will abridge this moment of my life, which could well fill a chapter.

Adrienne was two months older than me, and would turn 18 in October. She was French Canadian, with brown eyes and long black hair. When I saw her in the shop that day she was enough to make a lowly ordinary seaman dream things that would probably never eventuate. She certainly seemed well above our station. She attended university and was studying economics and other academic arts that had no meaning to me. No wonder she could deliver a broadside with such ferocity.

Adrienne was my first love. I have no idea what I had to attract this young lady, but there was chemistry. When we arrived at their mansion, her father made it plain I was not good enough for his daughter. They argued in French before he left the room screeching words I could not understand. Adrienne said she was not to bring me home again, and should she insist on seeing me her father would withdraw her income. I suggested I should go, but in defiance she kept me on the couch with her until the early morning. I thought it prudent to make an early exit, so as not to antagonise her dad any further. I was on cloud nine as the taxi wound its way back to the port. Bob was eager to hear the outcome. "Did yer score?"

Many seamen depart ports wearing their hearts on their sleeves. I was afflicted by the love-sick blues as we departed Montreal, much to the amusement of the mess. I had promised her a swift return and letters of love.

The weather on the run to Liverpool was the opposite of our outward-bound trip. The western had become an angry ocean and we were battened down until we reached the Irish Sea. Channel night was celebrated with gusto and arrival in Liverpool the following morning saw many of us still two parts to the weather. Adrienne had been busy with the pen and there were two letters awaiting me. Unfortunately I had not put my thoughts to paper yet.

Arrival in Liverpool saw the Scotland Road tailors aboard with their samples of cloth for making suits. They were amazing guys. One of the best suits I ever owned was made overnight there. An Italian 'bum freezer' short jacket and high lapels (after the Beatles' style) was made overnight and came aboard for me to wear down to London the next morning, complemented with a pair of outrageous pointed Italian shoes.

My head was still full of Adrienne and I had a mission in my mind to join the first ship going to Montreal when we got back down to London. Bob decided I was a nutcase and reckoned his next trip was going to be Australia and New Zealand. Such was the banter as we waited for the CPR paymasters and Board of Trade officials to arrive. Pay-off always reminded me of a conveyor belt. We would line up, collect our wages, then move along to the shipping master, sign off articles and collect our discharge books. Last was an official from the National Union of Seamen (NUS). There were union fees to be paid and he was there to make sure we were financially up to date by stamping our union books before we joined our next vessel.

As I collected my wages and signed off, I fronted up to the NUS official to pay the arrears in fees. "We are collecting a five shilling donation for Tom Yates's daughter's wedding present," he said.

Attached to my fees was a five bob wedding donation, which felt more like a levy than a donation. I could feel my outrage and my mouth spewed forth expletives, turning white-collar heads as well as everyone else's in the room.

"Fuck Yates, we never see him and I don't know his daughter!" I said.

The stunned NUS official was obviously taken aback and could only reply that every member was donating.

"Yates earns far more money than me and he ain't getting any of my money!" I retorted.

I paid the union fees I owed and pocketed the five bob. I surprised myself and though it was a trivial challenge to the union, I class this event as my first involvement in the body supposedly looking after our conditions and wages. No one minds donating to a worthy cause, but it must be the individual's choice. I had nothing against Tom Yates or his daughter, but she and her upcoming wedding meant nothing to me.

The official said he would be reporting this to London. My mouth ran away with me and I said I would tell Yates myself to stop cadging off hard-working union members. The explanation was that a motion for a voluntary donation had been struck, but some officials were exceeding the agreed motion by making it compulsory.

Yates was the boss of the National Union of Seamen in 1958. He and his cronies worked in Maritime House, Clapham. He was a faceless union leader that we in the rank-and-file only knew by name. But isn't that true of many union leaders, even today, who look down on their members with an imperious air. Still, the feelings I had towards the NUS during my maturing years at sea became more positive, especially with NUS officials in the Royal Dock branch. Sam McCluskey who died in 1995, God bless his soul, was the catering advocate. My good friend Roger Wilkins, who enjoyed puffing on the end of his pipe, guaranteed you a face full of smoke, but saved my bacon a couple of times. I attended union meetings in the port of London, which sadly attracted an average of ten members from 20,000 in the London branch. I was to support Paddy Neary's reform movement, which threatened to split the union in 1960. Bill Hogarth led the seamen's strike in 1966 as NUS president, an event I was part of. My affinity for the NUS and later the New Zealand Seafarers' Union (NZSU) was an important part of my sea-going career.

My refusal to donate was supported by one or two but the majority of members — including my mate Bob — handed over their five shillings, lemming-like.

The four-hour journey from Liverpool to London is a tale on its own if you can remember it. Many seamen boarded the train in Liverpool with all their faculties, but arrived in London in an inebriated haze, having to be helped off the train with an "Oh, where's me gear?" Of course our antics did not go down well with the travelling public — they must have thought us an unruly rabble.

On the way to London I had decided to go home. Lugging my case to Camberley was a forlorn exercise. No one was there. It was a Saturday so they could have been anywhere. My impetuous nature led me to jump back on the train and get myself down to Custom House and book into the Stornaway Castle. The telephone had been in vogue for decades, but it never occurred to my numbskull brain to use it. I left a note telling of my presence at Chapel Pines and caught the bus to Camberley Station, arriving in late afternoon in Custom House pretty knackered. I was to meet Bob on Monday morning to see what was in the offing at the Pool. In the meantime I was going to acquaint myself with the watering holes around the Royal Docks.

ten

THE ROYAL DOCKS WERE A part of London that had their own unique spirit. There was no other place that came close to the character of this corner of London. It supported thousands of tradesmen and dockers and the add-on industries that keep the centre of commerce going. Into this rare atmosphere were added the 'lodgers', seamen of all shapes and sizes, creeds and colours. Their focus was the many vessels that offered employment to exotic destinations around the globe. Leisure time for the seafaring fraternity was not spent musing around museums or having tea and cucumber sandwiches with the local padre. So it is important I recount the memorable pubs from Canning Town to North Woolwich and Custom House that were frequented by seafarers in the heydays of the '50s and '60s. One of them was to become famous, making the West End of London green with envy.

Slap next door to the Stornaway Castle were the 'Spanish Steps'. God knows where the 'Spanish' part of the name came in, but seafarers knew it as the Steps. They answered the prayers of those needing a livener after a hard night, as they could just fall out of their bunks and stagger into the Steps on opening time.

The bar stretched the full length of a house and was separated halfway along by steps leading to the upper part of the bar. At lunchtime seamen met for a chinwag, but there was less life in the Steps at night. The real life was over North Woolwich where a number of public houses suffered the bulk of seafarer patronage.

On my arrival in 1958 the Roundhouse pub seemed to be the flavour of the time. Many a seaman has had a last quaff of Charringtons in the Roundhouse on Manor Way before departing for faraway places. You could walk to this pub while your vessel was waiting in the locks before entering the Thames.

Across the locks on the corner of Albert and Pier Roads was the Royal Standard, used by the locals. If you turned right on Pier Road and turned again right on reaching Woodman Street there was a pub called the Royal Oak, a grotty little place opposite the Wicker Gate entrance to the King George Dock. Since the Royal Oak was isolated in the back streets of council housing, I could never figure out how it became a favourite with seafarers. The Oak was so small it could hardly accommodate the patronage that it attracted.

The publicans, Danny and Rene Cousins, were a couple who we at sea could relate to. They enjoyed our company and of course there was a bonus as the tills rang profitably. Danny and Rene were astute operators and saw a future in attracting the sea-going fraternity to their ale house.

Within a year or two the legendary Kent Arms opened its doors for business. In the 1960s you could ask directions to North Woolwich, which is where the Kent stood, and you'd get a stupid look. But ask directions to the Kent and anyone could tell you. Many seamen will have memories of staggering out of the Kent Arms on closing time and walking just up the road to the fish and chip shop or in the opposite direction to the delights on offer at Stella Minge's abode. 'She' was a local transvestite who opened her home up for extended parties after closing time. She was a harmless old trannie and even had a jukebox in her lounge.

"Where did you end up last night?" Ribald banter would follow if you mentioned you woke up on the couch in the morning at Stella's.

The Kent Arms and its seafarer clientele became so well known, it was to attract film and TV celebrities and also some known villains from the underworld in its 1960s heydays.

There were other pubs such as the Three Crowns on Pier Road, and as you made your way to the Woolwich ferry, past North Woolwich Station, tucked in the corner was the Royal Pavilion with its large Courage beer sign arrayed on its roof. Canning Town had its iconic pub, the Bridge House. Patronised by the local girls, it was an obvious attraction for seamen. But even this pub was no match for the Kent Arms.

Kent Arms, 1962. Rene Cousins behind the bar, with a bunch of sailors including myself at the back, and Barry James with no teeth.

On my 1995 trek to old haunts in North Woolwich, the Kent Arms had been long demolished. Just round the corner on Pier Road I came across the once proud Three Crowns boarded up, still in its faded green décor. It was a beacon of yesteryear and a sad reminder that time had moved on.

I have no problem in devoting a chapter to a nostalgic walk back in time, which touches on names many seafarers and locals can relate to. Many of these old watering holes around the Royal Docks were built in the 19th century and there is nothing today that can surpass their charm. They were part and parcel of an era, the 'swinging '60s', that I was lucky to experience.

Service medal — this gong was given to seamen who served at least three years in the merchant navy before conscription ended in 1960.

eleven

Bob ARRIVED IN THE STORNAWAY Castle cafeteria on Monday morning. I had also sussed out a good feeder in the form of a transport café just past the Freemason's pub on Victoria Dock Road where a mixed grill cost only two and sixpence.

"You still going to see that bird in Canada?" Bob asked as we scuttled off down the Pool. Adrienne was a girl not easily forgotten, and I affirmed my intention to return to Montreal as soon as I could. He had made up his mind that his next job was going to be shipping out on a vessel to New Zealand.

Arriving at the Pool I scanned the board, hoping to see a Beaver boat listed. No such luck.

"Anything going to Canada?" I enquired.

"The *Tyrone*, due to sail for North America, Australia and New Zealand," the impatient clerk said. "Do you want it or not?"

Bollocks to him, I thought, and asked what company the ship belonged to and if it was cargo or passenger.

"Look, sonny, the chief officer is over there, go and ask him. Then join the queue again."

Bob was amused at this little git's ranting. I forfeited my place in the queue and sought the information from the horse's mouth. The *Tyrone* belonged to Avenue Steam Ship Company, which named all its vessels after Irish counties. It was a cargo vessel and the first port of call was going to be Corner Brook, Newfoundland, then Montreal, the USA and New Zealand. I lined up again, but Bob said he was off down the Albert Dock to join a Port Line vessel.

The impatient clerk had been replaced by a more congenial one who confirmed the SOS job was still available and signing on would take place in the Pool with the chief mate and shipping master present. I had never signed on a vessel this way but it was made up for by not having to do the usual foot-slog around the docks. After my medical I signed on the *Tyrone* for what was meant to be a three to four-month trip. Many of us who spent time in the KG5 Pool would remember the impatient shipping master whose stateliness earned him the title of 'Reggie the Rat'. Reggie came into his element when the saga of the reform movement reared its head two years later.

Bob and I had a farewell drink in the Royal Oak that evening. Both of us were off to the antipodes and hoped we would meet up there. He was a good shipmate but it was the last I was to see of him. Years later I learnt the sad news that his love of fast motorbikes had led to his death in Australia.

The *Tyrone*, at 5852 tons, was built in 1937 for the New Zealand Shipping Company and christened the *Kaikoura*. She was transferred to the Avenue Steam Ship Company in 1954. With five hatches and twelve derricks she was a holiday after the *Beaverburn*. She had a red funnel with black topping and the house flag emblazoned with a white background and a blue cross. In the middle of the cross was a diamond with a swan in the middle. It was known to the fraternity as the 'Hungry Goose Line'. I can attest the accuracy of that moniker.

The winches were driven by steam, a new concept for me. Though slower than electric power, the warm steam was a godsend when we were freezing our goolies off, moored in Canadian and American ports during the winters. The seamen's quarters were aft and the galley amidships. This meant the peggy had to lug the kits holding the food from the galley to our accommodation where it was put in the hot press. You can imagine what the tucker was like when the sea was temperamental! The hot press was also home to a nest of cockroaches, who somehow survived every attack we made on them. The tale of the hot press gets worse, when one of the ABs in an inebriated state mistook it for the heads. Nothing worse than having your grub peed on.

On the corner of Freemason's Rd — a favourite watering hole for the Stornaway seamen.

When the Port of London Sun tugs mosey up alongside the vessel you know your time is up and it's time to let go the mooring ropes. We sailed from Victoria Dock to Liverpool to pick up general cargo. My cabin-mate was a Dutchman named Gus. Obese and short of breath, he was probably at the end of his career. The sea had not been good for his health. Unfortunately he and I didn't see eye to eye. His personal cleanliness was appalling, and a shower was a treat. It was usual for ordinary seamen to reside in the same cabin. They must have taken one look at Gus and palmed him off on me.

I was put on a watch and Gus grabbed the day-worker position. On leaving Liverpool we headed for Corner Brook. The *Tyrone* wasn't exactly a greyhound of the ocean, plodding on at her top speed of 13 knots. It was still summer as we neared Newfoundland.

Most people who lived in Corner Brook were employed by the paper conglomerate, Bowater. It was here that we heard that we would be going on the MANZ run — Montreal–Australia–New Zealand. This meant doing a double header from North America to down under, extending our voyage from three months to almost a year. Hitherto I had thought the metaphor 'shanghaied' related to some place in China.

We had signed two-year articles, as all foreign trade ships did, and this company took the contract literally. Some cursed the company after the skipper broke the news, but I found it amusing since I had no ties. I was not popular that day.

The other OS, Ricky, the deck boy Allan and I were easily the youngest in a crew of ancient mariners. They were mainly Irishmen and Geordies, plus a couple of highlanders, all in their thirties and older. I was a few months off my eighteenth birthday with Rick eighteen already and Allan just sixteen and on his maiden voyage.

Corner Brook seemed pretty bleak. The milkbar cowboys were everywhere, as were the girls in what must have been the 'in' place. My mind was on Montreal and Adrienne. I had penned a letter of undying love in London as soon as I secured a job on the *Tyrone*. Ricky had looks that attracted girls and I watched his success in the local milkbar. The following morning he complained of getting romantic underneath the house he was taken to, when the cold night air froze his arse off.

"Serves you right," chimed in the highland fossil, wishing he were young again.

Having loaded the paper rolls for Newark and Newport News, our next port of call was Trois-Rivières. As soon as we arrived in Montreal I was on the phone to Adrienne. Apparently she had not told her parents I was due in port, so she could discount the bad feeling her liaison with me brought between her and her father. Our reunion went well for the first two nights when we crept into the spacious living room. I skulked out in the early morning hours, clutching my shoes as she called a taxi. We had it all down pat until the third night, our last in port.

We spent the evening at our favourite milkbar and then made our way to her house. There were no lights on; she thought her parents had gone to bed. We were well under way when the slam of a car door and the distinct rasp of her father's voice panicked us into a scramble for clothes.

There was no escape. The living room light went on. At once her father realised that her innocence was gone, as we held what clothing we had mustered. The look on her parents' faces was one I can well comprehend today. I was bundled out on my ear accompanied by French and English expletives, and threatened with arrest by the Mounties. The baubles she was to inherit once again came under threat.

I tried to contact Adrienne before we left Montreal but her mother seemed to own the phone. My words were silently listened to, and with no answer I was cut off. I was annoyed and my immature mutterings of 'rich bastards' won me no favour. We slid away from the wharf next morning for the States before I had regained contact. The tale of my being caught and unceremoniously heaved out of her house made me a subject of hilarity in the mess. I took their piss-taking with a pinch of salt, and retorted by suggesting at least I didn't have to use the trusty hand.

I was to learn that getting emotional about a relationship is a foolish course. I was to see Adrienne one more time before she lit out of my life. She gave me the order of the boot in a 'Dear John' letter, saying how much she loved her parents and did not want to hurt them. Her dad's threat against her inheritance had won the day. On our return trip to Montreal.I tried to renew our relationship by going straight to the lions' den, her home. She came outside and I could feel her politeness had a barb, which suggested my pauper status was an embarrassment to her. I was hard hit and wandered away from her house feeling robbed.

Later in London, having just completed the MANZ run on the *Tyrone*, I went over to the Maritime Museum in Greenwich. There was always something new to see there and I loved browsing this museum. The familiar French-Canadian twang of "Dave" sounded in my ears. Adrienne looked particularly mature and beautiful. Hanging off her arm was a bespectacled guy whom she introduced, telling him I was a seaman. I felt like telling him I was the very sailor who had dropped anchor at her house in Montreal before her dad gave me the heave-ho, but I kept my mouth shut and let her fill me in as to what she was doing in the UK. She told me she was enrolled at the London School of Economics and had been in Britain for three months. Her beau spoke with a plummy accent, which would have pleased her dad immensely.

I spoiled this meeting by opening my gob. "I hope Papa approves of him," I said.

The *Tyrone*, my first vessel to New Zealand. They said it was a three-month trip and we came home eleven months later — a shanghai job.
VH Young

She ignored my sarcasm and like the artefacts that surrounded us, our liaison was consigned to history. I have no idea how her life has treated her, but I hope it has been as rewarding as mine.

Newark was at this time the main port for New York, and the largest on the east coast. We had a consignment of paper to unload from our Canadian ports and we spent a couple of days there, before heading to Baltimore where we loaded American products for New Zealand.

Our last port of call in the States was Newport News. I was amazed to see hundreds of obsolete World War II naval vessels anchored in long lines. Each vessel was kept to a serviceable standard and could be ready for sea in a very short time. The same set-up could be seen in San Francisco, in the port of Oakland where over 400 World War II Liberty Boats were anchored and could be ready for sea within 24 hours.

We headed for the Panama Canal at 13 knots, after loading cargo in Newport News. Seamen had yarned about the Panama and Suez canals in the messrooms on other vessels, and here I was about to journey through one of them. It sounded strange to me — I had never been through the canal, so I thought the mules used to attach the ships were of the animal variety. We were due to dock for an overnight stay at Colón near the city of Cristobal.

Panama Canal connects the Atlantic and Pacific oceans across the isthmus from Cristobal on the Atlantic side to Balboa on the Pacific. The 82km were first excavated by the French before the turn of the 20th century, with many deaths from yellow fever and other diseases. Finance ran out and put a stop to the French excavations. The involvement of the United States in the building of the canal is very complicated, but it was their army engineers who completed the job in 1914. The canal zone, as it was called, came under the protectorate of the United States. It was not until 1979 that sovereignty of the canal zone was transferred to Panama.

My first impression of Colón was its humidity. The mosquitoes threatened to eat you alive. But who could forget the run ashore? An advance on our wages of £5 per man was offered to any crew member who wanted to sample the delights ashore. On my wages of £24/12/6 a month I had to watch my spending, as the currency was the American dollar, and with the exchange rate at US$2.40 to the pound, a few quid didn't go far. With spirits high we set off to explore the tropical surroundings.

It seemed that if you made it as far as the Doghouse Bar you didn't have to go any further. The rum & coke and the girls were perfect for a bunch of randy sailors. Latin ladies are very beguiling and the temptation to go upstairs with one of these perfumed beauties for $5 a romp was heavy. Of course there was an added expense of buying the lady a drink, which was twice as dear and might only be water.

I don't remember getting back to the ship, and not a dime could I find in my pockets the following morning. I was hauled back to the ship by one of the ABs who reckoned I fell off my seat. Rum & coke was a concoction that had a lethal effect on me. A post-mortem of the night's events always followed among the crowd the next morning.

"A fiddler's elbow had nothing on that arse!"

"My señorita was like a buck rabbit!"

"Hope you get a dose!" were some of the sentiments parleyed back and forth. I'm thankful that political correctness was still in its dad's bag in Baghdad in the '50s and '60s. A hangover from a night out in Colón and the sweltering heat of the morning was not a mixture that you wanted on your maiden transit through the Panama Canal.

The first locks on the Atlantic side were the Gatun Locks, which lifted vessels 25 metres above sea level into the Gatun Lake. The mules were iron mules that ran on rail lines and attached to the ship by steel hawsers. There were four mules; two up forward on either side of the bow, and two aft. They acted just like tugs, but on land. After the Gatun Lake we entered the Galliard Cut and came to the Pedro Miguel Lock, lowering us into the Miraflores Lake. We then entered the double Miraflores

Locks and ended up in the Gulf of Panama. The transit through the Canal took eight hours. It was a fascinating passage, spoiled only by the mozzies.

The first city in New Zealand we were to visit was Auckland, nearly a month away for the old plodder. When she hit bad weather her stern lifted high out of the water, exposing the screw, which meant no sleep for us. She handled bad weather all right but there was little progress on the miles sailed. The Pacific was more settled than the Atlantic and we spent the days getting in plenty of overtime, stripping the derricks down to the metal with 'scabby annies' — chipping machines. Many arguments took place between Gus and me, as he was too lazy to take off his work clothes in the changing room, and would litter the cabin floor with chippings.

There was no TV or video on board in those days. We had a small recreation room, but most of the crew favoured the messroom for a yarn. Those who had been to New Zealand before gave glowing accounts of their time on the coast. I heard tales of Maori princesses with snake hips, and all the other fantasies that invade the mind when the fair sex is thousands of miles out of reach. Yet I still pictured New Zealand as another England away in the South Seas.

The excitement went up a notch as the loom of Auckland's lights appeared on the horizon. Anchor was dropped and the pilot would be aboard in the morning for docking. There was a bridge being built that would span the Waitemata Harbour, to connect Auckland City with its North Shore neighbours. The newspaper of the day reported that scrap metal sent from New Zealand to Japan had been returned as iron girders for construction of the Auckland Harbour Bridge.

Around that time the papers reported foul murder on the vessel, *Monowai*; a cook had taken a knife to a crew member. Funnels of familiar shipping lines from the UK were visible around the wharves, notably the Blue Star funnel. I was a regular visitor to a pie-cart stationed in Queen Street. The pies were far more filling than the fare on the ship. The Ambassador pub across from the wharf was a favourite for a lunchtime session. It was patronised by seamen and wharfies, with a chequered black and white ceramic floor that was covered in sawdust to keep you from slipping on the beer-soaked deck. And the closing time of six o'clock only encouraged the guzzling of grog to beat the deadline. It seemed a more ancient system than even our pub hours at home.

But for this youngster my introduction to New Zealand erased the image I previously had. The Kiwis were an open people, and their friendliness was refreshing after the stodgy old class system of Britain. I was especially intrigued with the Maori guys, who brought new meaning into the teddy boy style. They wore red jackets with black drainpipe trousers and brothel-creeper shoes.

Ricky and I got friendly with an OS on the Shaw Savill cargo vessel *Canopic* and sauntered aboard with our carry-out of beer from the bottle store. I had never

The Teddy Boy look —
on the *Tyrone*, 1958.

seen such enormous bottles of beer, let alone the half-gallon jars carried out at closing time. Party time was after 6pm it seemed.

The *Canopic* recreation room was a mass of men and women gyrating to a local singer's version of an Elvis song, 'Lawdy Miss Clawdy'. As the beer flowed, so did our mouths, and my Cockney accent had the birds stumped.

"I thought you were Maori!" was parroted in my lughole for the umpteenth time.

"Never heard of the *Tyrone*. Is it a pommy ship?"

I was given a lecture by this bird, who told me quite firmly that she only went with English jokers. She must have thought I was putting on my born-and-bred accent. Only after confirming I was a pom did she change her mind. The *Tyrone* was two berths along and she asked if I had any drink on board. But the thought of that great heaving unwashed mass that I shared the cabin with would have put paid to any desiring thoughts I had. In the morning I was skint, what with a taxi to her flat and another back to the ship.

One could talk about the girls of the Kiwi coast all day. It was they who encouraged the majority of British seamen to make the long haul across the globe to these enchanting islands. Girls who went aboard ships were frowned upon by the locals as being loose or to some, prostituting themselves. Seamen are used to paying for the services of women in most ports around the world, and indeed have been to most of the red light districts on the continent, in South and Central America and Asia. New Zealand women who enjoyed our company never asked a penny. Free love was an obvious attraction. The accusations were myths, conjured up by miffed local guys. I don't know why the women thought poms were better than their own men.

It was the golden era in which hundreds of ships from Britain came to New Zealand shores and stayed in port for weeks at a time. The pubs closed at six, but ship bars were open until late. Not everyone had a family to go home to. Single people looked for entertainment and company to fill their evenings. People found all manner of amusement and in the ports there was no doubt that a lot of ladies enjoyed the hospitality provided by visiting seafarers and their ships. The need to seek entertainment aboard vessels declined after 1967, when the 'six o'clock swill' was abolished, and 10pm closing was legislated. We still had our bevy of belles climbing ship gangways.

Drinking and driving was not a big deal in those days and I can attest to many hairy rides where the driver was seeing double. Six o'clock closing seemed to encourage New Zealanders to rush into the pubs after finishing work at 5 and quaff as much grog as they could, then jump in their vehicles and drive home. It was of no concern to seafarers — none of us gave a thought to the sins of drink-driving.

On my final sailing from the UK in 1969, I sensed that things had changed. We knew that containerisation of cargo was about to impact on us, and it did. Conventional vessels, whose slow mode cargo operations using derricks or cranes were no match for the speedy system of containerised cargo, were eventually phased out by the shipowners. Container vessels were in and out of ports in a day, leaving no time to stretch the sea legs, or sample the delights ashore. And from the seafarer's perspective, the stay on the Kiwi coast had gone forever.

But way back in 1958, I was not thinking of events in the future, and why should I, when the present was enough. The image of Adrienne in Montreal seemed far away as I looked forward to Saturday nights jive at the Auckland Trades Hall. The place was packed and Johnny Devlin, New Zealand's answer to Elvis, set the place alight. Those Maori guys were natural rock and rollers.

Wellington is one of the most picturesque harbours in the world. I had sailed into quite a few harbours, yet to this raw youngster Port Nicholson, with its surrounding hills sprinkled with houses, left an impression of quaintness and beauty. I had been to Rio de Janeiro and gaped at Sugarloaf Mountain, topped by the statue of Christ. It was a harbour to behold. Yet to me, Wellington had its own character. It was the harbour which was to be my haven for 34 years, and my impressions have not changed.

The clatter of trams on Wellington's narrow streets seemed to fill my ears. The Waterloo became our lunchtime watering hole where we would meet guys off other home boats and, ours being a dry ship, we had to find out on what vessel the nightly knees-up would take place. Cash was low and I was forced to hock off my Cowboy King denims to keep up with the night life.

On Dixon Street there was a coffee bar called the Man Friday where coffee could become lethal. The Sorrento on Ghuznee Street and the Casa Fontana were coffee bars that could have put the real pubs out of business. They were popular meeting places to jack up women for parties. There was a house near the top of Taranaki Street (where a school stands today) which left me with some memories.

I have not forgotten the names of the ladies who lived there, and if you happen to read this book please accept my thanks for the hospitality you gave to many seafarers. I don't mean this in any way other than sincerely – I genuinely enjoyed the company.

Lyttelton was a one-horse town with about seven pubs. We youngsters gave cheek to a publican, who threatened us with a baseball bat if we didn't vacate his grotty little pub. We were well under the weather, so we made our way to the Royal Hotel, from which we were immediately barred.

On Saturday night we tried our luck in Christchurch and ended up in a jive club. They seemed to have them everywhere in New Zealand. I think it was actually called the Teenage Club — no one bothered to check that our bottles of coke were laced with Captain Morgan. The band sounded great. Some beady eyes spied our rum and we were escorted out, just as things began to liven up.

In this port on our second trip to New Zealand there was a tragedy. The *Tyrone* was moored on the opposite side of the wharf to the coaster *Holmburn*. Because of our close wharfage, crews from both ships had become drinking pals and most were ensconced up the road in the Royal. We youngsters had been barred from all drinking establishments and relegated to the only milkbar up the hill because of our behaviour. Some time during the evening the *Holmburn* caught fire. The only crew aboard were the master and chief steward. Both perished, and it was suggested that their attempted escape was thwarted because the portholes were too small to exit through. The New Zealand Ministry of Transport said that all new coastal vessels had to have portholes big enough to escape through in an emergency. Somehow that legislation was lost in time. On the Cook Strait ferries I was later to sail on, there was no way a body could fit through those portholes.

Chic's pub at the end of the wharf in Port Chalmers was handy enough for those who still had money, but I was bereft and didn't want to hock off my last pair of jeans. Our last port of call was Bluff, the southernmost port of the world. As usual it had its selection of watering holes, such as the Golden Age. Our stay in this somewhat isolated port turned out to be enjoyable for me. A car ride to Invercargill was the highlight, thanks to a couple of siblings from the Johnstone family whose friendship was to last into the early 1960s.

New Zealanders are noted for their laid-back demeanour and because they are the first to hold the hand out in friendship. My first trip to this country opened my eyes. We left New Zealand for North American ports having spent five weeks in idyllic surroundings. My trips to South Africa had made me mindful that the colour of your skin could have a detrimental effect on your place in society. The inclusiveness of all New Zealanders was very noticeable even to these young eyes. I left feeling New Zealand was a unique one-class society, and had integrated its indigenous peoples. My home country was more modern, but was steeped in traditions of privilege, which looked decidedly antiquated against New Zealand's approach to people.

When we arrived in Balboa, on the Pacific side of the Panama Canal, nearly three months had passed since we were last there. Our interest was the mail the pilot brought aboard with him — his bag held not only company business, but also letters of undying love from romances hatched on the Kiwi coast. There is nothing like receiving a missive from a wife or a girlfriend on reaching your next port. Some of these Kiwi lasses had a way with the pen and could melt the socks off an Eskimo. I was certainly naïve. A girl said she loved me and wrote the acronym 'swalk' (sealed with a loving kiss) on the envelope. The ribald warnings around the messroom from veterans of the Kiwi coast suggesting my girlfriend had probably shacked up with a Geordie off another ship the day we sailed, were soundly rejected by me. Blimey, I was thick in them days.

Our schedule included the ports of Newark and Boston. We discharged the last of our cargo in Montreal and loaded paper in Halifax, Nova Scotia and St John. We got to Montreal just before the big freeze and I was tempted to contact Adrienne, not a smart option after her missive which clearly terminated our relationship. My persistent phone calls won me no reply, and perhaps fate dealt me a hand for the better; I left Montreal none the wiser.

Halifax felt like the Arctic. My old duffle coat was no match for the zero temperatures. There was a well known clothing store by the name of Gars that sold fur lined jackets, which were more appropriate for the Canadian winter. The purchase emptied my pocket of dollars but it was well worth it when I trudged up to Monkey Island on lookout duties during those cold nights.

I was not prepared for what I was to witness across the Mason-Dixon line, the pre-Civil War demarcation that divided the southern slave states from the northern free states. The American Civil War may have been a victory for the abolition of slavery, but little else had changed. Everything was still literally seen in black and white.

My first experience was at the pilotage on arrival in Charleston. I was standing by the ladder as the pilot climbed aboard.

"Good morning, boy," said the overweight pilot as he gained the foredeck.

"Who the fuck are you calling a boy?" I snarled.

The pilot, who was obviously not used to having a 'boy' swear at him, reported my greeting on the bridge. The skipper reprimanded me for swearing, but nothing more came of it. A walk ashore soon explained the pilot's attitude. I had not studied American history or the slave trade that all the so-called civilised nations participated in during the 17th and 18th centuries. I had experienced one brand of racial intolerance in South Africa, yet here was a country that had put itself up as the leader of the free world. So what was I to make of notices that read 'Whites Only' on diners and public buildings? Even the pavements had a sign requiring coloured folk to keep to one side.

Memorabilia: an 1806 coin from the era of George III.

Our last stop on the east coast was Savannah, the main port for the state of Georgia, which became the thirteenth colony during the reign of King George III of England, hence its name. The transatlantic slave trade was at its peak and millions of Africans passed through the port of Savannah in chains on their way to serve their masters on one of the cotton or rice plantations.

Savannah's history was not on our minds as two compatriots and I boarded a bus downtown. Two of us took the last seats, leaving the third shipmate standing. We sat there innocently, waiting for the bus to move.

I was tapped on the shoulder by some guy who said I had to stand up and go to the back of the bus. The driver bellowed that he wasn't moving until I vacated my seat to the white passengers who were standing. My complexion meant I was subject to a segregation law, which required me to vacate my seat should any white commuters be standing. At first we took no notice.

A black man came up to me and offered his seat at the back of the bus, saying he would be getting off at the next stop. It was one of my own shipmates who caught on to the meaning of the bus driver's outburst.

"'E ain't a negro! We're British!"

My shipmate's Cockney accent left them in no doubt of that. All three of us got off the bus effing and blinding at the driver, and much to the delight of the coloured commuters, giving the two-finger to all and sundry as the bus pulled away.

We walked off into town and oddly enough my dusky self seated on a milkbar stool among the locals caused no hostility, but plenty of looks. My two shipmates decided it would be fun to see how far we could push the system: never mind I was the butt of their amusement. Our Cockney accents drew attention and "I just love that accent," was a common remark.

We got into trouble, making light of a system that was deeply rooted among the Savannah gentry. When you ask your hosts whether they are Ku Klux Klan members they are inclined to get testy. One guy quoted verses from the Bible and was quite adamant that it was God's will the white man should lord it over any other race. Telling him he was full of what made the garden grow was not the most diplomatic way of expressing one's opinion. How were we to know our Bible-bashing friend was high up in the police force?

We had outworn our welcome and took comfort in the safety of the vessel. Savannah seemed to me to be in a time warp. The opinions we were subjected to were from a time long past.

Having experienced the stateside brand of apartheid, I was keen to read about the daily grind that coloured folk had to go through to win racial equality. At that time, Martin Luther King was becoming prominent, having brought about the boycotting of public transport by the blacks in Montgomery two years earlier. The boycott caused a problem for the public transport, as they were forced to integrate their system for all colours. I saw no evidence anywhere else I had been to in the USA of signs openly promoting segregation between blacks and whites as I had witnessed in Charleston and Savannah. I just happened to be caught up in an era when history was taking place in the USA. The civil rights movement was about to take off. The momentum it gathered through the '60s finally saw the southern states conforming to the ideals of the Founding Fathers, eloquently penned in the Bill of Rights, but seldom adhered to in practice — 'That all men are by nature equally free and independent.'

As a seaman, you witness the systems of other countries. You may not like them, and you may express disapproval. Savannah, with its segregation notices and plantation mentality was an insult to any sane mind. I left there mature enough to be shocked into wondering why a supposedly civilised nation had fought a Civil War to abolish slavery, yet had still not found the key to racial equality 100 years later. It hit me even more than South Africa. I felt insulted that my dark skin would be represented as a threat to society — only those it affected could feel the insult personally.

There was a sense of relief as we sailed into the South Atlantic air; a cleansing of the mind if you like. The port of Cristobal and the Panama Canal awaited us. I had subbed most of my wages buying denim jeans to sell on the Kiwi coast and hopefully I would have a few quid in the kitty for a night ashore in the Doghouse Bar in Cristobal. Once again we were allowed an advance of £5 for the night ashore. It was every skipper's nightmare to find half his crew shacked up with those alluring Latin bargirls when it was time to let the ropes go.

The *Tyrone* was the longest time I had been at sea without seeing land. The Pacific usually had more reasonable weather than the Atlantic, but on this occasion we were plagued by bad weather, finding ourselves doing two miles forward and one back. Her little Doxford engines negotiated the 6000 miles of the Pacific, arriving in Auckland again after about 40 days. My overweight cabin-mate Gus had experienced some heart problems and was rushed off to the company doctor who put him in hospital for observation. We were told he was to join the vessel at another port. In those days crew members who were invalided off were never replaced, nor was there remuneration for sailing short-handed. On this occasion Gus rejoined the vessel before we left the New Zealand coast but he was only allowed to do light duties.

We were well into 1959 and my 18th birthday had passed without ceremony during our long haul across the Pacific. Purchasing denims on the American coast proved to be a financial windfall, as did buying the Kiwi dockworkers favourite fag, the Woodbine, which were sold on tick from the slop chest and came in boxes of 50. A tin of Capstan tobacco was also popular among the 'roll your own' fraternity.

I was amazed at the number of British ships that graced the ports of New Zealand. Crews of Shaw Savill, Blue Star, Port Line and New Zealand Shipping Company vessels vied to impress the girls that their vessel was the best 'party boat'. When told what vessel I was on, the stock answer would be, "Never heard of it." I made a mental note to make sure I was on one of the premier line ships when I next came out to New Zealand.

A run ashore was gauged by the number of females one managed to impress. I was certainly influenced by this and the New Zealand experience was an adventure I was not to forget. Our homeward-bound journey was going to be via the Suez, calling into the Italian ports of Naples and Genoa, before finally finishing with engines in Liverpool. So cynical were the crowd by this time we took the homeward-bound schedule with a pinch of salt, secretly guessing that we would probably end up doing another trip to the States. The cargo being loaded scotched our cynicism as commodities marked for Liverpool swung on board to the delight of us all. I thought I was so lucky getting to go through two famous canals all in one trip.

The Suez Canal was a very different experience from the Panama. The dhows, the bum-boats and the odd shackle dropped from the ship's decks, not to mention the legendary Egyptians known as 'Jock McGregor' and 'George Robey' and co who would come on board to entertain us, all went in to make a passage through the Suez special.

The Straits of Messina are one of the most spectacular and beautiful settings I had seen in my short time at sea. The southern tip of Italy was starboard, and Sicily on our portside. The straits at their narrowest point are two miles wide. On watch one night I witnessed the dramatic display of the volcano on the island of Stromboli. I had never seen a volcano before, let alone an active one. The pronounced pong that permeated the ship out in the Tyrrhenian Sea came from the City of Naples, according to those who were familiar with the Italian coast. Every port has its aromas and, not to be unkind to this historic city, Naples's was probably the worst.

We focused on a very narrow agenda when hitting the ports of the world where the fair sex hung out. We were young, and a discerning seafarer is a rare sight. History was (and still is) a favourite subject of mine. I rue the missed opportunities afforded me to explore the places and browse the museums that told of Italy's past and the Roman Empire. I would kick myself in later years as I forked out hard-earned currency to browse the glory of Rome.

Liverpool was a welcome sight as the Mersey tugs hitched onto us fore and aft. The *Tyrone* had arrived home. Our trip around the world had taken just over eleven months. After paying my union dues, all I had to show for nearly a year's work was £42. But the experience I gained and the memories of faraway places outweighed the material rewards. With no time for Scotland Road vendors this trip I jumped on the first train to London, and arrived feeling quite merry on good old British Rail grog at Euston Station four hours later.

Four years later the *Tyrone* found herself in the knacker's yard. She was broken up in 1963.

twelve

The oceans have no compassion, no faith, no law, no memory…

— *Joseph Conrad*

NOTHING HAD CHANGED IN Custom House. The taxi I had commandeered at Plaistow Station dropped me off outside the Seamen's Mission. I was thankful that Mrs Harvey was not present when I handed my discharge book over at the reception desk. She had the knack of sniffing the alcohol on your breath.

"Have you been drinking?"

Yer, that's what seamen do, Mrs Harvey. Handing over your discharge book at the reception desk was proof you were the man in the photo and a bona fide seafarer. There were those who tried to pass themselves off as seamen until their seaman's bible was called for.

I missed the *Tyrone*. Being on a ship so long, you got used to the racket of the screws as they lifted out of the water. Even Gus, who at the beginning of the trip had an aversion to personal hygiene, gradually began to smell of roses. It was the closeness of living together for so long — friendships sprang up. Suddenly the voyage comes to an end and all you are left with is memories. There were many times I felt like I was in a happy time warp, and my release into the mainstream ashore was a rude awakening.

I was always going to jump on a train to Camberley to see my foster parents on returning to the UK. Unfortunately I was the world's worst procrastinator. I had not shown my face in three years, let alone picked up a phone. Nothing changed after my *Tyrone* journey. The guilt had set in and I had no excuse for not calling in to see the folk who had given their time to my youth.

I was not ready to go back to sea straight away. I decided to have a look further beyond Custom House and the Royal Docks, and took a tube to South Kensington where the museums are. It was impossible to look through all of them in one day, and I spent three days educating myself, which was a change for me. I spent another couple of days at the Imperial War Museum not far away on the Lambeth Road. I had been there before and my interest was in watching the old war footage at the museum's theatre. While scoffing a bacon sandwich in the transport café up the road from the Flying Tab-Nab one morning and planning where I was going to go, a familiar face from the *Highland Princess* walked in. Ted had been bosun's mate when I was transported home from Las Palmas as a DBS.

"Allo mate, what yer doin wiv yourself?"

I related my year's venture on the *Tyrone* and whiling my time away at various museums.

"What museums?" he asked incredulously. "I'm goin up the other end to the Two 'T's coffee bar in Soho to watch Hank Marvin and Jet Harris play this afternoon, wanna come wiv us?"

I was certainly into my music and there were some great homegrown artists around like Lonny Donegan and Tommy Steele.

"Why don't yer whip down the Pool, cos there is ordinary shite hawk's jobs on the *Princess,* I saw them on the board yesterday." Colourful name Ted had for ordinary seamen. He said he would get the bosun to stick me in his watch if I signed on, hoping to trap me further. "Wait until we get to Monte and go over the road to the Gobble Shop for a lunchtime sesh." He was talking about Montevideo, Uruguay. I won't elaborate on what the Gobble Shop had to offer, but I was guilty of foregoing my lunch under sufferance of the bosun's mate.

A few days later I signed aboard the *Highland Princess* tied up in the Victoria Dock, making my usual run to Gregory's to buy a pair of wranglers to sell if I got short of pesos.

The Board of Trade requires each vessel to hold a boat drill and fire emergency exercise before putting to sea, with BoT officials present to ensure the lifesaving gear is in working order. Most vessels have lifeboats that are power-operated. Wire falls are attached to davits and the boat, with the running part fixed to a drum on deck. A press of the button, and the electric motor operates the drum to which the fall is attached, lowering or lifting the boat. The *Highland Princess*, of 1932 vintage, had Clincher lifeboats rigged with rope-falls. It was a lifeboat drill that could have come out of the 1920s — no motorised units here. To simulate a real abandonment of the vessel the stewards posed as the passengers and filled the lifeboats, with a certified AB fore and aft and an officer in charge.

The boats were lowered by stag horn. We eased off the forward and aft falls around the horns to make sure they were lowered equally and the boat stayed level. To lift the laden boat we had to take the falls to the nearest windlass, which was on the foc's'le head. Those of us who had never been through this drill didn't have a clue what was demanded of us. Ted laughed his head off saying "I bet you ain't done a boat drill like that before!" He was right.

During one of our boat drills on the trip, we were to use 'Norwegian steam' to lift the boat. There were no passengers in the boat and we were told to man the falls and heave the boat up by hand.

The Royal Mail Line's passenger vessels were not noted for their majestic lines as were the Cunarders and Union Castle vessels. The *Highland* boat was distinguishable by two squat yellow funnels. The superstructure was prominently divided by a well-deck that separated the bridge and crew quarters from the passenger decks. The *Highland* boats were two-class vessel, first and third class passengers, transporting immigrants from Spain and Portugal to the east coast of South America and vice versa. Our itinerary included Boulogne, Vigo and Lisbon. At these ports we would pick up the bulk of our passengers then head on to Las Palmas for bunkers, before setting off across the Atlantic to Rio de Janeiro and Santos, and up the River Plate to Montevideo. We would spend most of our time loading chilled beef just across the Plate in Buenos Aires.

Ted was true to his word and I was put on his watch. The crew accommodation was in the foc's'le head. The bridge was above us and a forward well-deck separated our accommodation from the passenger quarters. The ordinary seamen's cabin was a four-berth affair: two bunks and a space between. It was cramped living but I was used to that by now. The number one hatch stood between the seamen's cabins starboard and the catering department on the portside. We were issued with company working fatigues and a jumper emblazoned with the house flag pennant. Most shipping companies issued their crews with jumpers sporting company logos. I wish I had kept them as a reminder of an age we will never see again, but my better half is thankful that they were not added to the memorabilia cluttering the house today.

On this vessel I first heard the term 'Black Pan' — a meal cooked for the men whose work commitments deprived them of tea. Black Pan was a condition won by the union whereby a meal would be cooked at 8pm for men coming off the four-to-eight watches. It was usually a big fry-up and most of the seamen who were up and about took advantage of the culinary delight, not just the 8pm watchmen.

Ted had been on the South American run for years and knew the American coast inside out. He could speak their lingo, and was greeted enthusiastically in each port. He had fallen in love with a bargirl from the Via Monte, Buenos Aires's red light district, and we were not to hear the last of it. He owned the latest gramophone record player and the voice of Slim Whitman's 'Rose-Marie I love you' echoed round the

Memorabilia — a sail barometer in my collection, made in Lisbon in the 17th century.

cabin. By the time we arrived on the South American coast we knew the words of that song off by heart. Another character was Black Angus, the lamp-trimmer. Angus hailed from Barra and believed in the practice of a couple of hours of sleep and the rest of the day working. I was to sail with him later when he was bosun on the *Deseado*.

The most important task on reaching Rio de Janeiro, after discharging the last of the cargo, was to clean the hatches for loading meat. Unlike New Zealand frozen lamb where the carcasses are stowed in the hold, chilled beef is hung up on meat hooks. There were thousands of meat hooks and all had to be sterilised before being used again.

Black Angus was the expert overseeing sterilisation. The hooks were assigned to 40-gallon drums to soak in a sterilising solution. Each of the 'tween decks in the hold were sealed with hatch boards which were scrubbed before any meat was loaded.

As we finished cleaning each of the hatch boards in the 'tweens, somebody left one of the boards off. We were at morning smoko sitting on the deck in Rio's stifling heat when I realised I had left my box of Players down the hold. I knew exactly where I left them. Without a thought for safety I bounded down the hold ladder with only the dim cluster lights to guide me. I forgot about the open hatch. I fell, and I was lucky the boards were in place on the next deck, as I could have fallen even further with fatal consequence. I landed on the next deck and suffered a broken nose and bruised bones.

Nobody knew that I had gone down the hatch. The 'tween deck I had fallen into was dark and I had lost my sense of direction. It seemed an eternity before I heard voices and cluster lights being turned on. My head felt like a sledge hammer had smashed it, but I managed to shout, gaining someone's attention. I made a frightening spectacle lying there — all hell broke loose when they found me. Gold braids appeared in droves, including the ship's doctor who would not let me be moved until he was sure my joints were working.

I was strapped to a stretcher and winched out by derrick to the deck above. The doctor snapped my nose back in place. I was given a rest and then began the questions. Why did you go down the hatch? Cigarettes? You're not supposed to be smoking down the hatch! The skipper wanted a written statement from me, and in turn the management would require a statement from the ship.

It was an episode that taught me that things can become very painful when you are thoughtless. The ship's doctor was a dapper chap without the airs and graces of others I have seen of that rank. When we sailed from Rio he informed me that female students from an American school were passengers going to Buenos Aires and then would be returning with the vessel. He was going to give them a tour of the hospital and I was to be on my best behaviour. Conscious that my two black eyes and swollen nose may frighten them off, I was not to keen on having an audience. It is no secret that Brazilian lasses have beautiful features. So I felt quite overwhelmed when girls from Bennett College in Rio surrounded my hospital bed. The doctor related my misfortune to them with a twinkle in his eyes. They greeted me as 'Daveed' and I focused my attention on Marcia Guttares. She and her friend had the doctor's permission to visit me in the morning and evenings for half an hour or so.

I was up and about before we reached Montevideo and Ted reckoned the elixir for my recovery lay in the Lighthouse Bar just over the road from where we were berthed. This was the famous Gobble Shop. I can already imagine the smile on the faces of those who are familiar with lunchtime forays to this establishment. I plead guilty in following tradition and taking Ted's recommendation.

Montevideo was the port that hosted the German pocket battleship *Graf Spee*. After overstaying its welcome in a neutral port, the majority of the crew were set ashore, and the *Graf Spee* sailed into history by being scuttled at the mouth of the River Plate to evade the wrath of allied warships waiting for her outside the port. A shop displayed photos of the battleship and its crew during their stay in Monte, and the top of its mast was still visible during my travels on the *Princess*.

Argentina had become a booming economy in the 1920s and was one of the richest countries in the world. Buenos Aires was known as the Paris of South America, with its wide boulevards and upmarket shops on the Corrientes. But shops and fashion were not my interest. We had slid into Buenos Aires to drop off our remaining passengers and discharge the rest of our cargo. Marcia and her fellow students were booked in to a hotel for the next two weeks.

The chaperones who accompanied the teenage students had eyes like hawks. While I was in the ship's hospital Marcia was free to come and chat. After my discharge it was impossible to find a corner to meet. The master-at-arms was vigilant and the only excuse for being on passenger decks was if we had work to do. I managed to spend an evening with her under the eyes of her chaperones, sipping cokes in the hotel lounge. I had one of those feelings that she was far above my station and I was just a plaything for a rich kid.

They were to travel to the interior as guests on a ranch, which suited me. Via Monte was the red light attraction for us in Buenos Aires, with countless bars and bargirls whose main object was to fleece as many drinks from their clients as they could, and if you had any pesos left over they had to cover the cost of a hotel room if 'jiggy-jig' was part of your plans.

A civilian government was in power in 1959 led by Arturo Frondizi, but the military were never far from the seat of power. The army and navy had overthrown

Juan Perón in 1955, but they had no answer to the Perónist supporters who ran the trade unions. We could feel the tension among the differing communist and Perónist wharfies who worked in separate cargo holds. Ashore it was more visible, with vigilantes patrolling the city streets like the Gestapo. They swaggered around the bars dressed in shiny boots that reached the crotch and black Napoleon hats, armed with machine guns and a threatening attitude.

If a vigilante asked you for a fag you gave him one. To refuse was not an option. The bargirls were not allowed to leave the bars until 4am, which put clients off if they wanted to go to a hotel — it was hardly an all-nighter. Mariñeiros (the naval counterpart to the vigilantes) guarded the docks. There was also a fluctuation in currency. You were rich one day and poor the next. One day I got 144 pesos for a pound; the next day it could be twenty pesos more or less. The rampant inflation was a stark contrast to the heydays of the 1920s.

We moved to La Plata, a few kilometres out of Buenos Aires to load beef and all the other commodities the poor old cow offered. The first thing that caught you was the nauseating hum of the place. Dock Sud was the home of the Vesty-owned meat processing company and slaughterhouses. Ted's girlfriend had a brother working at the La Plata meat factory who arranged an invite for a few of us to have a look at how a living cow is processed into by-products. The slaughterhouse made me chunder. You would have to be a nutcase to work there. I didn't stay long enough to witness the procedure of killing the cow because of the cloying smell of blood. They stunned the animal electrically then bounced a pointed hammer on its skull, killing it. It seemed an antiquated method but no one protested. Apart from the chilled carcass, other canned products like corned beef were processed. Even the poor old hooves were boiled up and made into soap.

Leather from the pelt was a lucrative trade. Fur-lined boots and leather jackets from Buenos Aires were a favourite purchase for seamen. I could well have missed the meat factory tour without any regrets, but it did not stop me from tasting the iconic Beefy Loma, Argentina's answer to the steak sandwich: thick cuts of prime beef marinated in garlic between thick bread. I was not a fan of garlic in those days but the many Beefy Lomas I consumed soon changed my mind.

The Vesty Brothers meat company had a presence in Argentina on the scale of what P&O was to Australia. The brothers were sent to South America to make their fortune. They initially exported game birds to Liverpool, which led to beef export. They started buying and running their own cattle ranches and eventually a meat processing factory at Dock Sud. To export their beef to the UK and the continent they commissioned their own vessels, and began the famous Blue Star Line, and complemented their business with a chain of retail butchers throughout the UK under the name of Dewhurst.

They did not have South America to themselves. Competition from the giant American meat packing company Swift-Armour helped fill the holds with canned meat products such as corned beef and offals.

My broken nose was on the mend and the bruising around my eyes had almost disappeared by the time we were due to leave Buenos Aires — Marcia remarked on it when she returned from the interior. Our communication was good since she spoke English with an American accent. I found us a meeting place on the poop deck above the third class bar. My clumsy hands wandered in seaman-like fashion, and I hoped she wouldn't object. Blimey, you would think I was with one of the Vestal virgins. She made it quite clear she was not a bargirl and left me standing on my own. Why do we seamen think we are God's gift to women? I was punished for my transgressions, and it highlighted the macho attitudes towards women in the messrooms. Maturity eventually changed my attitude and I learned that showing respect was far more appealing to women.

The homeward journey from Buenos Aires involved a temperature sounding on the deck of our cabin. A refrigerating engineer would come into our cabin during the night as the chilled beef had to be kept at a certain temperature. The flashing of his torch in the cabin woke those of us who were off watch. I told Ted that this was ridiculous and he said there had been no complaints on previous trips.

My rebellious mind kicked in. When the reefer (refrigeration) engineer made his rounds on the twelve-to-four watch one morning he was greeted by a locked cabin door. We had discussed among ourselves how we could bring attention to this issue. One of our cabin-mates was on the twelve-to-four watch and he was ordered to open the cabin door. He couldn't, since we held the key inside. The temperature sounding was more important than crew getting proper sleep and entrance was gained after the banging on the door and commotion outside had woken other crew members.

We had no union convenors in those days who could advocate for us. In the morning the bosun wanted to know who the bright spark that locked the door was, and stared straight at me.

The four of us were hauled before the skipper and chief engineer to explain our skulduggery. Not one of the gold braids saw our point of view. The cargo was far more important. Readings had to be taken every watch and that was that. There was no attempt to find a solution we could all live with. We were warned by the master that we would be logged with sabotaging the cargo should we continue to stop the engineer. Eighteen-year-old kids supposedly had no sensible ideas according to their reckoning. We were dismissed with a flea in our ears, lucky to get away with a warning.

In a funny way it showed a glaring need for worker representation. We had no choice under sufferance of the skipper's threat but to put up with nightly disturbance to our sleep. Help came from an unexpected quarter. The reefer engineers were sympathetic and made it clear they would not enjoy being woken up at 2 each morning. A compromise was struck, and instead of the 2am sounding, it was put back to midnight or the change of watches. It wasn't much, but we saw it as a victory against the master on the bridge.

The master on any vessel is the shipowner's representative and in charge of all he surveys on board, including his crew. I certainly respected his authority, as did most seamen. After all, anything that went wrong, they would be responsible. Some masters were aloof and downright imperious to the point where a powdered wig, breeches and buckled shoes would not be out of place. Most were modern and outgoing skippers who were not afraid to communicate with their crew, and they commanded our respect. The divide between the officer class and the ratings had always been there. It was no big deal being referred to by my surname, but I often had the rejoinder, "Mr Share, if you don't mind." After all, I didn't call the officers by their surnames.

The officers ate in one messroom and the ratings in another. A steward was appointed as 'Captain's Tiger' to look after his needs, which included making his bunk and keeping the cabin clean. The officers' steward looked after their needs. Later when I joined my first vessel on the New Zealand coast I was surprised by a laid-back attitude between the ratings and officers. First names were used and familiarity was a matter of course. However the same separate messing arrangements took place on the home boats.

In the 1990s this all changed. New management who took over the Cook Strait ferries decided to pull down the barriers that separated officers' and ratings' messrooms, and integrated them so we ate together like one big family. There were a few detractors on both sides who preferred the status quo but most of us were amused at the turn of events. Fears that somehow eating ship's duff with ratings would reduce upper deck authority were quickly dispelled, and we all got on with our shipboard lives in a more communal spirit.

Our temperature readings issue went down well in the messroom. It was a small victory over 'them'. On return to Rio, Marcia and her party of students disembarked. We exchanged addresses but I was hopelessly out of my depth with this academically-minded girl. Her parents owned showjumping horses, and my knowledge of horses went as far as cowboys and Indians. Her other interests were over my head, which made difficult any future liaison with her.

My broken nose looked more respectable by the time we left the South American coast, but I was experiencing an airway blockage as though the nose was not set right. I informed the ship's doctor who dismissed it as part of the swelling that would clear. Later on a slight blockage on the left nasal passage was still apparent, but I ignored advice to have it set properly. To wit, I have reached my pensionable age and the slightly disjointed snoz is a reminder not to venture into dark places.

The Royal Docks were a welcome sight, with the trip lasting exactly two months. Ted had been talking me into signing back on for the next voyage. I had nothing against him, but I had an issue with a cabin that houses a sounding. I enjoyed the South American east coast, and I was told the west coast was even better. The gauge was women, of course. I strode down the gangway lugging my worldly possessions on my back, my pockets flush once again and my thoughts on the next ship to the west coast.

The *Highland Princess*, at 14,000 tons, had plied the UK-South American trade for 30 years by the time I paid off her. A year later she was sold to Greek owners and renamed *Mariana*.

thirteen

MY STAY ASHORE WOULD ALWAYS be governed by financial limitations. I had no one to keep except myself and 'thrifty' was not part of my vocabulary. Being a happy-go-lucky person who lived life from day to day, I enjoyed the few days my pay-off afforded me. Sure, I cringe today at the thought of squandering the quid that took months to earn, but no one could accuse me of keeping my money prisoner. There were always seamen I had sailed with who were now 'on the beach' or booked in at the Mission. We congregated in the Steps in Custom House and would earbash each other on the latest shipping news. We always knew that when the coffers began to get low we could present ourselves at the Pool, choose what part of the globe we wanted to visit, and unlike ashore, find food and bedding supplied by an employer.

It took me just a week to arrive at that position. My intention was to seek out a ship going to the west coast of South America. Pacific Steam Navigation Company (PSNC) traded on that route. I could not afford to hang around. Since there were no jobs going to my preferred destination, I inquired where the *Wairangi* was going. The answer came: South Africa, Australia and New Zealand — about a five-month trip, according to the Pool official.

So began my long association with the Shaw Savill Line. I was shunted off down to their office in the King George Dock to see the hiring manager. Apparently Shaw Savill required a closer perusal of discharge books, and on reaching their office I was greeted by a Mr Pook. Pooky was a large man, sporting a moustache and a posh accent that would have sounded right in an RAF officers' mess, but seemed rather out of place in London's East End dockyards. Perusing my discharge book, he noted I had not sailed with Shaw Savill before.

He got carried away regaling me with stories about a holiday he had in Australia, before reminding himself that I was waiting for a yea or nay as to whether I had a berth aboard one of his vessels. I liked the cut of his jib on the many occasions I met him. The loud guffaws that rumbled from him after cracking some of the worst jokes in history had those present in fits of laughter. Not the joke, his laugh.

The *Wairangi*, 13,400 tons, was built in 1942, requisitioned by the MoT for war service and named the *Empire Grace*. She was renamed *Wairangi* and began her career with her parent company in 1946.

Our outward route took us to Cape Town and Durban. Nothing had changed in Yarpieland since my last visit. Four million whites held 22 million of their fellow citizens in penury and the world of 1959 was not interested.

The *Wairangi* was a six-hatch cargo vessel with twenty derricks and the gear to overhaul once clear of Durban and in the tropics of the Indian Ocean. Australia was a new destination for me. My excitement mounted as the ship's radio picked up the vocabulary unique to Australians, where women are 'sheilas' and the English are 'pommies'.

Fremantle, 20km from the state capital of Perth, was the front gate to Australia. My first impression was of the easy and outgoing nature of the Aussies. Their forefathers had etched out a land far from the stiff lip of the mother country. In town we explored the pubs and it didn't take us long to sniff out Cleo's, where the local sheilas gathered to meet the latest talent in town.

"G'day cobber, what tribe do you belong to?"

Fits of laughter from my shipmates as I answered the enquirer, an aborigine who thought I might be part of his clan.

"I'm from the Cockney tribe, mate."

My answer didn't seem to amuse him and his mates. They lacked humour and became aggressive. The barman saw what was happening and chucked them out.

"They don't like poms, so watch it when you come out of the pub."

We were all full of Swan Lager, the local brew, by the time we left Cleo's. We were no use to the sheilas, nor did we take heed of the barman's warning. Luckily our antagonists were gone and I could swear I had just turned in when the call of turn-to reached the ears.

Young minds are easily impressed and our short stay in Fremantle had done just that. Australia seemed to me just like New Zealand. Both had their indigenous people, both had an easygoing friendliness that highlighted how hampered we Brits were in our upstairs and downstairs mindset. I had heard the Aussies and Kiwis referred to as rowdy and uncouth antipodeans. If this was once a dumping ground for all the crims in 18th-century Britain, then I identified with these ex-poms.

Victoria Dock in Port Melbourne saw us dock just down from Shaw Savill's *Karamea*, a real antique with a classic counter stern from the 1920s. The lads on that vessel were certainly not ancient and there were familiar faces on both ships, enough to warrant a get together in the nearest watering hole, the Pier Hotel. We discovered St Kilda, Melbourne's red light district. Our mission centred on a dance hall called the Sound Lounge on the seafront. Bottles of rum disguised as coke were sneaked past the doorman and all eyes focused on the array of sheilas that graced the dance hall, who we wasted no time in chatting up.

Bringing women aboard ships was permissible if the master and port authority allowed it. I sailed with one skipper who would not let any female aboard his vessel, but most were modern-thinking and realised the crew needed to let off steam, a concession that we knew went with responsibility. As long as you did your day's work and females were not running around the deck during cargo operations, everyone was happy. Women were not allowed to remain aboard once the vessel went to sea, though I'm sure many seamen were guilty of ringbolting their sea wives around the coasts of Australia and New Zealand. I found it wise to arm myself with a visitor pass before coming ashore each night, just in case.

The Sound Lounge was a magnet for the young and the restless who enjoyed rock and rolling to the latest tunes. We had decided on a party aboard the *Wairangi* and a tarpaulin muster had been called for to help pay for the grog. A muster was a contribution from each crew member to a common kitty. The only thing lacking was the women. The Pier Hotel had its selection, but there was a more elegant choice in the Sound Lounge. We had our party and unhappily there were some who ignored the rules about having women aboard. Captain Forbes-Moffat was a fair skipper, but strict on discipline. He decided to hold his weekly inspection of the ship's accommodation the following morning. One AB forgot to hide his bird in the cabin wardrobe, and the damage was done when the skipper opened the cabin door and was greeted with those untimely words, "Who the fuck are you? Piss off, I'm tired." Yer well, you could understand old Forbes's ire. Passes were suspended, and no women were allowed aboard the vessel. We left Melbourne wondering how we could retrieve the situation.

I had seen pictures of the famous Sydney Harbour Bridge, but there was nothing more thrilling for me at that time than actually sailing under it. It is an awesome sight that you hold in your mind through the span of time. The Sydney Opera House would not dominate the harbour landscape for another fourteen years, though its foundations had been laid earlier that year in 1959.

The main landmarks we had eyes for, of course, were those in skirts. A pub near the Piermont Bridge called the Bunch of Grapes held all our desires, we were told, so we made our way ashore in anticipation of what we would find there. I met Shirley, the current 'shore bosun' who seemed to know more about the cargo gear on a ship than we did. Being a coloured youngster I was given much attention by the aboriginal ladies — trying to disengage myself was a hard proposition.

My so-called mates decided to visit a bar across the Piermont Bridge called Montgomery's, leaving me on my own. Each time I suggested that I had to go, my glass was filled by Shirley. I was never going to escape her clutches. She wanted to stay aboard the vessel during our stop in Sydney, and I was to be her host.

It was Captain Forbes-Moffat's edict of no more women that saved the day. I had no ship's pass to show the bloke at the gate and even Shirley, who was known to him, was more than his job's worth to let through. I promised I would be in the Bunch the following night as I left her at the gate and quietly let out a sigh of relief.

Those of us who knew Shirley shared some good laughs with this lady who popped up in the main ports of Australia. Later on, I heard she had returned to her roots in the outback and had died. As it was, I gave the Bunch a miss the next night and visited the old seamen's watering hole, Montgomery's. Its claim to fame was a collection of ships' lifebelts displayed around the four walls. I would love to hear the tales those four walls could tell me of the years when seafarers were its main clientele. I have some memories of my own within those walls, but not on this trip.

With cargo operations complete in Sydney, we looked forward to the New Zealand coast. We were to load meat, wool and dairy products at various North and South Island ports. I had seen my wealth shrink on the Australian coast and when the subs list came round I was not sure whether I would get the advance against my wages.

The heads of Wellington were sighted and we were soon in the embrace of its picturesque harbour. I could see the many funnels of the shipping companies peering above the cargo sheds.

I need not have worried about my money, since we were introduced to a uniquely Kiwi concept. There was a shortage of what Kiwis called 'wharfies', that we would call dockers. To take up this shortfall, ship crews were offered work for generous remuneration. Some of us hard-up Brits would feel very affluent after a stint on the wharf. They called us 'seagulls'. The offer came down to the messroom that labour was required on the wharf from 6 to 9pm each evening for three New Zealand pounds per night. The remuneration kept my account in the black. The

The *Wairangi*, formerly the *Empire Grace*, took me to Australia for the first time.
VH Young

money was paid to the shipping company who allotted each crew member the rightful amount against his account.

At six each evening we had to report to the pick-up office with our employment slip and be sent to a vessel. I found myself on the wharf one night stacking lamb carcasses into a cargo net, and the following night down a hold freezing my cobblers off as I stowed boxes of butter. I noticed a strong union bond among the Kiwi wharfies, and when they called smoko you didn't pick up another carton of butter or carcass of lamb — you stopped work. By nine o'clock we were away and three quid richer. Six o'clock closing was still in and the good thing about seagulling on one of the home boats was that you could suss out whether there was a party aboard. As long as you were from another home boat you could usually contribute to a muster to buy some booze from the chief steward and join the revelries. It was too far to walk back to the *Wairangi*, so chatty but happy was the order of the night.

Napier didn't offer the same money-spinner. The port was almost empty, with just our vessel, a federal boat and a Kiwi coaster on the wharfs. I had not been to Napier before and knew nothing about the earthquake that struck in 1931, or that this town held some of the best examples of art deco architecture. To me it was a dead arse run ashore with no set hangouts to meet girls, or any dance halls like Wellington and Auckland. The end quarter of 1959 may have seen Napier in the grip of conservatism, but I am only expressing my first impressions. I am aware that many of us young seafarers judged a port only by the cut of a female skirt. Culturally bereft — the way of the seafarer.

I celebrated my 19th birthday in Lyttelton, on my best behaviour as it was only a year since I was banned from the many pubs of this port. The skipper, Forbes-Moffat, was intent that females were not to be permitted aboard his vessel. A birthday party aboard was out of the question and we kind of got lost in the village that night, ending up at a local resident's home where a party got under way.

"Get up Dave, it's bleeding ten o'clock!"

The half-gallon jar on its side took my eye, as did the wooden crates filled with empty beer bottles. On the couch, leaning against me was a girl also in an alcoholic haze, who could well have been born in 1859. At least we were dressed, which meant I was celibate on my big day. It must have been a good night since there were bodies lying around in odd poses.

My state was not the immediate problem. I had missed turn-to, meaning two of the ABs and I were in trouble. When I got back to the ship, Forbes-Moffat listened to me waffle on about my birthday and found no justification as to why I was late aboard. I sustained my first logging, forfeiting a day and a half pay for missing half a day's work. "Robbery with violence!" I fumed.

It was a warning to keep my nose clean for the rest of the voyage. Another visit to Forbesy could result in a DR. The remainder of the New Zealand trip went without incident and after topping off in Port Chalmers a few days later we sailed for Panama, Curaçao and London. Shipping companies tried to avoid being in port over Christmas since it would cost them two days alongside the wharf with their vessel idle. Christmas Day at sea is a tame affair, with most missing their family and children. It was just another day at sea, as was the event of bringing in the New Year. We had steering and lookout duties that required every watch-keeper to have his full faculties.

In late January 1960 the *Wairangi* rounded the Nore and the smell of the Thames entered our nostrils, four months since we had left our berth in King George Dock. Who better to greet us than the plummy voice of Mr Pook, who had scanned the list of those wanting to resign and noted my name missing. He told me that the *Waiwera* would be picking up for a home trade run around the continent in a week if I wanted a job. The incident in Lyttelton had no effect on my discharge book, and the two VGs were a welcome sight. I told Pooky I was thinking of getting my AB's certificate this time off, and was to let him know if I was available within the next two days. He was the only crew administration officer I dealt with who had a personal touch with the men, a contrast to the aloofness of one officer of another company who thought his excrement had no aroma. Some got so carried away with their authority to hire or fire, they put themselves up to be ridiculed and became the butt of some jokes. To seamen they were just the office boys.

The *Wairangi* served seventeen years with Shaw Savill before going aground in Stockholm in 1963. The damage she sustained made her uneconomical to repair and she was taken to the breakers that same year.

I had been at sea for three and a quarter years and almost had enough sea time in for my able seaman rating; it was astute to do something about it. My financial situation precluded me from waiting for the next AB's course, but there was an alternative remedy that would take only a day. It involved a rail trip to Great Yarmouth on the East Anglia coast, where the certified Board of Trade examiner lived. I was lucky to call at a time just after New Year when his schedule had eased off. If I made it on the morrow I would be the first cab off the rank at 9am. I did not need any prompting and rushed down to Liverpool Street Station to buy a ticket to Yarmouth. It took a couple of hours from London to Yarmouth and I searched for bed and breakfast accommodation near the examiner's office.

I was in and out of the examiner's office by half past nine, holding an able seaman certificate. By mid-afternoon I was in the KG5 Shaw Savill Office seeking Mr Pook out for the job on the *Waiwera* he had spoken of. I shoved my brand new certificate in front of him.

You have to laugh at this guy. "Yes, very good, what is it?"

When I told him he said he could not change my rating, and suggested I go to the Pool to get it authenticated. He examined my discharge book and said, "Are you sure you have four years sea time in?" Also missing was a lifeboat certificate, he reminded me.

It was a bit of a downer after thinking I would be signing on as an AB. I had passed only one half of the AB's certificate and needed to sit my lifeboat ticket. It could not be taken in one day, and I was having too much fun to devote a few days in a lifeboat and secure a full certification. In fact, it took only a day to finally take the certificate on Auckland harbour in 1966. I was rated an efficient deck hand (EDH) later on, which was a bit lower than the AB rating, and a couple of quid difference in the monthly wages.

Mr Pook was correct in pointing out I was short in sea time to secure an AB rating. Without asking whether I wanted the home trade run as an SOS on *Waiwera*, he went on to tell me what ports she was going to on the continent. Signing on was to take place in the morning and that was that. I never got a word in.

There is no doubt that 'round the land' runs were handy fillers if you needed quick cash or were waiting for a certain ship to sign on to. These jobs involved vessels that had just arrived from overseas and the crew had paid off or gone on leave. She would have cargo to unload in British and continental ports, and required a fresh crew. Home trade articles are signed and the duration of these articles would determine how long the unloading and the loading of cargo for foreign destinations took, but it was never more than six months. As soon as the ship reached her last loading port before setting off overseas the home trade crew could sign off, or if an individual wished he could go deep sea on her as long as a berth was available.

I had not ventured around the continent before but I had heard about Hamburg and its street of bawdyhouses. Rotterdam I had passed on my way to Schiedam aboard the *Pass of Leny*. Antwerp had its red light district, but it also had a beer, Stella Artois, that was worth getting a hangover for. While I was far from being a connoisseur, I found the Belgian brew far more agreeable than the German Beck and Dutch Heineken.

Hamburg had obviously picked itself up after the war. The German mark had a pocket-emptying effect on our sterling — the exchange rate was nine marks to the pound, and the cost of living in Germany was higher than ours, which showed in our purchasing power. That didn't stop us from rushing ashore and hailing a taxi to Hamburg's red light district, St Pauli. Its most notorious street was the Reeperbahn where striptease clubs, peep shows and brothels were to be found.

We made straight for the WinkelStrasse, a small sidestreet where prostitutes were on show for customers behind windows. It was a men-only affair with women and children barred. Herbert Strasse was its proper name, and I believe 'Winkel' had had more to do with a pet name for a part of the male anatomy given by seamen. I was somewhat disappointed with what was on show — it seemed more like a cattle market. The first few windows had lovelies decked out in skimpy lingerie and provocative poses. I noticed the ladies behind the windows got progressively older as I moved down the street.

The final windows had us in fits of laughter. Ladies long past their best were trying to reinvent the past, hoping to attract an equally ancient seaman or two.

We made our way to a bar full of girls too pricey for our pockets. The Beatles had not hit the charts yet and nor were they living in Hamburg at this time. On a later visit to Hamburg in 1960 I heard that the Liverpool band was performing at the Kaiserkeller club in St Pauli. I never went but some of the lads who were there said they were great. On a round-the-land trip a year later I was to see the Beatles perform at the Top Ten Club in Hamburg. They had not made their entry onto the world stage yet. Little did we figure these four lads would set the trend in the '60s for youngsters across the world not only in fashion and Mod haircuts but also opinions, encouraging rebelliousness against the old ways of thinking. I felt the change deeply between the young who at last had found a voice, and the established people who through no fault of their own had only memories of wars.

There were other bands that also helped bring us out of our post-war morbidity. It was an exciting time, but not all was a bed of roses. With the new freedom of expression came the proliferation of drugs. Some of those expressions became skewed up with people who believed world peace would reign as long as everybody came under the effect of marijuana.

"Make love, not war," was the cry. Music has always influenced world trends since the advent of flappers in the 1920s — so it was in the swinging '60s.

During my first trip to Hamburg, two of us jumped into a taxi on the Reeperbahn, rather inebriated. The Hamburg docks are vast and we were speeding along a dock road when the cab driver had a fit and the taxi was filled with his shouting of "*Stanke! Stanke!*" The cab came to a screeching halt and next thing I knew I was hauled out of the cab by the scruff of my neck and dumped on the ground. The same treatment was meted to my mate and the cab took off with a stream of Teutonic abuse.

"What did we do?" I asked.

"I farted," my mate confessed.

Drunk as we were, we rolled around on the dock road in a fit of laughter. It was a freezing cold night in January.

"Ain't these krauts got any sense of humour?"

We picked ourselves up, having no idea where we were. It seemed to be a busy road with a steady stream of cars. It slowly reached our intoxicated minds that we didn't have a mark between us. We laughed that we had been saved from a worser fate by a fart.

An AB spotted us, and asked us why we were stranded on the dock road. By the time the *Waiwera* came into view the three of us were in gales of laughter. That became the talking point of the vessel in the days following and the ship comedians had a field day. No crew member would hazard a taxi ride with us in Rotterdam or Antwerp.

We docked in Liverpool in early February. The *Waiwera* was topping off her cargo for Australia and New Zealand and would be leaving in four days. The continental trip had brought the crowd together and I decided to keep with it and signed deep sea articles. I had grown fond of the lands down under and their laid-back lifestyles. The crowd was made up of Scouses and Southern English gentlemen. I always enjoyed the company of Liverpudlian seamen because of their great sense of humour.

Liverpool at this time was the cradle of militancy within the NUS. Rumours were rife about a reform movement being developed to challenge the existing Seamen's Union, and heave out its inert executive. The leader of the reform movement, Paddy Neary, came on board to give us a rundown on what he proposed. He was a passionate speaker and I was impressed with his idea of a convenor or delegate aboard every ship advocating for NUS members. There were some serious anomalies that were not being addressed, such as union agents in various ports around the world coming aboard and going straight to the skipper's cabin for a friendly chat and a noggin or two, before coming below to see the members he was paid to advocate for. Needless to say I became an instant disciple and bought a reform movement badge to demonstrate my support.

Before signing deep sea articles on the *Waiwera* I questioned why I could not sign on as an EDH. After all, I had a certificate that was validated by a recognised Board of Trade examiner. I agreed that I was short of sea time and my lifeboat certificate would be required for a full AB's licence, but that should make no difference to the EDH rating. I was simply offered the option of the senior ordinary seaman berth, or signing off. My mistake was signing on as SOS under home trade articles in London in the first instance. Mr Pook had wanted to fill the lower rating and I felt conned. But the crowd were my type and I didn't want to miss the camaraderie that had sprung up on our short trip around the land.

We sailed from Liverpool on a freezing mid-February evening, to arrive back in the same port on a fine summer's morning five months later. The voyage had taken us to the Cape of Good Hope, and on to Melbourne and Sydney. On the

New Zealand coast an engineroom greaser and a steward had taken off after their girlfriends and had 'forgotten' to return to the ship. They were posted as deserters and would eventually be picked up by the police and deported back to the UK. The trip was repetitive — the same ports, the same women, and the same watering holes as I went to before. The crowd lived up to my expectations of camaraderie, and it was always a shame when we said our goodbyes on completion of the voyage.

Jumping ship or 'skinning out' in Australia or New Zealand was common with British and foreign seamen. I should know, since I was a statistic in those occurrences. Usually the impetus for jumping ship was a woman. Both these nations were magnets to simple working folk like us. Our crowded little island in the other hemisphere, weighed down with its Empire building and the aristocracy bleeding the public purse, could not equal the simple but attractive lifestyle and superior wages. The Common Market was a decade away and when countries had dedicated markets to which they could sell all their products (as did New Zealand and Australia), it was no wonder they had not a care in the world.

The 12,000-ton refrigerated and general cargo ship *Waiwera* had a good crowd on it. Built in 1944, her service with Shaw Savill ended in 1967 when she was sold to Greek owners and renamed the *Julia*.
VH Young

fourteen

WITH PLENTY OF OVERTIME, MY FIVE MONTHS ON THE *Waiwera* had been a money-spinner. I was still as spendthrift as I had been as a deck boy. I booked in to Stornaway Castle after the long train ride from Liverpool. Dumping my gear in the room, I made for the Steps to check out the faces.

As it was evening most of the seamen would be over in Woolwich at the Royal Oak. Always the Rockefeller on pay-off day, I took the luxury of a taxi to Woolwich. It seemed like I had been away from the Royal Docks for years. Six months had lapsed and it was good to see familiar funnels as I walked down Woodman Street and into the Royal Oak.

Among a row of council houses, the only thing suggesting this was a public house was a sign hung over the entrance. The Oak was filled to capacity and I spied a few old heads, abuzz with the events taking place in Liverpool. The reform movement had reached London. I proudly displayed the movement badge on my jean jacket lapel.

"Fucking hell, don't show that badge round here, Dave!" called one of the boys.

They all agreed that we needed to chuck the old guard out, as they were the ones who sat on their fat arses, giving the shipowners *carte blanche* over our conditions and wages. But apparently it was unwise to wear the movement badge openly, especially in the Pool. A rumour was abroad that Reggie the Rat, at the behest of the shipowners, was refusing employment to 'militants' who displayed the badge. The shipowners and their lackeys still had the upper hand, but the rise of the reform movement was a threat to the power they enjoyed.

An executive member of the NUS who I knew as Roger sat with smoke billowing from his pipe, which was a bit much in a confined space. Roger Wilkins was an amiable old codger happily waiting for his retirement. He shared the Royal Dock union office with NUS catering boss Sam McCluskey. Roger warned that the reform movement was doomed to failure. I answered that the movement was built on dissatisfaction with the executive who had their heads up the shipowners' arses while doing nothing for the members. Talking shop while drinking is never the best idea. Roger's observations were aggressively refuted by some of the lads and he was told in no uncertain terms that he was full of shit. Emotions ran high and Danny the publican had to step in to quieten things down.

That movement badge stayed on my lapel for all to see, and the more the pints went down the more intimidating it got for some members. A fight ensued, which resulted in me and my old chum Bob, as well as other supporters of Mr Neary, being ejected.

There was no such thing as unity in the NUS at that time. Non-Pool contracts (freelance seaman such as I) had no loyalty to the Pool or the shipowners. But there were many seamen who had Pool contracts and still others who were company men contracted to a shipping company of their choice. I could never understand how you could be contracted to the Pool or a company and still be a loyal union member.

Be that as it may, I didn't actually begin the fight. The sight of my movement badge had an effect on some whose faculties had long been dimmed by booze.

Next lunchtime I was back at the Oak, pleading innocence in the previous night's scuffle. The publican's wife Rene was apologetic; her husband had given strict orders that myself, Bob, and a number of others were barred for a week. That was a bit strong, I suggested, since we never started the fight! Danny appeared while we were talking and confirmed our ban.

"Well, fuck you then, you can have all the scabby arse bastards, and the rest of us will black this pub and drink in the Three Crowns!"

This threat, coming from a more clued-up union member than I, must have sounded like treason to Danny. Our ban was downgraded to one night. We strode round to the Crowns with an air of militancy, guffawing over our victory.

The incident at the Oak had given me more recognition than I deserved. The seafaring fraternity residing in and around the docks had heard about the fight, and everyone had an opinion about the reform movement.

It was July 1960 when Bob and I called in at the dockers' canteen for a greasy banger and onion roll and a cuppa. Sitting there puffing away on his trademark pipe was Roger Wilkins.

"What you got in there, Roger? Sandwiches?" Bob was referring to Roger's briefcase.

"You two going down the Pool?"

We nodded.

"I would advise you not to be showing that badge." He pointed at my lapel.

The rebel in me wanted to ignore his advice. Bob was more thoughtful and the badge was put out of sight until we had done our business at the Pool.

Roger Wilkins suggested we attend the union meeting next morning at 10. We said we would be there just to placate Roger, who was a nice guy but was part of the cabal that the movement denounced.

KG5 Pool was busy as usual. On the board was a selection of jobs. In my hand was the certificate of my new rating. I was three months away from my fourth year of sea service.

The *Gothic* was my choice but Bob was not keen on a passenger vessel.

"Too much bullshit on 'em," he reckoned.

True enough, I thought, especially one that had carried the Royal retinue a few years before.

"Lift your lapel!" ordered Reggie the Rat as I fronted up at the counter.

"What are you, a copper?" I retorted. I knew what he was looking for and thankfully I had avoided trouble by listening to Bob's advice. My AB's certificate was recognised and Reggie handed me a chit stating my rating as an efficient deck hand (EDH) for the *Gothic*. Having passed my medical, I made my way down the docks to the Shaw Savill office to present my Pool chit to Pooky.

"How did the *Waiwera* trip go? Bit longer than I thought it would be. Five months eh? Oh, good show, you're an EDH now!"

I couldn't get a word in edgewise as he went on. At last I butted in with "When does she sign on, Mr Pook?"

"Oh yes, you'll want to know that."

Old Pooky never failed to put a smile on my dial and I walked out of the office knowing I had thrown off my OS rating and would be signing on in a couple of days as an EDH.

Shaw Savill ran a joint passenger service with the White Star Line between 1880 and 1933. Notable was the trio of Olympic class vessels, the most famous being the *Titanic*. Her sister ship *Britannic* was a hospital ship in World War I, but only saw nine months' service before following her sister's fate when she hit a mine in the Aegean. The *Olympic*, on the other hand, enjoyed a full life. When Shaw Savill took control after the collapse of the White Star Line in 1933, the company continued using the '-ic' suffix. A few of the vessels had Maori names such as the *Wairangi* and *Waiwera*.

Most celebrated of the vessels in my era was the *Gothic*. In 1951 she was fitted out for use as the Royal Yacht to take King George VI and Queen Elizabeth on a tour of the Commonwealth, but the king's death led to the tour being cancelled. She was instead given the privilege of fulfilling her role as Royal Yacht for Queen Elizabeth's Commonwealth tour in 1954. Her hull was painted white and carried the Royals and their retinue to the antipodes.

The crew berths were aft, below the poop deck. Sharing the cabin was a fully certified AB nicknamed 'The Professor'. You came across all kinds of characters at sea. Most were unassuming guys who eked out a living on the briny as did I. Occasionally you came across a character who stood out from the rest. The Professor was one of those people who could have you in fits of laughter one

Such was the discipline on the *Gothic*, it seemed they thought the Queen was still aboard. The *Gothic* ended life in a Taiwanese scrapyard in 1969, after a fire in the Pacific. Temporary repairs were made in Wellington but full repair proved uneconomic.
VH Young

minute, and the next have you in a serious discussion. He hailed from the town of Battle, the location of the Battle of Hastings. But William the Conqueror was, in Ray's words, "that French git who came over here and killed our king." He might have swallowed *Encyclopaedia Britannica* with his knowledge. He recited the union rules word for word and could interpret their meaning in language we lesser mortals could understand. He was eccentric but brilliantly versed, and he seemed out of place swinging in a bosun's chair up a Sampson post. We were on the same watch together and he would spend hours talking about current affairs. Like me, he was an avid supporter of the reform movement which was set up, as he put it, to oust those carpetbaggers in Clapham.

He also knew how to keep a quid prisoner. We would be in a pub, and each of us would put our hands in our pockets when it was our round. It gradually dawned on us that he drank but never bought.

"Oh, is it my turn already?" he would say innocently. I'm sure the face on the pound note was shedding tears of joy as he released it over the counter.

On arrival in Auckland I sensed that the reform movement had became more militant. There were calls from the UK for a national seafarer strike against the shipowners. Ray became the voice on the *Gothic*, urging action. The majority of us were in support. A minority urged caution since the action proposed was not sanctioned by the NUS. Should we walk off the vessel we were threatened with charges of mutiny.

There was a lot of liaising with crews from other UK vessels in port and Ray advised us that he had been in touch with New Zealand Seamen's Union delegates in Auckland. No move was taken in Auckland, which was a disappointment to the headstrong among us. A watering hole by the name of Ma Gleason's had something to do with this. Gleason's was the 'in' pub and the Orange dance hall was where we could swing the night away after the pubs closed at six.

We were not told when the action would take place until the very day. This, Ray said, was to thwart the shipowners and officers making counter-preparations.

It came in Wellington. Most of us walked off the vessel brimming with militancy, fists held high in defiance. The shipowners' answer was to pull the gangway up on each vessel, preventing crew members from returning aboard that night. The Mexicali coffee bar in Victoria Street became a refuge for stranded seamen, and it stayed open all night.

A girlfriend from my previous trip to Wellington on the *Waiwera* had a live-in job as a housemaid at a city hotel, and kindly solved my problem, bless her. There was a huge meeting outside the Waterloo Hotel, where speakers on the back of a truck assured us that our cause was just. As we cheered and waved clenched hands, a heady atmosphere reigned, helped by Waterloo Hotel comestibles. Members of the New Zealand Seamen's Union were in support, although I am not quite sure whether Fintan Patrick Walsh, the boss of that union, approved of the reform movement, which was trying to oust an elected union. The NZSCo passenger vessel *Rangitiki* moored at Aotea Quay did not join the action, but as is always the case they were happy to pocket the fruits of a campaign that others fought for. Those of us who were in our element on the day of action were not quite as active the next morning as we strode up the gangway, which had been lowered for the start of cargo work. The company made sure it got its recompense. We were each fined a day's pay and, to rub it in, suffered another day's forfeiture. There was argument from some of the crew who said they were not part of the unofficial strike, so why should they be penalised? They were mostly company men who were upset at having their names in the log book.

It was November 1960 as channel night was celebrated. Our day of action in Wellington a few weeks previous had not damaged my opportunity for another trip. I enjoyed my time aboard the *Gothic* but I made no commitment to rejoin her. She was in port too long for my pocket anyway.

fifteen

W E HEARD THE REFORM MOVEMENT had taken a bit of flak after the action. The seat of dissent was in Liverpool. Reform leader Paddy Neary was jailed for a couple of months. Gordon Norris was also a prominent player in the south, along with Jim Slater who would later become NUS secretary-general. I believe the action gave the executive a big fright, although it would be another six years before they decided to get off their backsides and challenge the shipowners. The dispute between factions of the NUS in 1960 was a good starting point for my future interest in the union movement.

Just three days after paying off the *Gothic* I presented my credentials at the KG5 Pool. It was winter in the UK, it was brass monkey weather and I wondered what I was hanging around for when I could be in the tropics. I discarded Shaw Savill in favour of the New Zealand Shipping Company. After the mandatory medical I trotted off to its office, halfway down the Royal Albert Dock. As I stepped through the door a voice said,

"Yes, what do you want? Your office is down further."

The voice belonged to a character known as Ginger Moxley. He must have thought I was a lascar seaman who had strayed into the wrong office and was referring me to the British India Shipping office further down the dock. I laid my discharge book on the counter, and took pleasure in noting the shock on his face when he heard his 'lascar' reply in a pure Cockney accent.

He scrutinised my discharge book as though it might be a forgery. My mission was a berth on the immigrant-carrying passenger ship *Rangitata*.

"Why did you leave Shaw Savill?" he asked suspiciously.

I was a freelance seaman. What did it have to do with him, I thought, but it was smarter not to take umbrage with those handing out jobs, and so I controlled myself. "No reason, just wanted to get out of the cold weather."

My reply satisfied his curiosity and I was told to be on board the following morning for signing on. As I retrieved my discharge book, I couldn't help ask, "Does the company supply tin cans for the bog house?"

The quip went over his head and he replied that I would have to ask about that on board. Lascars carrying tin cans for toilet use were a common sight around the docks.

The *Rangitata* (16,900 gross tons) plied the UK-NZ immigrant service with her sister *Rangitiki*. Both vessels made their maiden voyages in 1929, with capacity for 120 first class and around 280 tourist class passengers. During the war, the government used both as troop carriers with berths for 2600 each.

The seamen's accommodation on this old banger was under the foc's'le. Each seaman was outfitted with company gear including the much-prized woollen jerseys with the crossed house flags depicting the Federal Steam Navigation Company and its parent NZSCo. Toilet paper was supplied and there was therefore no need for tin cans. The seamen were from around London and the east counties mixed with a sprinkling of 'Stornawegians' including the bosun.

The bosun and I never saw eye to eye, even from when I was part of the forward crew letting go the moorings on that cold day in November 1960. Whilst coiling the ropes the crew were prattling on about various things as is usual. Seamen have plenty to talk about and 'taking the rise' was a common occurrence that you either accepted or you let it eat you. Somebody suggested that the company bosun looked so old that they must have dug him up from the Pyramids. Unfortunately he overheard this and was not amused by our guffawing. Thinking I was the one who made the remark, he warned me that he would be watching me. I retorted by asking him if he was part of the KGB. This didn't go down well, and set the scene for a finale in Wellington.

I was appointed to the four-to-eight watch. Each morning between six and seven o'clock we were tasked with washing down the petty officers' accommodation on the forward well-deck. Portholes were open as we were in the warm Pacific. Anyone with an ounce of brain would not attempt to wash down the housing until you had made sure the portholes were closed, but not on this morning. A stream of

The *Rangitata*, which I jumped to stay in New Zealand in 1960.
VH Young

abuse was directed at the man on the hose by the bosun whose head was framed by the porthole. He caught the deluge of water full in the face. Luckily it was one of his countrymen on the end of the hose.

"Och, Mac, a bit of water will nae harm ye!"

The rest of us thought it a great joke, which caused McIvor the bosun to come running out onto the deck blaspheming at anyone but his mate on the hose. It was the fastest I saw this guy move and I thought he was going to have a heart attack when someone called out that he needed a shower anyway.

A few bosuns I sailed with took their position of authority too seriously. They were usually company employees and would remain there for life. They knew every nook and cranny and the running of their vessel. That was acknowledged in the main by the seamen under them. But there were a few who showed no trust in their charges and meddled in everything, ingratiating themselves to the mate, whom they were answerable to, by dobbing in their men on disputes that could have been settled below decks. It made for an unhappy crowd and was not good for the smooth running of a vessel. Happily they were few and far between. The majority of bosuns would give the crowd jobs to do and trust their crew to complete them without standing over them. McIvor had no people skills, but in 1960 that was not a requirement of a seaman's CV.

Pitcairn Island was a mandatory visit by company vessels, to offload stores and dunnage used for cargo stowage which contributed to the building of houses. Pitcairn Island lies approximately halfway between Panama and New Zealand. Discovered in 1769 by the British, the island was given the surname of an officer on that voyage. I had read about the *Bounty* mutiny and here I was in person staring at this historic landscape wondering how those guys in 1789 managed to survive on such an isolated place. There were no port facilities or anchorage in Bounty Bay so the islanders had to manoeuvre their longboats out to the *Rangitata*. With them came their handicrafts, which were swooped on by passengers eager for a souvenir from this remote British outpost.

I made sure that I bought a carved flying fish as a memento of my visit. The ship was only a few hours there before we were farewelling the islanders and getting under way for Wellington.

As soon as we reached Wellington the ritual of painting the ship's hull began. Stages were rigged on both sides of the bow. I think most of us on deck spent half our sea careers hanging off stages over the wall or swinging aloft on bosun's chairs up masts or Sampson posts. A touch of vertigo had no place at sea.

We were halfway along the ship's hull one morning when my stage mate and I turned to after breakfast to find our stage was missing. In its place another stage had been rigged up, but it had a crack going the whole length of it. There was no way I was going to sit on that. Not only were we painting on the shore-side, but I doubt whether my mate or me would get up off the wharf should the stage collapse under our combined weight. The safety of the crew and passengers was a requirement of the shipowner, but safety was not in the bosun's vocabulary. Today's safety requirements on all aspects of operation aboard vessels are very strict and have to be adhered to. We had no recourse as we do today to a union convenor or delegate who we could call on to advocate and declare the stage unsafe.

McIvor was either blind or ignorant and threatened to take both of us before the chief mate. Our refusal led him to put his threat into action.

I was quite sure the mate would agree with us once he had seen the stage, and urged him to come down on the deck and see for himself our reason for refusing to work. His reaction was disappointing. He came out with the stock line, "You do as the bosun tells you."

I lost my cool and yelled out expletives as I exited the cabin, slamming the mate's door behind me. I got into my go-ashore gear and hot-footed it over to the Waterloo Hotel. I got talking to a guy who was sailing on the Picton ferry that evening to go tobacco picking in Motueka in the South Island. The money one could earn sounded impressive and I made up my mind to go. The last I saw of the *Rangitata* and her bosun was from the deck of the Cook Strait ferry *Tamahine*. I had deserted my vessel and knew not what the future held.

sixteen

M Y ADVENTURE ON THE SOUTH ISLAND began in mid-January 1961. I was twenty and mature enough to know what I was doing. Jumping ship meant I had to change my name to evade detection. I was an illegal person and the shipping company was duty-bound to inform the police of my desertion. None of these matters had much effect on me at the time except the adoption of a pseudonym.

'Davy Jones' sounded right to me as there was a nautical ring to it. My Waterloo Hotel friend had led me thus far to a small town where he had promised there was plenty of work and money to be made in the tobacco fields. Our travel ended at the Swan Hotel on the main street of Motueka.

Apparently this was the place to sound out which farms were looking for workers. My friend seemed to know everyone and I was soon offered work on a hop farm at nearby Riwaka as well as a tobacco farm in Kaiteriteri, near the sea but further from Motueka. The seaside sounded like my kind of place, so I made a phone call to the farmer to secure the job.

I told my employer that I was a novice as far as tobacco picking went and he said that was okay, I would soon learn. He came in to town to pick me up. For the next two months Davy Jones learnt the art of tobacco picking. The farm was idyllic, not far from the golden sands of Kaiteriteri beach, a bit of paradise. It had not been exploited by developers as it has been today.

Mr and Mrs Stebbings were a lovely old farming couple. My alias Davy Jones led them to nickname me 'Locker' and my Cockney accent at first had them in a quandary, as they thought from looking at me that I was Maori. My story was that I had been fishing out of Wellington and had come to New Zealand with my family when I was a child. We had our own living quarters and vegetables were easily obtainable from the garden, with a dairy just down the road.

I got an annoying tobacco rash on my arms, but the itching was soothed by calamine lotion. On Friday evenings we would go into Motueka with our wages and visit the Swan Hotel. Parties were the weekend preoccupation at the farms. One Saturday we were drinking in a pub called the Rat Hole at the bottom of Takaka hill. We decided to go to a party, which meant driving over the hill. Our transport was a 1929 Dodge truck which we loaded up with half-gallons of beer.

My compadres were too pissed to drive and the job was left to me. I had 'driven' the *Queen Mary* and other ships but never a 1929 Dodge or any other form of land-based transport.

"It's easy!" they said. "You drive and I'll do the gears."

So off we chugged with the rattle of half-gees in the back. The pedals on the floor had me baffled, not to mention the gearstick I was supposed to operate as my passengers snored.

I managed to steer the old jalopy to the top of the hill, free of trouble. The fun began on the descent as the old girl began to pick up speed. Without the aid of a gyrocompass, my steering was hopeless. We finished nose down in a ditch on the side of the road with the horrendous sounds of half-gee bottles shattering at the after-end.

No one seemed upset about the fate of our transport; it was the destruction of most of our grog that bought tears to our eyes. We were lucky to be pulled out of the ditch by a passing motorist who was on his way to the same party as we were. A few dents were all the damage sustained. We transferred the few intact jars of beer to his car and arrived safely at our destination. Its owner picked up the Dodge once he had regained his full faculties. Imagine leaving a classic vehicle on the side of the road today and hoping it would still be there in the morning.

I felt safe from the law, tucked away on this isolated tobacco farm. That I was a jumped seaman didn't really bother me. I was having a great time earning good money, accommodation all found, so what more could I want? But one day Mr

The *Ruahine*. We arrived in Tahiti when Marlon Brando
was making *Mutiny on the Bounty*, 1962.
VH Young

Stebbings introduced me to his son who was home for a few days. Unfortunately for me, he was in the police force. He was an amiable guy, but my Cockney accent probably led him to question the story I had given his father. My luck had run out and I was called up to the house. The son explained that he knew I was wanted for deserting my ship, and he had told his superior that I was working for his parents on their farm. He had asked if I could be held in detention there whilst awaiting deportation, but permission had been refused.

After saying my goodbyes I was taken to the Nelson police station. They held me in custody for five days when, as luck would have it, I was to replace a seaman who was reported missing from the *Ruahine*, due to depart from Wellington to London. I was lucky in the fact I could work my way home and earn some cash instead of being deported as a DBS on a shilling a month.

I was transported to Wellington with a policeman in tow and escorted to the *Ruahine* on sailing day. My two months ashore, though illegal, was a rewarding experience. Impetuous as my walking off a vessel had been, it sat well with my spirit. The friendly people with whom I came into contact around the tobacco and hop farms of Motueka made for a memorable interlude during my short stay.

The *Ruahine* was a one-class vessel with a capacity of 250 passengers. At 17,800 tons she was a bit larger than the *Rangitata*. The *Ruahine* made her maiden voyage in 1951. She also had a more eventful homeward-bound service, calling at Tahiti, Pitcairn, through the Panama, then on to Port Everglades and Bermuda, to Southampton and London.

Now I had to put aside memories and repair the damage caused by my impulsiveness. Fitting in with the crowd presented no problem. My fellow seafarers were curious and wanted my reasons for jumping ship. They assumed a woman was my reason: "What was the name of the bird?"

After stating my refusal to work on a damaged stage, I got an unexpected visit from a so-called sea lawyer who reckoned I had a good case and should write a report to the union, and that he would help me compose the letter. I had reservations and told him that those wankers wouldn't lift a finger to help me. But it could do no harm and a report was drawn up on our way to Tahiti.

Tahiti is the largest of over 100 islands that make up French Polynesia. Fletcher Christian and his mutineers from the *Bounty* sought refuge on this island after setting adrift the infamous Captain Bligh and eighteen of his crew on an epic 5600km open-boat voyage to Timor. The mutineers who opted to stay in Tahiti instead of settling in the haven of Pitcairn were caught by the long arm of British justice and returned to England where the gallows were waiting.

We slipped into steamy Papeete early in the morning, looking forward to going ashore. We had heard that *Mutiny on the Bounty* was being shot and Marlon Brando was in town. We couldn't get off the ship quick enough. Motor scooters were on hire so we could visit the Lafayette nightclub up the hill, or the more popular Quinn's. Marlon Brando went to Quinn's and those of us who were in the bar that night were lucky enough to meet and have a drink with him. Trevor Howard, the British actor in the role of Captain Bligh, never showed his face.

I had seen posters depicting beautiful Tahitian wahine with grass skirts and shapely bodies, and hoped to see them in the flesh. I did see some and they looked the part when they were facing the wrong way, with that lovely long black hair down to the waist. That was until they turned around.

"I don't think they've got a set of teeth between them!"

It blew our perception of Tahiti. Perhaps we were not in the right place or the tourist department had snatched all the ones on the posters and had hidden them somewhere on the island.

There was a furore over the motor scooters some of the crew had hired. Some had jumped on them pissed after vacating the Lafayette and either crashed them down the hill or in one case driven the scooter into the drink. I only had the money that I earned on the tobacco farm, which on the exchange rate did not go very far in Quinn's. I wondered whether the mutineers on the *Bounty* jumped ship when they encountered these toothless beauties. Since that visit I have returned to the island and can attest with my own eyes that the posters were in fact genuine.

On my return I was offered my berth for the next trip but Mr Moxley nipped this in the bud. That was a pity since another trip on the *Ruahine* would cover up the 'Voyage Not Completed' (VNC) stamped in my discharge book. My union fees were in arrears for the two months I had spent ashore in New Zealand. A hasty trip to the Pool was the answer but I did not look forward to handing my discharge book to Reggie the Rat when I got there.

Yet it was nice to be back in my old stamping ground, among the hustle and bustle of the docks. My friend the sea lawyer accompanied me with the letter he had drafted to the union office. Roger Wilkins, sitting in a cloud of smoke, read my letter and to my surprise cursed the fact that the bosun, a member of the union, should be reporting one of his fellow members to those up on the bridge. The only thing lacking in my report was a signed witness to the unsafe state of the stage in question. He asked that I leave the letter with him, saying he would take it from there. Should I run into difficulty at the Pool when I went for my next job, I should report to him. I thanked my friend for his help and looked at the piddling amount I had paid off with, resolving that the Pool would be my next destination after stowing my bag in Stornaway Castle.

The shipping company sends a report to the shipping master when an employee has misbehaved, which could result in a bad discharge. It certainly brought me grief on my visit to the Pool that morning. I was informed that I was barred from employment on any vessel going to New Zealand for six months. The majority of vessels on the board were heading to that part of the world, so that didn't give me much of a choice. To me it sounded pretty stupid as an itinerary could be changed at any time on a vessel and I could find myself in New Zealand again.

Whether the New Zealand authorities had any input into my six-month penalty I did not know. I reported to Roger Wilkins and he suggested that I should leave it at that. Covering up the VNC was the easiest way to solve a bad discharge, he said. I agreed and promised I would attend the union meeting next morning.

The union meeting was an eye-opener. 20,000 NUS members sailed from the combined docks in London, but only a handful attended the meeting. The reform movement had been thoroughly dismissed by the majority, we were told, and I detected some smugness from our speaker. The question of having convenors aboard vessels was on the agenda. I pointed out that the shipowners had too much power and it was about time members had some protection aboard. I surprised myself by asking why NUS officials in New Zealand made a beeline for the captain's cabin on coming aboard the vessel, before seeing the members they were supposed to be advocating for. My observation was ignored and I saw no change on my following trips to New Zealand. But the convenor system did eventuate in 1962.

My saga on the *Rangitata* had a sequel some twenty or more years later while I was a crew member aboard the New Zealand Rail ferry *Aratika*. The chief officer who presided over the 1960 event on the *Rangitata* had followed the track of many seamen in making a new life in New Zealand, working on the coast. He well remembered the event and suggested that had I not slammed the door in his face things would have been different. That of course did not answer the question of unsafe practices, but the past is the past and it stays there. There was no umbrage taken and we got on well.

The demise of the *Rangitata* came just two years later in 1962 when she was sent to Yugoslavian shipbreakers in Split and scrapped. The *Ruahine* survived a little longer, being sold to the Chinese and renamed the *Oriental Rio* in 1968. She was restyled to carry 220 passengers on world cruises before going to the knackers in 1974.

seventeen

I HAD NEVER HEARD OF the Saint Line, let alone the *St Thomas*. I assumed I was off to Buenos Aires, which seemed boring after three years on the Australia-New Zealand run. But it was a chance to cover up the VNC that stood out like a sore thumb in my discharge book.

I had to be accepted by the chief officer first, so my hopes were not high. The *St Thomas* was loading cargo in the Victoria Dock and the first thing I noticed was that she looked very modern, especially with the flash funnel, a squat affair with the radar scanner on the forward end. There was also a pong about this ship that was giving my nose a bit of GBH. Blimey, it hummed. On her previous trip she had been to the west coast of South America and had returned with a cargo of guano, or bird shit, used as a fertiliser for its high nitrogen content.

The mate studied my discharge book and asked me about the VNC. I didn't want to give a long-winded account so I told him I'd had too much to drink and missed the ship. He was good-natured about it and suggested that I wouldn't want to do the same in Buenos Aires. You're bleeding right, I thought.

Her modern lines belied her age; she had made her maiden voyage in 1948. There was accommodation for twelve but I never spotted any passengers. Why would anyone want to pay money for a passage on this chatty old tub? The galley was manned by a couple of Chinese cooks. She had five hatches and fourteen derricks, a holiday camp compared to some of the heavy lift jobs I had been on. The bosun was an Irishman and the crew were a mixture from all over the country. Included in the crew were four officer cadets. One had to feel sorry for them, as they were the dogsbodies to senior officers and got all the shitty jobs. All officers went through that stage during their apprenticeship.

I went to see Roger Wilkins at the union office to thank him for his help and to tell him I had found a job to South America. My time ashore, as always, was spent doing the rounds of the pubs and getting up to date with the latest news at home and abroad. Danny and Rene told me they were moving to the Kent Arms, a larger pub on North Woolwich Road, since the Royal Oak was too small to service the growing clientele. Otherwise, nothing had changed around the Royals.

We pulled out of Victoria Dock in April 1961 for a continental tour before embarking for South America. Antwerp, Rotterdam and Hamburg were on the

The *St Thomas*, a flash-looking ship for her time.

itinerary. The Beatles were still a small-time band performing at the Top Ten Club in Hamburg, alongside many other bands that were to become household names. For many of us the Beatles were the only attraction in Hamburg. On this occasion I came to Hamburg skint, which was a disaster. I didn't have money for the price of a beer let alone the entrance fee to go to watch the Beatles at the Top Ten. I was really pissed off at missing the mop tops. At least I had the pleasure of having seen them on my previous visit before the world had claimed them.

Rio held no secrets for me; I had seen most of this vibrant city on trips before. I had to laugh at our novice cadets who were in awe of the beautiful women who graced the white sands of Copacabana. They reminded me of myself on my first time there, gawking at the delights. A couple of the cadets ignored the warning from those of us who had been to the Cages in the red light district before. Their clothes were nicked along with their money while they romped with the girls. The law does not allow you to walk naked in public but fortune came to their rescue when they discovered the thieves had left their underpants. Our nightwatchman told us it was a hilarious sight to see two sailors jumping out of a cop car in just their underwear. The youngsters got a right old ribbing from us in the days that followed.

Buenos Aires, however, was to make me the laughing stock of the vessel. The Via Monte had not changed since my last visit two years before. The militia strutted the girly bars with their usual swagger. My eyes took in the pretty Latino ladies of the night, but their asking price was too much for my pocket. I left the girly bar fuelled with rum & coke, telling the lads I was going back to the ship.

I hailed what I thought was a taxi, which was in fact a police vehicle. A guy in a peak cap got out saying something I couldn't understand, then opened the door and shoved me in. The fact that I was pissed didn't help the situation.

The car was stopped and I was ordered out. They made me empty my pockets and relieved me of the few pesos I had left. My wristwatch was also confiscated before I was locked up in the 'Wall'.

The Wall was made of brick, with alcoves and iron grille doors. They could lock you in those holding cells if you came to their attention. There were no toilet facilities and no bunk to lay one's weary body on. A hard concrete floor was my bed for the remainder of the night.

The roar of traffic woke me from my drunken haze and I was frozen cold. My surroundings brought me out of my stupor. The pedestrians stared vacantly as I ranted and raved. "Anyone speak bloody English around here?"

I had to relieve myself against the wall and as much as I needed to, there was no way I was going to take a shit in full view of the public. By chance my ranting got the attention of a passing American. I gave him the name of my ship and he said he would get word to the vessel. It seemed ages before a police vehicle pulled up outside my cage — out jumped the chief steward and the coppers. I could only be thankful to the American who had taken pity on me.

I was let know how lucky I was when I arrived back on the vessel. Since my money had been taken off me the chief steward paid my fine for being drunk, as well as 'accommodation fees'. I had struck a rogue element of the Buenos Aires police force. Seamen have been found floating in the dock sometimes so I guess I got off cheaply.

The cadets got plenty of mileage from of my night of internment and reminded me at every possible opportunity. I decided that the Catholic Mission was a safer venue and attended the Saturday night dance. Alcohol was strictly prohibited and the matronly dancing partners were not exactly my cup of tea. At least I left the Mission with all my faculties, the Mission bus taking all us happy sailors to their vessels.

The voyage of convenience had taken just over three months by the time the *St Thomas* returned to the humdrum of the Royal Docks. The *Ruahine* and the *St Thomas* had covered my VNC but anything going to the antipodes was still off limits for another three months. My gallivanting around in the ports on the South American coast had not helped towards a substantial pay-off day for me but what else was new?

Dowdy old London had been waking up for some time with a culture that would put her on the globe as the swinging city of the world. People in a variety of industries collectively gave us the impetus for new thinking. Musicians had opened up our minds to the fact that we had a voice, that those in power could not say how we should live our lives. Fashion changed the way we thought about ourselves. Men lost the cuffs on their pants, and hemlines on dresses were hitched above the knees. Our hairstyles went from short back and sides to mop tops and long hair. On the down side, drugs like LSD were introduced, sending some users into a drugged-up haze. The young at heart fought for peace and told their governments in no uncertain terms by demonstrating their opposition. Sons and daughters drove the social and cultural revolution that was to reject the old lifestyles of their mothers and fathers.

Pop groups such as the Beatles, the Animals, and Bob Dylan had a big impact on the youth of the day. Mary Quant, Marianne Faithfull and Carnaby Street were the centres of Mod culture and the rebellious millions who mimicked them enjoyed the new-found freedoms that came with the lifestyle. It was a great time to be a British seaman, to witness the youngsters in countries embracing the lifestyle revolution of Britain.

My next ship was unexpected, considering the antipodes was prohibited. I happened to be in the Steps with some of the lads having our usual chinwag when someone put the word out that the *Dominion Monarch* was short of seamen and was due to sail the following day for South Africa, Australia and New Zealand.

What could I lose by putting my book over the counter? I could have gone to see Pooky but my ban came from the shipping master, and it was he who had the last say. I made my way down to the Pool that afternoon and was pleased to see no sign of Reggie the Rat. Handing my book over to the shipping clerk, I daringly asked for a job on the DM. There was nothing to give him an instant history of

The *Dominion Monarch*, nicknamed the 'Dominion Maniac'.
I managed to get as far as Lyttelton before jumping her.
VH Young

my employment, only the discharge book which recorded my previous trip on the *St Thomas* resulting in two VGs. The clerk said they were desperate to fill the DM and wrote out a chit to Mr Pook. I exited the Pool, as I didn't want Reggie to spoil my good fortune.

Pooky greeted me, wanting to know where I had been. "Good lord, what happened in Wellington?" He had spied my VNC and before I could answer he was giving me instructions to sign on the morning of sailing day, 8 August.

The *Dominion Monarch* (27,000 tons) was the largest quadruple-screw motor vessel in the world. This two-funnel beauty made her maiden voyage in 1939 for Shaw Savill and recorded the fastest trip from London to Fremantle in 23 days. After war duties as a troop ship, she resumed commercial duties in 1948 calling at Cape Town, Fremantle, Melbourne, Sydney, Wellington, Auckland and Lyttelton. She had accommodation for 500 first class passengers, and conveyed them across the oceans at a cruising speed of 19 knots. Her six holds carried general cargoes outward-bound, and on return to the UK carried meat and dairy products.

She was nicknamed the 'Dominion Maniac' because of the boisterous crews who sailed her. Boisterous may be too kind a word to describe some of the nutcases who stepped aboard that vessel. Her crews had earned notoriety on the New Zealand coast with the port authorities and the law. "Lock up your shops and women before they arrive!" went the cry.

Kitted out with the much-prized Shaw Savill jumper, I was delighted with my good fortune. The Royal Navy hat those on deck had to wear was not quite so flash. They were discarded into the Thames the night we sailed for Southampton. The exercise was foolish since the article that was given free on joining cost us each ten shillings to replace, and we were logged a day's pay for throwing ship property over the wall. Not a bad start to the trip.

Everyone was mindful that this princess of the oceans was on her second-to-last voyage before being sent to Seattle as floating accommodation for the 1962 World Fair.

My cabin-mate 'Tiny' was anything but small. The DM was made for him, I reckoned. As we departed from Southampton the streamers and well-wishers on the dock brought back memories. This great port had seen millions depart for a new life abroad on these leviathans.

My mooring station was aft and I was assigned the twelve-to-four watch. Our accommodation was two-berth, on the portside. We had a night in Cape Town before setting course for Fremantle. One of our seamen, Jesse, whom I had seen in the pubs around the Royal Docks, had stayed away from the Pig & Whistle to give the booze the flick. Unfortunately his quest to dry out took a turn for the worse and he succumbed to delirium tremens, known to sailors as the dreaded DTs.

He was on our watch and we all had an interest in his progress. One night he was not to be found on our midnight turn-to. Tiny found him in the seamen's washhouse lying fully booted and spurred in one of the tubs.

It was fortunate there was no water in the bath. The withdrawal from alcohol was taking its toll and he was shunted off to the ship's hospital, and eventually taken ashore in Fremantle in a bad way.

After the short trip across the Tasman we arrived in Wellington. I didn't see any shops closing on account of the Dominion Maniac, nor did I perceive any lack of women. The highlight of our stay was the *Dominion Monarch* ball at Trades Hall. Anyone who was anyone in Wellington attended the ball, which saw the drag queens from the DM decked out in their finery.

I got the feeling that Kiwis were not quite ready to accept such ostentatious display. There were echoes of disapproval from a weekly rag that dug up all the dirt; the journalism read like a version of our Sunday *News of the World* in the UK.

I wasn't interested in the ball as I had been taken by a young lady who worked in a milkbar next to the Roxy picture house on Willis Street. Her goal was to save enough money to go to the UK. The milkbar job was an extension of her day job, which meant she worked long hours.

Flying to destinations around the world was far too dear for the working class in those days. It was cheaper to book a passage on one of the many liners that pulled into port. She had booked a fare on a Dutch liner and I promised I would keep in touch. I left Wellington thinking I had found love, amusing Tiny who reckoned some hairy-arsed AB was already chatting her up.

Our arrival in Lyttelton meant plenty of service for the pubs of this small town. My baseball bat-wielding publican from the Royal who had banned me a few years before had been replaced. The British Hotel had not reached its premier status at this time. A ship from the New Zealand Navy arrived in port a week later and this was cause for some of the hotheads to start a riot. It began in the pub and ended up on the street. Bodies went flying everywhere and baton-wielding Navy patrolmen got stuck in, as did the police who called for reinforcements from Christchurch. Tiny restrained me from taking part when the call came. He said the stewards had started the fracas, so let them be carted off to the nick. It was good advice — quite a few of the crew spent the night in the slammer.

The night before the DM left New Zealand we heard about a party being thrown at a house up the hill. A bunch of us arrived with our carry-outs at the venue, which clearly could not accommodate the numbers arriving. This was the last thing I observed — I succumbed to a night of top shelf liquor. Someone was shaking the life out of me, and echoing in my ears were the frantic words, "We've missed the bloody ship, it's sailed on us!"

On the *Hurunui* we took the first shipment of meat and wool
from New Zealand to the USSR.
VH Young

The words woke me up and I looked out of the window to a view of the harbour.
No *Dominion Monarch*, only the ferry *Hinemoa* and a couple of home boats along
the dock. Shit! I thought. What was I to do now?

Our host Alan was on the *Maori,* which ran in conjunction from Lyttelton to
Wellington with the *Hinemoa.* He offered to ringbolt us to Wellington that night.
Three others, all stewards, had also missed the ship. We ringbolted to Wellington
and were wary of lawmen since we were now in the country illegally.

Leaving my fellow seamen, I made tracks to my girlfriend's flat up the top of
Willis Street. She had gone to work and I had to spend the day wandering around
Wellington until her arrival. She was amazed to see me, but she was saving for
her trip to Europe and I sensed that my unexpected appearance interfered with
her plans. She put me up but I knew I would have to clear out. Anyway, she was
too near the city for my liking.

I searched the paper for a job and found one requiring labourers for drain-
laying in the new suburb of Porirua. The only clothes I had were the ones I went
ashore in. The boss, an Irishman, picked me up early the following morning, took
a look at my jeans and jacket and asked me if I had any working gear. I stuck out
like a sore thumb and it didn't take him long to figure out I was a jumped seaman.
Paddy told me not to worry, as he'd had other jumped seamen work for him. That
made me feel better, as did the pair of overalls he gave me.

One of the guys had a spare room at the house he was renting and I moved
in, sharing the bills. My girlfriend was much happier now that I had a job and

my own accommodation, but we grew apart as the months went by and we saw no future in the relationship. One day we were doing drainage in another new suburb, Titahi Bay. Paddy came running over, exclaiming there was a policeman who had come to see me — at times like these you need a Mintie.

I was taken to the lock-up in Wellington and Paddy promised to speak up for me in court the following morning. But I had broken my contract, and the shipping company demanded my return. Judge Scully sentenced me to be held in Mount Crawford until a ship was available to deport me. Paddy did his best, saying he would take guardianship of me until a vessel was found. The court rejected the offer and I was shunted up the hill. It was one of the lowest days of my life.

Not long after, James K Baxter was to write about the same judge: "… Skully sits like Rhadamanthus/Weighing the guts of the poor in his scales/And handing out fines not one of them can pay, /And riding the drunks with a saddle of iron/ And treating the Islanders like idiot children,/I must thank Mr Skully for the opportunity/Of completing my Marxist education …"

I was put in a dormitory cell. Jumped seamen flowed through the prison and didn't stay long, a fellow guest of Her Majesty's assured me.

The lock-up was unfamiliar territory and I was shit-scared. Paddy visited me with fags, which were gold in the nick. He bemoaned the useless twit who he had hired in my place and said he would visit the following week. The inmate who told me I would not be there long came up trumps and Paddy never had a chance to visit again. A lucky star had come to my rescue. I was to sign on the NZSCo vessel *Hurunui* bound for London instead of being deported.

Usually the company to whom you were originally contracted, Shaw Savill in my case, would repatriate you home, so it was a surprise to be signing on a different company — not that I minded. I had overstayed my welcome by four months and it was good to be standing on the deck of a ship again. I also became part of an historical event on that day, 3 April 1962, when the *Hurunui* sailed from Wellington on her landmark trip carrying the very first shipment of New Zealand meat and wool to Leningrad in Soviet Russia. I worked all the overtime on offer to boost my pay-off. I was looking forward to seeing what it would be like in Russia. Don't jump ship there, they reckoned.

The Kiel Canal, the only transit to the Baltic Sea and Leningrad, has a lock at each end of its 58-mile stretch. It was a disappointment — there was nothing much to see but grazing land. Leningrad (now St Petersburg) lies in a bay at the top of the Gulf of Finland. It has a fabulous history and is obviously a city to explore with its palaces and buildings if you can, but we were in the Cold War era which unfortunately prevented such activities. A shipboard celebration in the officers' accommodation marked this first for New Zealand-Soviet trade.

My pay-off came to a tidy sum thanks to all the overtime. My arrears in union fees were also substantial, and Roger Wilkins groaned when he saw another VNC in my discharge book. He reckoned I was a serial ship-jumper and I should forget about the Kiwi coast. He told me to tell him when I was ready to go to the Pool. I was quite sure I would need his help.

The *Dominion Monarch* at Glasgow wharf, Wellington, 1950s.
Alexander Turnbull Library F20505 1/2Δ

eighteen

B Y THIS TIME THE KENT Arms had overtaken the Royal Oak as the preferred watering hole for seamen. I had reached age 21, which empowered me to run my life as I saw fit, and I managed to stretch my shore leave to over a month. I was beginning to be smarter with money but I had a long way to go. My stay was lengthened by a tryst with a girl I met in the Kent Arms. I also went to union meetings, which attracted the usual dismal handful of members from the port. If I needed advocacy for my sins, it was only right I should take an interest in union affairs.

I was at the meeting in the NUS dock office when it was announced that the shipowners had bent to the union's drive to have convenors on each vessel, to be the eyes and ears of the union. I asked who they envisaged should take the position of convenor since it was a very important jobs. If company contract men took on the advocacy for the union, how would that stand against their loyalty to the company? This would be a conflict of interest. I proposed that unestablished seafarers, not contracted to a company or the Pool, should fill the convenor's position. I was only one voice, and more powerful voices conducting the meeting dismissed my concerns. To them, winning a concession over the shipowners was more important. I could understand their excitement since it was a milestone for the union and they wanted it implemented as soon as possible with no complications.

After a month ashore my finances were low and I knew I had to get back to sea pronto. The *Hurunui* was my last discharge, recording two VGs. I did not bother to ask any help from the union and looked through the jobs advertised on the Pool board. I was pushing my luck if I chose any ships going to the South Pacific, so I opted for a vessel on a home trade run before going deep sea. The Pacific Steam Navigation vessel *Cuzco* was due to sail for Liverpool that night.

"I'll take it," I said before the clerk could get a closer look at my discharge book. He was desperate to fill the job and I was just as pleased to avoid the hassle that my VNC might bring. The mate gave my discharge book closer scrutiny, but was more interested as to whether I had my gear aboard. I didn't but that would be no problem as it was just over the road at Stornaway Castle.

What a line-up of ports we were designated to call at. Liverpool for a week was a hectic affair. I met a girl at the Clock pub opposite the Locarno dance hall.

Scouse birds are a bossy lot, said in the nicest possible way. She lived in the local housing estate in Huyton and was a real earbasher. I was ordered what time to pick her up each evening. My hair needed cutting, she complained. Didn't I have any clothes other than that jeans and jacket? Nor do you take a lady from the Huyton housing estate to the seafarer's favourite pub, Ma Booth's on the waterfront. She was quite put out that I should take her into the rough and tumble of a dock bar. The Magic Clock in the market, patronised by dandies, or the Legs of Man, were more preferable to her.

I found out early that my randy hands could only stray so far before I was threatened with a kick in the cobblers. She was very attractive in her tight sack dress, turning eyes wherever we went. My attempts to meet her demands came to nought. I was surely not versed in the ways of courting, which of course was what she wanted and I was too blind to see. Anyway, at 21, I had no interest in a long-term relationship. The only romance for me was the sea. She took me to see her parents the night before we sailed. I became a right little Romeo promising to write to her everyday.

Having signed deep sea articles we slid down the Mersey into the Irish Sea for Las Palmas and the Spanish Main. The seamen were mostly the 'Birkenhead Navy', what we Cockneys called a Scouse crowd. I was the only Londoner to sign on deep sea. Scouse crowds are a good laugh and I enjoyed their company if you could get a word in edgewise.

Those who had been to the west coast before advised us novices to stock up on smellies like aftershave lotions that we could sell to the local males who used them as a lure for their señoritas. Also on our shopping list were cheap perfumes that we could use as barter with the prostitutes.

As usual we were assigned to watches. My life had taken a few twists and turns I could have done without the past six months, and it was good to put it behind me and get back into the business of going to sea. The open waters had that effect for me — they were an elixir that could wash away any depressing moments.

Taking bunkers in Las Palmas, we headed into the Caribbean, for the Colombian port of Barranquilla. The first things you noticed were the stifling heat and the mozzies that bit the hell out of you. Our second Caribbean port was Cartagena de Indias. Here was the real Spanish Main with a lot of history behind it. The huge Spanish treasure fleets of the 16th century sailed from here to Spain. That was of course if they could elude that Elizabethan seadog, Sir Francis Drake, who sacked Cartagena in 1580.

The fortifications the Spanish built to protect them from British privateers were still evident. I would have loved to be a crew member on one of those marauders in those days.

Our next Colombian port was Buenaventura on the Pacific. It required us to transit the Panama, but before that we had a stop in Cristobal, which meant a run ashore to the Zanzibar. I enjoyed the attention of the señoritas there but always ran out of dollars before I could get more intimate. For these girls prostitution was purely a way to exist, unlike the prosperous European nations where I assumed it was a matter of choice. There was no such thing as free love; I never heard of any sailor I sailed with who could melt the heart of those Latin beauties, but that is not to say it couldn't happen. An offer of financial security and a haven anywhere but Panama would probably have caught their interest, since it was the reason they spent their nights in a bar.

For jack tars thousands of miles from home I will make no bones, they were welcome company. Some of them were real fiery, especially if any another señorita muscled in on their client, as I saw in a Valparaiso bar.

There were some wise heads on the *Cuzco* who had seen it all before and told us there were better sights to see once we were on the west coast. They would rather have a clear head going through the canal the next day and save the dollars than have a night ashore in Cristobal. The advice never washed with me or the other youngsters and we hared off ashore as though it was the last time we would hit land. No one showed any sympathy for the hangovers we endured as *Cuzco* made her way across Limón Bay to the Gatun Locks in the stifling heat. Those bleeding mozzies seemed to be attracted to those who sweated rum & coke.

Our list of ports on the west coast was heavy, and sometimes we did two a day. Buenaventura on Colombia's Pacific coast was notable for the animals on sale on the dockside — tiger cubs, grass monkeys and parrots were all on show.

I handed over a carton of Lucky Strikes for a grass monkey, thinking I had got myself a bargain. I named him Speedy Gonzales because there was no way you could catch this mischievous little bugger. I put him in the cabin and forgot to tell my cabin-mate. Speedy gave him a near heart attack when he opened the door and the young fellow made all haste in his escape from the cabin.

When I returned from ashore to find no Speedy I was pissed off. I looked everywhere except up the mainmast. There at the very top, surveying all around him, was 200 fags worth of monkey.

"How the fuck am I going to get him down?" I cried.

Some smart-arse suggested I lash a banana to a halyard and coax him down that way. The nightwatchman would keep an eye on him, he said, and I turned in.

Speedy was nowhere to be found in the morning. The watchman said he must have gone while he was cooking his supper. The ship left Buenaventura at noon and Speedy, I assumed, had signed off before we left. That was until the chief steward found him in his cabin helping himself to the fruit bowl. Reporting his finding to the skipper, he told me I should set Speedy free at the next port as I would not be allowed to bring him into the UK, and anyway he wasn't going to have the rest of the crew bothered by the young fellow. A cabin was a cruel place to confine young Speedy, who I had bought without thinking how I would look after him.

The chief steward took a shine to Speedy and relieved me of responsibility for his welfare, and even offered me the 200 fags I paid for him. Speedy and the chief seemed to have an affinity that had us all amazed. He could be sat on his favourite perch, the top of the mast, and at a call from the chief steward he would scamper down and find solace on his shoulder. Contrary to the captain telling me that entry into the UK would not be allowed, Speedy, as far as I know, was still with the chief steward when we got back to Liverpool. It was a happy ending I assume but I have seen some unhappy endings for animals that could not cope with leaving the tropics and surviving in Atlantic temperatures.

The *Cuzco's* next stop was the small port of Esmeraldas in Ecuador. You could not help noticing the ethnicity of the people here. The majority were negro folk who somehow looked out of place. Colombia also had a negro minority but the indigenous South Americans were made up from Indian tribes. I had to read up the history of Esmeraldas to get the answer. A Spanish slave ship beached on this part of the Ecuadorian coast in the 16th century. The slaves were sent into the interior to find help but never returned. Can you blame them! Eventually the slaves took over this part of Ecuador and founded Esmeraldas. Today the port, Guayaquil, is Ecuador's chief petroleum terminal.

In Guayaquil the population was the customary mix of Spanish, Mestizo and African. I wondered what beasties were below the surface of the Daule River because the mosquitoes were lethal above. Guayaquil is close to the equator and had the most uncomfortable heat I have ever experienced.

I was amazed at the rolls of American $20 bills that were carried by some of the locals. The sailors pawned their perfume and nylons for cash and souvenirs. The Ecuadorian money was Mickey Mouse currency and had no value outside that country.

I was warned the dollars could be counterfeit so I never parted with my Bond Street smellies. Speedy caused a riot almost when he snatched a wad of dollars from one local. Somehow he had escaped the chief steward, presenting himself on deck while our Latin friend flashed the wedge. Speedy must have thought the notes were food as he perched himself on the ship's highest point to enjoy a feast.

It was enough to bring tears to your eyes, watching shreds of $20 bills float down through the air. Nothing could console the owner of the money. The movement of cargo stopped, with the local dockworkers finding the funny side of Speedy's antics. I almost had a bowel movement when a knife was produced by the owner, bringing him to the attention of the *policia* on the wharf. They rushed up the gangway with guns drawn and restrained him. Speedy decided the notes were not to his taste, and hundreds of dollars floated anywhere but into its owner's hands.

Unperturbed by the near riot he had caused, Speedy scampered down the mast to resume his mischief. Oh, to be a monkey, imagine what you could get away with! I could sympathise with the unfortunate man who was escorted off by the lawmen. The chief steward had no inkling of what his monkey had done until later when he discovered Speedy had climbed out of an open porthole. I reckoned he would make a great lookout on his favourite perch.

Although Sir Francis Drake gave the Spaniards a headache with his raids on their townships on the Caribbean mainland of South America, I was not aware he had caused havoc around the Pacific coast. Quaffing *cerveza* in one girly bar, the women were still raving on about the 'Engleesh pirate Drake' sacking Guayaquil nearly 400 years before. Boy, some of those señoritas can give you a right old earbashing and you couldn't understand a word until they squeezed the crown jewels and offered a jiggy-jig. Pleading poverty brought another round of abuse, which went in one ear and out the other.

Our next destination was Chimbote in Peru, a small fishing port. We were there for only a few hours loading fishmeal and canned fish before sailing to Callao 400km down the coast. Chimbote today is Peru's largest fishing port with modern canning factories.

Callao is just 15km from Lima. It was founded in 1535 when Philip of Spain had a fortress built in his name, the Castillo de Real Felipe, which is still prominent as you come into Callao. The port itself grew to be the premier city for Spanish trade in the Pacific coast of South America.

I offloaded some of my bottles of aftershave to boost my finances, which had been sorely diminished in Guayaquil, and we went to Lima that night to see the sights. There I was given a potent nectar called anisette, a clear liquor with the plant inside the bottle. When the bottle was empty it could be filled with water. As its name implies, it tastes like aniseed. The crystals of the anisette plant would dissolve and a free bottle would be created within a day or two.

It was highly illegal to bring this drink into the UK. Anisette was lethal to unsuspecting victims. Also, I believe, those in power did not like the thought of the minions making two bottles of booze out of one.

We got to the big smoke via a corrupt taxi driver who tried charging the earth but could not fool the Scouses who had made the trip many times. The red light district had plenty of bars and we were soon in their favourite bar with the dishy girls of the night. A glass of anisette was put in front of me. My señorita pointed at the glass saying 'mucho loco' — the drink would send me mad.

As I woke up in the morning I heard the voice of my cabin-mate screeching in my ear that it was morning smoko. A sweet cloying taste invaded my palate and the real world came into focus.

I remembered very little of my night out in Lima. My wad of notes had gone, and I was thankful to my mates for shoving me in a taxi and getting me back to the ship in one piece. You could always be assured that missing hours would be related to you with glee by those not afflicted. I had been rescued from the bed of my señorita in the upper floors of the bar. The story went that she had returned to the bar complaining to her boss that I had flaked out on her and she couldn't wake me. She complained to my mates, who went aloft and got me respectable before taking me back to the vessel. That didn't stop her from emptying my pockets. It was probably the most expensive time I had spent with a lady of the night without gratification. Never again would I quaff this exotic liquor that has the ability to take a day or two out of your life. The bosun nodded knowingly at my late arrival on deck. He had seen it all before.

We made our way along the coast of Peru to the small port of Pisco, but spent only a few hours there. The same was the case with our next ports Matarani and nearby Mollendo. Arica, our first port in northern Chile, had just held the preliminary rounds of the 1962 World Soccer Cup matches a month before. The ports of Iquique and Antofagasta had saltpetre, guano and copper as exports. Chances of getting ashore were few and far between after Callao. I stayed aboard after my foray into Lima. I was waiting for Valparaiso where we were due to stay for three days. I hoped my cache of cologne would bring in enough funds to keep me going.

Valparaiso has to be one of the best runs ashore on the west coast according to the benchmarks of wine, women and song. The renowned city lived up to its

The name *Cuzco* came from the capital city of the Incan empire.
We must have visited every port on the west coast of South America.
VH Young

reputation. There was no anisette or any other strange liquor this time. Selling all my smellies, I went ashore with a pocketful of pesos and headed for the hot spots, and managed to keep my faculties for the two nights there. It was so cheap that creeping into the arms of a girl of your fancy never broke the bank. I left Valparaiso thinking the Chilean folk were the gentlest people I had encountered.

The name General Bernardo O'Higgins Riquelme was advertised everywhere. The surname looked out of place in a Spanish society and I wondered why an Irishman was revered in Chile. I was to learn he was the illegitimate son of Ambrosio O'Higgins, a Spanish officer of Irish ancestry. He was the liberator of Chile, who won independence from Spain in 1817. He ruled Chile until 1823 when he was deposed.

Our last call on the west coast was Talcahuano, the port for Concepción 15km up the road. In safe Talcahuano Bay, it was touted as the best harbour in Chile, and probably why it was chosen as their naval base. We sailed for Panama with hatches full of guano and fishmeal.

Halfway up the coast I had an uncomfortable twinge in me John Thomas. Venereal diseases were a hazard hardy seadogs had to expect if we were to spend time in the bawdy districts of foreign lands, but it was very disconcerting for a first-timer. I was ashamed and wanted to keep it under wraps. I snuck up to the mate to report my malady, and he passed me on to the chief steward.

"You're the second one who's been up here. Where did you catch it?"

Who bloody well cared where I caught it! I just wanted it out of my system. Under Speedy's disapproving eye the chief explained that he would put me on the list to visit the pox doctor when we reached Curaçao in the Caribbean in a few days.

"There will probably be more of you, there always is," he said as I departed. One would rather not advertise afflictions of that variety.

By lunchtime I had been found out, and became the butt of bawdy ribbing. Shipmates will not let you forget your misery. More terrifying was the 'umbrella' treatment I was told I could expect. It was described as a small device that is inserted in the penile canal that opens up like an umbrella to be slowly withdrawn, extracting the impurities. It sounded dreadful and I reported back to the chief steward to take my name off the doctor's list. I was not aware of the seriousness of VD and the chief sent me packing with a flea in my ear and told me to take my affliction seriously. I departed his cabin in no doubt I was in for the umbrella treatment once we hit dry ground.

Curaçao, part of the Dutch Antilles, was the bunkering port for many vessels in that part of the world. Cargo vessels usually bunkered at the oil berth in Curaçao Bay. Ruins of a fortress built by the 17th-century buccaneer Henry Morgan lie just above the bay. Passenger vessels would dock in Willemstad, so that they could sample the delights of this small Dutch outpost.

Three of us jumped in the agent's car, not to sample the delights of Willemstad, but to visit the pox doctor. The umbrella treatment that I was fearful of never took place: instead a needle of penicillin was produced. As I pulled up my pants I wondered if that was all there was to the treatment. To my relief we were in and out and were cautioned that no alcohol was to be taken until the condition cleared. But three years later I was to experience the fearful umbrella treatment in savage El Salvador. By this time I had a more mature view of the gravity of sexually communicable diseases.

The *Cuzco* arrived back in Liverpool, with our voyage taking just over two months. Apart from the disease I got in some floozie's bed, the trip and the crew were magic. Though the itinerary of going in and out of so many ports was hectic I was impressed with the west coast of South America — it was far superior to the east coast run from Rio to Buenos Aires. My reasoning was very narrow: wine, women and song. But what other reasons would cause sane men to spend weeks in an iron tub rocking around the oceans of the world?

My discharge book was looking less like a crime magazine, my latest trip listing a couple of VGs. I had written a letter to my Liverpool girlfriend and posted it from Valparaiso giving her the estimated arrival time of the *Cuzco*. My belated missive garnered no reply, possibly due to the mail from far-off countries in those days. I had stopped peeing razor blades, which suggested the penicillin had done its work. However, it was stupid for me to pursue her. I boarded the train for the four-hour ride to London and Stornaway Castle.

nineteen

In London I jumped on a District Line tube for Plaistow, took the No 69 double-decker down to Custom House, dumped my bags at the Flying Tab-Nab and booked in for the week. I didn't want to see the girl I had met on my previous stay until I had confirmed that I was cured. Nor did I want to go to the Royal Albert VD clinic in case shipboard acquaintances might spot me. News travels fast in the seafaring community. The doctor in Canning Town confirmed that all was okay but advised me to take precautions for another week.

If I ventured into the Kent Arms or got out and about around the docks, I was bound to bump into someone who knew her. While I was travelling, one of her siblings spotted me. There was no use hiding now, I was sprung.

"Why didn't you write? Why didn't you come round?"

Women have this awful knack of reading a guy's mind. Nor could she get her head around the unexpected fervour I now showed for Alcoholics Anonymous. She was happy just staying on a couple of Babychams all evening while my glass of orange was questioned by guys who knew me better.

I could not blame her for thinking that I had suddenly lost my marbles when I returned to the Flying Angel for the night. I kept to the doctor's advice for the week and put up with all the grief of a hidden agenda. I got my clearance and announced to my lady friend (much to her amusement) that I was giving up my AA support to go on the piss. As for what else, we would wait for what the night brought.

My funds were in good order since my leisure time had been a cheap affair on the orange juice. After a month of abstinence, it didn't take me long until I was back in the groove and swinging the night away. In fact, I should be saying, twisting the night away. Chubby Checker was in with his 1961 hit 'Let's twist again' which he followed up with his 'Limbo Rock' in '62. I wasn't going to get a hernia for Chubby or anyone else, trying to go below the bar.

The revolution was still raging in Britain and it seemed like we were all making up time. Vespa and Lambretta scooters became the in-thing to be seen around on with a bird on the back. The young became either Mods or Rockers. These groups were to do battle in Hastings a year later and it would seem the Mods held sway if fashion gave a verdict.

I began to get itchy feet and three weeks ashore seemed far too long. Finally I'd had enough and cleared off down the Pool. There was no sign of Reggie the Rat as I pulled my eyes from the board showing the ships on offer. Nor were there ships running down to the west coast of South America.

I met a ghost from the past. This guy was certifiable for the nut house I reckoned. He pointed to the board.

"*Sugar Producer*, going to the West Indies, three month trip, sign on tomorrow," he said.

"Fuck the West Indies, what do I want to go down there for?" I replied.

"Come on, Dave, let's have a laugh!"

"No, I don't fancy a tanker." I was quite certain about this.

"It ain't a tanker, you wanker, it's a sugar boat! Carries bleeding sugar."

"Has it got derricks?"

"Course it has."

And so the man from the *Dominion Monarch* convinced me that three months with him would return me to my sanity. His name was Harry: he was the laugh of the messroom, and talk about pulling birds. He was a real handsome geezer and had a charm with females that none of us on the DM could match, a roguish persona was obviously endearing. So I jumped into the fire as it was and handed over my discharge book.

"*Sugar Producer*," I said.

"It's down the Tate & Lyle wharf in Silvertown. Go and see the doctor first," said the clerk as he made out a chit for me to see the mate on board.

Harry had a car, which was an advantage. The copper at the gate asked what business we two villains had. "The *Sugar Producer*," we sang in unison, showing him our chits from the Pool. We passed the chief officer's inspection and would sign on the morrow.

"Let's go in the Jubilee," said Harry, but it was lunchtime and crowded with workers from the Tate & Lyle sugar factory. He dropped me off at the Steps and I promised to meet him at the Two Puddings in Stratford that evening for a last drink before sailing. I would not be popular with the lady friend when I told her I would be off to sea in the next couple of days. What did she expect anyway? I'm a seaman, I told myself. Women can be the devil's own.

"You can go to the Pudding on your own," she replied.

There was no convincing her I was almost broke and had to start work again. The finances would need an advance note when I signed on just to keep me going. She got over her tantrum and off we went down to the Two Puddings on the Stratford Broadway. The band was playing Bobby Darren's hit song 'Things' when we got there. It was one of my favourites at the time, as was Gene Pitney's

'Liberty Valance'. Harry was in fine form, and I looked forward to the trip we were about to embark on.

Silvertown Services Shipping Ltd acquired three ships in 1951 for the sugar trade: the *Sugar Transporter, Producer* and *Refiner*. In 1956 the company went into bulk carriage of molasses and raw sugar and engaged the Athel Line to manage the heavy bulk ships. In 1961 both companies united under the Sugar Line, sailing from the Tate & Lyle Company factory at Clyde wharf Silvertown E16.

The *Producer* had three holds. The middle one was a double, serviced by ten derricks on the ratchet system, which is used to lift or lower a derrick over the part of the hold that is being worked. The concertina lids were heavy and the derrick had to be in exactly the right spot to lower the lids when closing up. McGregor hatch covers were still a dream in those days. There were two tarpaulin covers to each hatch and they were a nightmare to spread in Canada's wintry weather.

Two incidents marked this trip. First was the two most powerful nations in the world eyeballing each other with the threat of nuclear weapons. The other was unexpected and the saddest event of my sea-going career up to that time. It was a funny old trip. We were to be hopping around the West Indies, Canada and the east coast and gulf states of America.

The United States had caught the Russians placing missiles on Cuba that were capable of reaching the American mainland. Soviet vessels were photographed with missiles on their decks and were ordered by President Kennedy to turn around. American jets buzzed each vessel, making sure they were not carrying any weapons. The *Producer* happened to be right in the firing line and Captain Cassidy ordered us to display the Union Jack along the hull to appease the itchy fingers of the jet pilots who flew around the vessel at mast height. Old Khrushchev

The *Sugar Producer*. "Display the Union Jack over the side!" cried the captain. It was the time of the Cuban missile crisis.
VH Young

had the world on edge. In the end the Russians backed down and we breathed a sigh of relief. We thought it was great fun being buzzed and stuck two fingers in V-signs at the pilots. Had we known the gravity of the situation we may not have been so frivolous.

Our itinerary took us from Montego Bay to Montreal with a load of sugar. After discharging it we had to clean the hatches out for our next cargo, which was paper for Baltimore in Maryland. I couldn't stand the cloying smell of sugar after washing out the holds.

Harry and I were always first ashore to suss out the crumpet. The last time I was in Montreal I was a milkbar cowboy. This time my age meant I could down a few mugs of Moose and Labatt's grog in Joe Beef's. I could never get over those Canucks tipping salt in their beer. What a disgusting custom!

We had to make haste from one pub because this guy's wife had the hots for Harry and was getting upset. It wasn't Harry's fault since we were drinking with the crowd, minding our own business, when this geezer butts in warning Harry to keep his eyes off his missus. That had us up in arms and a battery of swearwords followed. It attracted a lot of unknown faces around our table and the barman advised us to vacate the bar while the going was good. I suggested to Harry he cover up his boat race so we could have a decent drink.

It was the beginning of November in Canada, and talk about freezing your cobblers off when battening up the hatches. My earlier visits should have had me used to the Canadian winters, but I don't know of any mates who ever got used to it. We sailed for Baltimore with our holds full of paper, then light-shipped over to Port of Spain for another cargo of sugar. This time the sugar was bound for the port of Corpus Christi in Texas. We had three days here. Four of us went ashore that evening, made friends with the locals and got the taste for the Lone Star beer. I don't know what it is with Yanks but they just love Limey accents. All we'd have to do was speak and another round of beer would arrive at the table.

The outcome of our foray ashore was a visit from the sheriff and his deputy a day and a half later. Texas was the place to spin bullshit and our tall stories had the locals mesmerised until the law sauntered in. The locals all seemed to know the sheriff who was shaking his head at us.

"When are you folks going back to your ship?" he drawled.

The skipper had put a call out that he had four missing seamen. The deputy sheriff knew where to find us, saying we'd had enough and he would take us back to the vessel. He waited while we had the cheek to buy a case of Lone Star beer each. Shaking hands with the barkeep and the locals we boarded the paddy wagon. The hardest part of the journey was staggering up the gangway with a carton of beer.

The mate was standing up the top of the gangway watching the performance. We knew we had to front the skipper and he was one of those chief mates who never made an issue of things. The four of us stood waiting in the skipper's cabin. I couldn't believe the bullshit Harry was spinning as to why we were a day and a half late. He must have thought we were still in the bar talking to the locals. I burst out laughing at the outrageous tale he was trying to tell the skipper: something about the four of us being taken hostage by Apache Indians. Even the skipper had a crack by asking if we spied Geronimo.

More unbelievable was the punishment. If we shared the cartons of beer we had bought ashore with the crew the incident would lie in abeyance for the rest of the trip. What more could you ask.

Just down from Corpus Christi is the port of Brownsville on the Texas-Mexico border. We were there a short time to unload the remainder of our cargo. I was pissed off at not getting ashore because it was my turn as nightwatchman. I tried palming the job onto others, but to no avail.

We found you could cross the border and do shopping or have a drink in a Mexican cantina. Harry and a few others took the piss out of me for having to stay aboard as they scooted down the gangway to explore Brownsville. By morning Harry was dead, murdered by a Mexican. I heard the story in brief from those who were with him that night. They had ventured over the border to a cantina. The barmaid took a shine to Harry, which brought animosity from her boyfriend. A missile was thrown at the bar mirror, shattering the glass into shards and cutting the barmaid. Harry chased and caught the culprit, who turned out to be the boyfriend. He stabbed Harry with a knife.

The police took the murderer into custody. Harry was laid to rest in England. There was no such thing as counselling in those days. As his cabin-mate it was left to me to clear his belongings and pass them on to the chief steward. Those of us who lived below decks and enjoyed his company were reminded of him every day by an empty chair in the messroom, and we were left to deal with the grief alone. The men who were there at the time of Harry's death put in reports and answered many questions.

We left Brownsville in shock. Seamen are like a family on board and tragic events like this were thankfully few.

We made our way to Georgetown on the South American coast to load sugar for Europe. We had one more stop in Haiti before making tracks for home.

Haiti has a colourful history. The Spanish, French and British all had a go at colonising it in the 18th century. A black army of ex-slaves, led by Toussaint L'Ouverture, defeated them all. Napoleon hoodwinked Toussaint by luring him to France for talks in 1802 and kept him captive, where he died in 1803.

I had the pleasure of reading the history of the greatest negro general of them all, Henri Christophe, who was not going to be a lackey of the French or any other power. From 1804 his army of slaves swept over all and he built a fortress overlooking Port-au-Prince, which deterred would-be invaders. He gained independence for his country from France in 1804, and made a deal with the European powers to send schoolteachers and doctors to help his people rise above illiteracy. In 1811 he declared himself King Henri I. Although he was dedicated to giving his subjects higher standards of living and education, his autocratic nature put him offside with others in powerful positions. He committed suicide in 1820 after being betrayed by his generals.

Port-au-Prince had not changed much from my observations on our short stay, and even now the Haitians still haven't found peace. I am not a historian but I have an affection for the underdog and for events that bring triumph over adversity. The American Revolution and the French Revolution were 18th-century milestones in history. We are flooded with history books of these events. For the black slaves who were shipped in fetters to the plantations of Carolina and the Caribbean, Haiti was their revolution.

I left Port-au-Prince with a knowledge of its impressive history but not much else. I wanted the trip to end. My 22nd birthday passed unheralded and Christmas day in the cold Atlantic was celebrated three days before arrival in London. We docked at the company wharf in Silvertown, having spent over three months in the Indies and America. Having completed pay-off, with my union dues paid up to date, I picked up my bag and walked down the gangway, not looking back.

News of Harry's death had preceded me and was the talk among the sea-going fraternity in Custom House. I didn't know his family but I had met his girlfriend the night before we sailed. His family would have been devastated. I was the target for news, but I had none. I wasn't there, I told them. Life had to move on and I saw the New Year in with a glass of rum. I'm sure Harry-boy would have been impressed, wherever he was.

My girlfriend didn't approve of my clearing off for months at a time. We had a spat when I joined the *Sugar Producer,* and I could detect a bit of animosity when she fished around to find out when I was going away next. My trip to the Pool after the New Year complicated that. It resulted in us going our separate ways. I couldn't understand why she demanded I drop the job I enjoyed just to come ashore, and do what? You can't live on love, I reasoned. Women have their own minds and no amount of argument would change hers. She accused me of being more in love with ships than with her and she was probably right. No matter how much I thought of her, the idea of going ashore to work gave me the shivers.

For the next month I did a series of home trade runs on various companies. I was thinking of a trip to the South American coast again until the newly acquired CPR vessel, the *Beaver Elm*, was advertised on the Pool board. Canadian Pacific had recently acquired some smaller vessels from the Norwegians after getting rid of their old 30 derrick ships like the *Beaverburn* I had sailed on a few years earlier. The *Elm's* sisters were the *Ash, Oak, Pine* and *Fir*. My discharge book was looking good again and I had no bother picking up the *Beaver Elm*. I lasted twenty days before going down in St Johns New Brunswick with a bug that had me sweating bucketloads in temperatures below freezing point. I was put in the local hospital for observation and doctors could not determine the cause of my malady. The *Elm* had departed while I was in hospital, rendering me a DBS. Repatriation on the *Beaver Pine* took ten days, across the western, to dock in Liverpool.

My wages had stopped once I had been paid off in St Johns. The shipowners never thought that their employees could suffer sickness, nor were there any provisions in the contract to allow wages to carry on when you had the misfortune to keel over. You were paid off and collected your shilling stipend, a gift from your employer to let you know they had your best interests in mind. They would never get away with being robber barons in today's world. Sickness is now permitted and wages are not cut off. That is not to say there are not some who would like to go back to the old ways.

I made immediate tracks to the place of employment. Finances were low, and this impressed on me that I had no time to tarry. The *Beaver Fir* had the initials HT chalked beside the name. Home trade runs were a great way to replenish the bank. I joined her in Antwerp and presented myself to the bosun who was Polish and the seamen who were Spanish. What was going on here? What were foreigners doing on one of our ships? These thoughts passed through my head as I changed into my work gear. I learned that Canadian Pacific engaged continental crews from the Rotterdam Pool on a couple of their vessels. Engaging foreign crews on British vessels was not new. P&O, British India, and a few other companies had reciprocal agreements with the country they traded with to engage their nationals. So why hadn't CPR engaged Canadians?

The answer wasn't available to me then and I really didn't care. I felt like a foreigner on one of our red duster ships and I was eager to get off. That opening came a week later in Liverpool where deep sea articles were to be signed. I paid off, flush with nine quid and a free train ticket down to London.

A quid was a quid in them days, and one could have a great night out on it. Beer was two and threepence a pint, fish and chips one and six, and a ninepence bacon sarney. British Rail was the dearest and they still held that status from what I could see 30 years later. The cost of living in Britain when I visited with my family in 1984 had risen remarkably. Time moves on and in the end everything is relative.

I was never to step aboard another CPR ship after that. Continental seamen didn't have the same camaraderie as British crews and my Cockney wit was not appreciated. The *Beaver Elm* (3950 tons) stayed with the company till 1971 when she was sold to Nanking Shipping Company and renamed *Hengshan*. The *Beaver Fir* (4530 tons) went a year later in 1972 to the Greek Arion Ship Company and was renamed the *Arion*.

Ashore, all hell was breaking loose with the dailies trumpeting on about a Tory MP John Profumo and a couple of dolly birds spiced up in a bit of how's your father with a Russian spy. It was the talk of Britain and the Kent Arms in Woolwich. You couldn't help listening to the banter by those claiming to have seen photos showing some aristocratic members in explicit sexual positions. We were all jealous we couldn't join in! For my part I couldn't care less what the rich and famous got up to. Hadn't that gone on for hundreds of years with that lot? Listening to Frankie Ifield's 'I remember you' and 'From a Jack to a King' were more pleasing to my ears.

The *Kenya Castle* (17,000 tons) along with her sisters the *Braemar* and *Rhodesia Castle* were the only three Union Castle passenger vessels that sailed out of the Pool in London. Much smaller than their counterparts in Southampton, they were known in the company as 'intermediate vessels'. The three ships were restyled in

The *Kenya Castle* took me on my first trip down the east coast of Africa. She was sold to the Greek Chandris Group in 1967 and given an extensive face-lift for the North American cruise service, renamed the *Amerikanis*. She was laid up in Greece during the mid-1980s and is probably razor blades by now.
VH Young

1961 and topped with domed funnels. They could accommodate 450 cabin class passengers.

I wondered if I needed to be humiliated once again by the regime that stood over the South Africans. Unlike the larger Castle passenger vessels from Southampton that ran to Durban via Cape Town return, the intermediate vessels had a much more interesting route via the Suez Canal. In late March 1963 when I joined the *Kenya Castle* in the King George V Dock, the company had revised their service to East Africa, going as far as Durban and then returning back up the East African coast. The ten-week round voyage looked pretty hectic to me as I perused the ports of call we were to make.

It was pleasing to see that on the *Kenya Castle* all victualling stayed in the messroom where it should be. There was no lining up for milk, tea and sugar as was the case on the larger vessels I had sailed on from Southampton. Cockneys, Geordies, Scouses, Scots, Irishmen, Welsh, Mooshes from Southampton: the babble of accents to be heard along the working alleyway told that the crew was from every corner of the British Isles.

The seamen were split into watches under a bosun's mate who was answerable to the bosun. The seamen's NUS convenor, Reg, was a company contract geezer from Birmingham who seemed to relish the position. I had always had serious doubts about company men being the advocates for union members and expressed that view loudly in the messroom. He had been the convenor on the *Kenya* since its inception, and I was told to butt out by those who knew him better. The convenor system was still a very new concept and the majority of union members had no interest in the position, so it was left to guys like Reg to sort out any disputes.

Reg was on the same four-to-eight watch as me and on the way down to Gibraltar he and I had a yarn about the doubts I had in London. A soft-spoken man a few years my senior, he agreed that there seemed to be a conflict of interest with him being a contract man and also the union boss aboard. He told me that I was not the first one to have a go, but no one else wanted to be the convenor so he had taken it up. His company contract would not interfere with union business, he said, and I went away wondering if I had been wrong. If there were no other things to be learned from the trip on the *Kenya Castle* then the quiet way that Reg conducted his advocacy was in itself a lesson for me. Our shortage of salt tablets in the tropics was soon replenished once Reg found out the supply had been commandeered above decks. Young and abrasive as I was at this juncture, it was from Reg I learnt that to be a union convenor one had to be credible to those you advocated for and believable to those on high. It meant preserving a clean all-round record of how you conducted yourself so no one could point the finger at you. It was advice I never forgot.

We arrived in Mombasa in sweltering heat. The excitement of a night ashore was strong as we rushed down below for a quick shower and into our go-ashore gear. My cabin-mate Billy P had already shown what a nutcase he was when he decided to pick up a chair outside one of the bars in Genoa's 'dirty mile' and heave it through the window. Full of eye-tye vino, he hoped to make his getaway in a taxi going past. Unfortunately the taxi driver had other ideas and took him as far as the nearest copper on duty. It was a costly exercise for him, with the damage deducted from his wages. I'm glad I wasn't with him. There was no way I would be around if he showed signs of that behaviour in Kenya.

Two huge elephant tusks in the form of an arch marked the gateway to the city of Mombasa. The Rainbow Bar was the favourite night-life venue. It looked a posh setting with a fountain in the centre and tables and chairs around it. 'We're all going on a summer holiday' was the favourite song of the night and it was played over and over. Billy P got himself wrapped up with one of the local maidens and was given a dose for unzipping his pants, complaining that it had spoiled his plans for any how's your father with those Durban birds on the beach. No sympathy was offered and we had a very subdued Billy for the next few weeks.

Zanzibar is an island 40km off the African coast, infamous for the huge slave market that operated there until after World War I. Slavery was meant to be abolished but under German rule it was allowed to carry on. Only when the British heaved the Germans out of East Africa during the Great War was a stop put to it. The Africans sold their prisoners taken in battle to the Arabs on Zanzibar who in turn sold them to the Europeans needing labour for their plantations in the Indian Ocean islands.

Dar-es-Salaam, further down the coast, was an anchor port where the passengers went ashore on a lighter to see the sights. All our passengers disembarked at Durban. It had been quite a while since I had last seen those divisive signboards. Conservative South Africa was a far cry from the 1960s revolution that was taking place in Britain and other western nations. Television was outlawed as an ungodly instrument, according to apartheid, and didn't make it into the public arena until 1976.

That didn't stop Billy P from going ashore. Because he was under medication for the handicap he had picked up in Mombasa, it prevented him from taking alcohol as well as forcing him to keep his pants zipped up. We went to a pub overlooking Durban harbour that he reckoned was full of women. A notice stating it was a European bar was dismissed by Billy and we were absorbed into the crowded pub without my dusky features being questioned.

The garden bar outside was crowded with women. One would think there were no men in Yarpieland. I'm quite sure Frankenstein's monster, had he shown his ugly mug, would have a couple of floozies on his arm. Erica, who came from Germiston, near Johannesburg, got into my vent. She came to Durban to surf and find work. She wanted to know all about England as she had booked a tourist class passage on the *Athlone Castle* later that year. She had no love for South African males and my Cockney accent seemed more agreeable to her.

When Erica suggested we take a taxi to her flat, no one was more surprised than I. I left Billy deep in conversation with his bird while I was about to test the racial barrier. I cannot report any dents in the apartheid armour after that climactic night. I arrived back on board to find Billy had already given a narrative on our night ashore. I could not help blurting out that I hoped he had kept himself to himself considering the malady he was carrying. His cries of outrage convinced others, but I never knew with him. Later on I was glad to hear that the QM had confirmed him coming aboard before midnight.

Erica was a nurse at Durban hospital and made no bones about hating South Africa. She was quite confident that she would find a nursing position in Britain or the continent and I had no doubt that her skills would be snapped up. Her parents were farmers as were her two brothers. She had no time for her brothers whom she referred to as ignorant Boers. She never once asked me where my dusky features came from. I could not have told her anyway.

The *Athlone Castle* whisked her off to the UK later on that year, and she ended up at St Thomas' Hospital in the South of London. We met by chance during the 1966 seamen's strike while I was handing out leaflets on the tube trains. She had time enough to say she was happily married with a family.

On the homeward trip we stopped in ports for a day to pick up passengers and cargo. We arrived in London early June where the Beatles had taken over the airwaves with 'Please please me' and 'From me to you'. The Rolling Stones had not yet made their mark but Elvis was telling us that 'You're the Devil in disguise'.

Pay-off day was always a drama on Castle boats because of the size of the crews. Billy had rid himself of the affliction and was his old self again. Too far away to go home to Sunderland, we both booked in to the Stornaway Castle and went next door to the Steps to earwig the latest gossip. Seamen are like old women wanting to hear all the scandals.

After a week ashore a six-week trip on the *Paraguay Star* took my fancy. Billy had opted for a Shaw Savill vessel on the Kiwi run. The *Paraguay Star* was a vessel built for the Blue Star Line in 1948. At 10,700 tons these refrigerated cargo vessels had accommodation for 50 first class passengers. As I joined her in the Vic Dock I was a rare non-company addition to the deck crew. Company men staffed these vessels and there was rarely a berth for 'outsiders'. The bosun was a

I did three trips on this vessel, the *Deseado*: two to South America, and one to collect apples in Tasmania. She was full of cockroaches, which might have tasted better than the food.
VH Young

highland man and made it clear from the start that I was an alien, filling in for his countryman who had taken leave that trip. I wasn't going to put up with that shit and asked him if he owned the fucking company. That got the crowd talking.

The majority of seamen took the job seriously because deck operations required us to be focused. Some went too far to impress the officers with the zealous handling of their charges. You'd think they owned part shares and were not lowly paid peons like the rest of us. My outburst seemed to mellow my antagonist and eventually we got along fine.

I had never been on a vessel that offered so much overtime. She called in at Recife and Salvador, two Brazilian ports I had not been to on previous trips on this coast. Rio, Santos, Monty and BA were old hat. In Buenos Aires cluster lights illuminated the ship's side while we toiled over the wall on stages painting the hull in its grey livery. It was all overtime, and there wasn't much you could do with the limit of a £5 sub you were permitted to withdraw. It was all worth the effort when I collected my pay-off on arrival in London — it was the largest amount I had ever paid off with.

The *Paraguay Star* met her end in London in 1969 when she was seriously damaged by fire. Beyond economic repair, she was taken to Hamburg and scrapped.

I sure felt like Jack the lad jumping out of the taxi, grabbing my sea bag and handing over a generous tip to the cab driver. My first chore was to go and buy one of those Beatle suits that had come into fashion. I saw what I wanted in Rose's clothes shop on the main street in East Ham. It looked real smart. The jacket was single-breasted with no collar. The pants were slim with no cuffs and the wide tie they wore in the 1950s had been replaced with the slim jim. I looked a mite out of place in my new get-up among the jeans and jacket brigade in the Kent Arms. Winkle-picker shoes had also made their way onto the fashion market. The name derived from the toe of the shoe coming to a point. The style looked ridiculous, but needless to say they became my next purchase.

The Great Train Robbery was all over the news and among the villains named in the heist was a geezer called Ronnie Biggs. A couple of pints of Charrington's had me taking note of a very attractive girl deep in talk with another female. Her eyes gave me a quick scan, and I hoped the cut of my trendy new jib might solicit more than just a quick look. The moment seemed right for me to butt in to the conversation. If I was rebuffed then it wouldn't be the end of the world. My appearance was welcomed with a wide smile, which brought me a sigh of relief. She told me about her family, who had lived around the Royal Docks all their lives. Her father worked in the docks, and had been a seaman. Our liaison was favourable and I was soon meeting the parents. Nothing like the friendliness of a Cockney family to warm the cockles of your heart!

She did not make a scene when I told her that it was time I got back to sea. My finances were dwindling and I had no intention of telling her I was almost skint after acting as though money was not a problem. Ain't it just the way we youngsters were when trying to impress the fair sex. She was no burden on my pockets, as I'm sure she would have been just as happy to take in a movie instead of the pub.

The *Deseado* (9600 tons) was the second vessel of Royal Mail Line to assume that name. I joined her in the Victoria Dock to be greeted by Black Angus, the lamp trimmer from the *Highland Princess*. He had stepped up a rung and was now bosun. A highland man, Angus was a hard taskmaster and liked his pound of flesh. That was okay with me since I saw nothing black in him. I got on well with him and I was to make four trips with him, along with the hundreds of cockroaches that daily invaded our food in the hot press.

The first trip was a bum feeder. Such were the complaints about the food, someone suggested that we sit the cook on his hot stove. Not a bad idea except it would have required the full deck to lift his fat body off the galley floor.

The outward-bound trip to the South American east coast was spent cleaning out the hatches for the loading of chilled beef. Derricks were topped at sea to lift out each wooden plug, tainted with the previous impurities. Every plug had to be cleaned, as did the meat hooks, which were soaked in a solution in a 40-gallon drum. Each hold had a number of decks and each deck had a number of plugs. It was enough to keep us busy until we reached the coast.

On our arrival in Buenos Aires, the port authorities inspected our cleaning before the loading commenced. The overtime was plentiful and pay-off day was good for my pocket. I signed home trade articles for the English and continent ports, giving me a week ashore.

The Beatles had taken the world by storm, and London had overtaken Paris as the fashion centre of the world. During my second trip on the *Deseado* while in the South Atlantic we heard that President Kennedy had been assassinated. My twenty-third birthday had passed unnoticed and we spent Christmas and New Year at sea. I was due to sail on the *Deseado* within the week, this time for Australia. The ship had been chartered by Shaw Savill to collect fruit from Melbourne, Sydney and the bulk from Tasmania. After this trip, and against all my better thinking I tried three months ashore to be with my girlfriend. It was not a happy intermission for me — I missed the sea, the freedom and the camaraderie that shore life could not offer.

The *Paraguay Star* offered plenty of overtime on the Argentina run.
VH Young

twenty

M Y FIRST JOB BACK AFTER three months ashore was a home trade run on the 9400-ton cargo ship *Oswestry Grange*. After calling in at Newport and Swansea we arrived in Liverpool, then once again I was on my way to South America, but not before calling in to Antwerp and Rotterdam.

The *Oswestry Grange* was a fine looking ship, as were most of the Houlder Brothers' vessels. A white Maltese cross on a red background stood out on her funnel. Houlders had a catastrophe in 1972 when their cargo vessel *Royston Grange* collided with the tanker *Tein Chee* in the fog-bound approaches to Montevideo. Oil surrounded the stricken *Royston Grange* and she lost her entire crew of 74 souls in a fire. One I knew from the *Dominion Monarch* a few years earlier. Fire at sea is a seamen's worst enemy. You can't call the fire station — *we* are the firemen at sea, and much emphasis is put on training for fighting shipboard fires.

The tragedy that befell the *Royston Grange* was numbing because they never had a chance to fight the fire. I was on the *Port Victor* in Wellington when another fire happened in 1968. The fire that could have been another *Royston Grange* engulfed my old vessel the *Gothic*. Though she was 1300km from New Zealand, her crew managed to put the fire out. There was loss of life but it was testimony to the training of the crew that they saved their vessel, and they could hold their heads high as she limped into Wellington Harbour under the command of Captain Agnew. The fire had caused so much damage to the bridge and the navigation system that repairs were not economic. It was a sad end for the only merchant navy vessel to be called the Royal Yacht.

In the beginning of 1965 I fronted up to the KG5 Pool and scanned the jobs on offer. There were plenty of ships going to Australia and New Zealand, but I had lost interest in that part of the world. It had been three years or more since I had travelled the South Pacific route. I had spent most of the last year with the Royal Mail Line so I chose another of their cargo vessels, *Loch Loyal*. I was happy with this company, even though they were bum feeders. It would be wrong of me to say that ship's cooks should be charged with grievous bodily harm, as was the case with our *Deseado* chef. They were the minority: most cooks could satisfy our bellies. On passenger vessels you had specialist chefs who were highly creative and efficient at satisfying the tastebuds of the punters.

The *Loch Loyal*, at 11,000 tons, was berthed in the Victoria Dock. The mate looking through my discharge book noted my trips on the *Deseado*, and declared one trip on that ship was enough for him. Apparently he had reservations about the *Deseado's* ritual of working derricks at sea. As the officer responsible for operations on deck I imagine it was a concern for him. But it was his other beef that was to become a big issue, something that governments all over the world would deny. He complained about the itchy insulation fluff that we had to sweep up on the bottom deck of the holds. I had noticed the skin irritation the glass fibres gave us on the *Highland Princess* and the *Deseado*. He mentioned the word 'asbestos' and how it would be the bloody death of us.

He seemed a friendly guy, which was unusual for a chief mate. I left his cabin having secured my berth and asbestos was not given another thought until years later when we heard workers who had had contact with it were dying of lung cancer. My mind went back to the words of the chief mate. It had me wondering whether this lethal material was used in reefer insulation. Mariners who came into contact with the insulation will remember the uncomfortable skin irritation it left. Oddly enough a Latin name for asbestos was *amiantus*, meaning 'undefiled'.

The *Loch Loyal* was a five-hatch cargo vessel that also accommodated twelve passengers. With a set of four derricks to each hatch and a jumbo lift stowed against the mainmast, she was no daddy's yacht. We were off to the Pacific coast of America via Bermuda and Panama: Los Angeles, San Francisco, Seattle, Portland and Vancouver were our ports of call on the west coast. It was obvious by the first few days at sea that the standard of grub had gone up a notch or three. Royal Mail Line employed cooks who could spoil the crowd. Old Charlie could have been 100 years old, but what a cook! He and his assistant came from Jamaica and were fixtures on the vessel for years. I enjoyed their company and their accents always had me in fits of laughter.

Crew cabins were two-berth and quite roomy. My cabin-mate Errol was from Margate and was younger than me. He was a studious guy, going for his second mate's ticket, and spent most of his time up on the bridge. Below decks there seemed to be a hatred of anyone who wanted to upskill themselves. I think it was just a hangover from the centuries of 'us against them'. So what if someone wanted to better himself? I thought it absurd that he should be a subject of derision around the messroom table. I had also begun my career intending to be part of the officer class.

Bermuda was too pricy for me even in them days. The island was developing into a tourist spot and the prices reflected it. A night in Panama's Zanzibar Club didn't help my finances and I suffered my usual Panama hangover the next morning.

My stay in Los Angeles was one of the few times I took an interest in what the place had to offer instead of seeking out bars and women. Errol had been here before and was clued up on all the attractions the city offered. The huge letters spelling out 'Hollywood' on the hillside caught my eye and I took an aimless tour that pointed out the various stars' palaces hidden behind forests of trees. Hollywood Boulevard and its Grauman's Chinese Theatre, the Walk of Fame where stars names were embedded in the sidewalk — I was not very impressed at all.

San Francisco was more interesting. We were berthed on the other side of the bridge in the port of Stockton, and all eyes focused on forbidding Alcatraz in the middle of the bay. Known as The Rock, it used to be a penitentiary that held some prisoners such as Al Capone and the Birdman of Alcatraz. The prison had been closed the previous year and the inmates transferred to the mainland.

The hippie era was nearly upon us and placards denounced the war with North Vietnam. Nobody at that time realised the outpouring of rage this war would bring. Unlike chic Los Angeles, I left 'Frisco thinking it was a pretty city with its trams and laid-back Bohemian style. Its vast bay and harbour were among the best in the world.

Portland, far into the hinterland up the Columbia River, seemed to be America's garden for exporting green peas. Vancouver was the vessel's last call. Paper was loaded and we set sail for Panama and home. By the time we docked in London the voyage had taken three months.

In 1969 the *Loch Loyal* sustained damage to her engine after a fire. She was sold to the Aegis Group in 1971 and renamed *Aegis Loyal*. The *Loch Loyal* was to be my swansong with the Royal Mail Line. Indeed it was only a few years later in 1968 the company transferred their three A-class passenger vessels, *Amazon, Arlanza*

The *Oswestry Grange*, from the same company as the ill-fated *Royston Grange*.
VH Young

Royal Mail's *Loch Loyal* took me to the
west coast of North America.
VH Young

and *Aragon* to the Shaw Savill Line. In the same year Royal Mail Line merged
with the Furness Withy Group. By 1972 this proud shipping line had become a
memory, after 140 years of service between Britain and the Americas.

It was April 1965 and there was no stopping the social revolution as more pop
bands and fashions came into being. Women wore their miniskirts higher and
their hair shorter. Men's hair went the other way, growing longer, and the new
term 'unisex' summed up the mid-1960s. A Geordie group called the Animals
threatened to top the Beatles with 'The House of the Rising Sun.' There were early
murmurs from union headquarters that they were going to seek union action to
cut our 56-hour week at sea down to 40 hours, in linc with shore workers. Yeah,
when pigs fly, I thought. I assumed they were banking on the support of the newly
elected Labour Party leader Harold Wilson, who we hoped was on course to defeat
the tired old Tories in the 1966 election.

Me and another local seafarer had decided on a drink in the New Gog pub on
Freemasons Road. I was waiting at the bar while the publican Paddy drew our
pints. A loud bang, which had us looking at each other wondering what caused

it, shattered the atmosphere. There was a scurry outside the pub door and the rev of engines as a car took off. Embedded in the front of the bar was a bullet. I was not in the line of fire but when it dawned on me what had caused the bang I was shocked. There was talk of the Kray twins paying a visit but that was only a rumour.

Paddy seemed to know who it was and cursed those bastards, saying that the bullet was meant for him. Soon the police were there in force and the pub was closed. Whoever fired the bullet was either a bad shot or giving a warning.

Some months later, after I returned from my next trip, the culprits had been collared. Two brothers, small-time crooks who Paddy had barred from the Gog for their behaviour were the villains; their retaliation came in the form of a bullet.

On the board at the Pool were chalked a number of vessels going to anywhere but the South American coast. Most berths were to Australia and New Zealand. The *Eleuthera* took my eye with its Spanish name. A number of ABs were wanted and she was berthed in Rotterdam. I was told she belonged to Pacific Steam Navigation, and was due to sail for the west coast of South America when she had finished loading on the continent. I couldn't pass my discharge book over the counter quick enough. A couple of coughs satisfied the Pool doctor that I was in good working order, and the PSNC crew administrator was on hand to give out the train and ferry tickets. From him I learnt the vessel was not heading for the South American coast but to Central America. Being a bit slow, I was trying to figure out the countries in that part of the globe. They were all funny sounding names like Nicaragua, Guatemala and Mexico. We were shoved on the train to Harwich for the ferry sailing that night.

Our administration officer in Rotterdam piled us on a bus to the local seamen's centre for breakfast, where we were palmed off with a bread roll and cheese and a cup of coffee. Bollocks to that! We let them know what we thought about bloody cheese rolls for breakfast. Bacon and eggs was more our style and panic set in with the office boy who was on a timetable to deliver us aboard. Poor guy looked rather panicky, watching the clock while we wolfed down plates of bacon, eggs and toast, plus the cheese rolls that were compliments of the stingy company. Served them right for being so cheap.

The *Eleuthera*, at 5400 tons, was small compared to other cargo ships I had sailed on. She was still relatively new, having made her maiden voyage in 1959. Our PSNC minder needn't have busted a boiler, since no one seemed remotely interested in the arrival of the crew. We rushed around below, hoping to secure what we thought were the best cabins and we usually got it wrong. Judging by the gear on deck it seemed we were in for an easy trip on the deck. We counted four hatches and twelve derricks, with a jumbo derrick affixed to the mainmast.

Her stern end told us she was Scouse, registered in Liverpool. The next morning the bosun, known as the Mad Piper, had a couple of us rig a stage to go over the stern end with a tin of turps and rags to clean off oil that had made the name illegible. The Mad Piper was a legend, hailing from the Western Isles. Out came the bagpipes when the whisky flowed and boy, what a racket it was.

Rotterdam held no novelty for me. I had been there many times, sampled the girly bars and endured the throb of my head after a night of Heineken. I was eager to get away from the hurly-burly of large ports and seek the serenity of the oceans. The huge Europoort on the North Sea, which the Dutch would have the foresight to build in anticipation of a larger volume of trade, was still ten years away.

The *Eleuthera* was certainly not built for speed. It plodded along at twelve to thirteen knots to Curaçao. There is a mysterious sea that stretches from the Azores to the West Indies called the Sargasso Sea, unique for the abundance of seaweed that floats on its surface. Sea turtles and other marine life abound in its warm waters. We know it as the 'Doldrums' but navigators through the centuries dreaded this part of the Atlantic because of its calms and the sea monsters that lived below. They called it The Sea of Lost Ships. Rather like the Bermuda Triangle, it has a history of vessels being found and the crew missing or found dead for no apparent reason. I have been through the Sargasso Sea many times and I found it the scariest bit of water in the world. Its calmness is deceptive and eerie.

On many occasions I was the subject of good-natured ribbing from the crowd whenever we entered the Doldrums. I had read stories about these waters and I was not surprised at the fear those old explorers recorded in their logbooks. There have been many attempts to solve the mystery of ships and aircraft that have gone missing in this area. Sceptics will always try to fit an earthly explanation to events and mysteries we fail to understand. I am blessed with an open mind. Even if 99% of mysteries have a solution, the one percent is good enough to suggest we don't have all the answers. The Sargasso Sea and its mysteries come within that one percent, in my thinking.

We spent the night bunkering in Curaçao. The long haul from Rotterdam had whetted our appetite for some shore leave. I had heard of Happy Valley on my previous calls to Curaçao but had never bothered to venture to the district. The taxi dropped us at this fenced-off complex that looked rather like the pictures I had seen of concentration camps.

Happy Valley was what its name implied — the bars were packed with women from all over the world. Its cosmopolitan attraction had me wondering some years later how on earth all these girls ended up on such a small island when big cities were more lucrative. But the migration of young ladies around the world was not on my mind that night. The tropical night air required me to buy copious amounts of nectar to quench my thirst, and the advances of our hostesses stopped as they probably decided there was no petrol in the engine where I was concerned.

Curaçao was a costly night out, and put paid to any thought of a run ashore in Cristobal. As we crossed the Panama Canal I looked forward to Puntarenas on the Pacific coast of Costa Rica. Any sailor worth his salt who is making his way to the west coast of South America never forgets to buy some bargaining goods before leaving home. Yardley's Bond Street perfumeries brought the biggest bang for your peso but locals eagerly snapped up any European toiletry brands.

We began unloading goods from Europe and loading wood and other commodities in Puntarenas. It was a sticky climate with plenty of mozzies to annoy you. There was not much else to report about this place except the stench of an ancient sewerage system.

Nicaragua's main port, Corinto, saw me go from riches to rags. My toiletry products were stacked on the cabin dresser below my porthole. You don't close the porthole in such humid conditions, but leaving it open was an invitation for light fingers. It was quite easy for anyone on the deck outside to stretch an arm through and take whatever was in reach. I was on deck and returned to find my smellies had been lifted. The west coast was notorious for 'tea leafs' and the amount of times I had been this way should have taught me better. That didn't stop me from exploding into diatribe.

We also went to a port that required skilful navigation to enter up a river enclosed by jungle on each side, till we arrived in what looked to me like a lake and anchored. The agent, dressed in a white suit and trilby hat, was conveyed to the vessel on a dugout log of wood, propelled by an outboard motor. We were anchored in this windless mosquito hole for three days loading wood. Other calls were made at Acajutla, the main port of El Salvador, at Champerico and San Jose in Mexico.

Returning through the Panama, our final destination before sailing for home was Puerto Rico. Mayaguez, meaning 'place of great waters', was a main port of the island in the 1960s. Its primary industry was sugarcane and agriculture. They also brewed potent rum, which was part of our cargo. I shall not explain how I got to know this drink but it was well above the percentage of alcohol permitted by UK standards of the day.

The *Eleuthera* berthed in Victoria Dock after another three-month trip. She was to part company with Pacific Steam Navigation in 1970, and was sold to Cypriot interests who renamed her *Mimi-M.*

I was getting fed up with the South American run and needed a change of scene. In the meantime I was to spend six weeks on ships around the land. They included my old deep-sea voyager *Oswestry Grange* on a run job to Liverpool.

Renewing my acquaintance with Shaw Savill, I collected the *Ionic* in Rotterdam, bringing her back to the Royal Docks in London. This was followed by a run up to Newcastle to deliver the *Cymric*. Mr Pook had left Shaw Savill during my four years' interlude with other shipping companies. Mr Starling, recently from the New Zealand Shipping Company office, had taken his place.

Whether or not we enjoyed each other's company on these run jobs, we all decided to sign foreign-going articles for the *Ionic's* forthcoming deep sea voyage to Australia. My cabin-mate Brian was from Poplar, just down the road from Canning Town, while the rest of the seafarers were from around London. She was to be one of the best crowds I sailed with on a four-month trip, bound via the Suez to Fremantle, Adelaide, Melbourne, Sydney and Hobart.

We called in to Hamburg and Bremerhaven to complete loading. One of the lads told us about a vendor whom he called the 'never never man' who would come aboard in here selling transistor radios, record players and guitars for his company, which required a deposit and the remainder to be paid in monthly instalments. The vendor reaped his reward with a commission on each article he sold.

We waited for the vendor to arrive at the ship. Portable transistor radios were a fairly new technology and lucrative money-spinners if you were short of cash on the Aussie coast. German electrical products were superior to the Japanese equivalents. The salesman duly arrived and it didn't matter to him if the deposit

The *Ionic*, or the 'Gin & Tonic', as some prefer.
VH Young

was as low as five shillings, because as long as he had your signature on his copy of the transaction he would be paid his commission, whether your debt was honoured or not.

We sailed from Bremerhaven with Blaupunkt radios blaring. Brian bought a Grundig turntable record player and I had to put up with Herman's Hermits' 'I'm Henry the VIII I am', and 'Mrs Brown you've got a lovely daughter' across the whole bleeding Indian Ocean. I felt like giving his 45s a passage through the porthole.

The highlight of the trip came in Sydney when the *Ionic* sailed for Hobart as the *Gin & Tonic*. While painting over the bow the 'I' was crossed, making the name 'Tonic', and mother's ruin was added. It did not go unnoticed by the mate taking the draft as we were leaving. The linesmen were in fits of laughter, which was the opposite of the captain's reaction. It was too late to throw a stage over to erase the offending title. The culprits faced the wrath of the ship's judge and jury. Those involved were logged and threatened with jail for altering the ship's name. How a skipper can threaten jail is beyond me. Things like this should be determined in a court of law.

Some of our skippers had no humour whatsoever. A DR was on the cards for the perpetrators. I was nowhere near there at the time. I was on the next stage and as Brian and I said to the mate (who was certain we were in the know), we were too busy painting to notice what others were doing.

The resolution of this incident came later in the voyage, after certain gold braids were spied in Genoa's 'Dirty Mile' with their arms round a couple of ladies of the night. I was not present but would have loved to have been there. The outcome was that there was no DR for our scribes, only a forfeiture because they had kept their noses clean.

Not many electrical goods bought in Bremerhaven made it back home. They probably sit as antiques in Australian homes today. Did we honour our transactions? I'm refusing to say. It was one of those trips that you wished could last another four months, such was the camaraderie within the deck crowd. Channel night was celebrated in usual fashion, and as the Harp Lager took effect we resolved to join the next ship *en masse*. This effusion was somewhat more muted in the morning as the vessel slowly manoeuvred in the Thames at Gallions Reach.

The *Ionic*, (11,200 tons), built in Birkenhead in the UK in 1959, was quite a work-up on deck, with six hatches and 22 derricks. She was the first of four sister ships, the others being *Icenic* 1960, *Illyric* 1960 and *Iberic* 1961. She was sold to Cypriot interests in 1978 who sent her to the knacker's yard a year later.

The *Doric* was due to go to Australia in a few weeks, Mr Starling informed us. For some it was too long to wait and for others it was perfect, and for me, well I would fill in the time by picking up home traders.

It was an exciting year for England as we were scheduled to hold the soccer World Cup in July 1966. The general election was also due and rumours abounded that the National Union of Seamen was going to call a national strike to secure a shorter working week. The Labour government claimed to be the workers' friend but we saw no friendly overtures from Harry Wilson.

Three of us had decided to wait for the *Doric* and in the meantime pick up a run job or two. Port Lines' *Port Victor* fitted our plan. London to Liverpool uses up a couple days or so. Later we picked up another run job to Liverpool on the *Salinas* belonging to PSNC.

The *Doric* (10,600 tons), built in 1949, was an older class vessel than the *Ionic*. Her itinerary was a copy of the previous trip — she was destined for Australia to load fruit. I was happy to observe that channel night frivolities on the *Ionic* had not been all Harp Lager talking. A further five 'Ionics' signed on, including Brian who didn't really fancy another Aussie run but reckoned another trip with us madmen was worth it.

We sailed to Southampton and the Juniper Berry. I was last here six years before and not much had changed, but the girls were six years older. We were there overnight before sailing for down under. When we hit Hobart it was a Sunday and we asked the local nurses and other ladies of that fair city aboard for a Sunday 'Oh come all ye faithful.' We were putting on side to impress the females when there was a knock on the cabin door and a loud voice telling us, "This is the police."

The third mate, who was one of the lads and wouldn't miss the company of the fair sex just because he wore gold braid, questioned what right they had to come aboard and round up the women. He went off to see the skipper. We wouldn't let the girls go even though the police threatened us with obstruction.

We were not expecting any sympathy from the captain, who arrived looking like thunder. Gee, I thought, here we go, another bleeding earbashing.

"This is British territory and you are trespassing on my vessel!"

Did we hear right? Here was a skipper telling the cops to clear off his vessel and leave the girls where they were. We could not believe our good fortune and our admiration for the captain soared.

The fact that we had girls aboard was not the focus of his attention. It was the way the cops came aboard without notifying him or any of the officers as to what their business was. Quite rightly it was his vessel and there was a notice on the gangway stating that no person was allowed aboard unless they were on business. The skipper made it plain that as long as there was no trouble and it did not interfere with the operation of the vessel then he had no problem with women coming aboard.

Boarding passes for non-crew members signed by the mate were the usual procedure on every vessel I was on. We all had our passes, of course, since the dock gatekeeper also had to be satisfied he wasn't letting anybody through his gate without authorisation.

The skipper became our hero, but this respect did not last long. In Sydney a female guest was caught in the chief mate's cabin. Nothing was nicked but that put paid to guests coming aboard for the duration of our stay.

We were well into the voyage when news came via the Australian unions that the British Seamen's Union had gone on strike. The strike applied only to vessels in British waters; vessels and crews in foreign ports were not to strike until their ships arrived back in the UK. That seemed daft to me, as I remembered the reform movement dispute in Wellington when we walked off our vessels. Unhappy as we were at the union's advice, we still had a contract to fulfil under the articles.

Our homeward journey included the Saudi Arabian port of Jedda in the Red Sea and Al Aqaba in Jordan. We were vaccinated against several diseases, yellow fever and smallpox to name a couple. Jedda was a mix of the ancient and the modern. Black shiny Cadillacs appeared alongside camels and donkeys. They still had public executions in Saudi Arabia and one had taken place the day before we arrived. I thought that sort of spectacle only happened in the Middle Ages, not the modern world. Al Aqaba is just across the gulf from the Israeli port, Eilat. Our consignment of frozen meat was unloaded at night and the meat conveyed to Amman by a fleet of army trucks.

Next was the Suez, then after calling in at Genoa and Marseilles we were lucky to get a berth on arrival in London because of the seamen's strike.

The *Doric* had three more years of plying the oceans before she met the scrapyard in 1969. On the Cook Strait ferry *Aratika* some twenty years later the skipper of the *Doric* who had stuck up for us in Hobart all those years ago, peered at the crew letting go the moorings on the foc's'le head.

"Is that chappie down there called Share?"

As I came off the foc's'le a voice shouted down from the bridge, "Dave, there's someone up here who wants to see you."

The boys joked it had to be a long-lost child looking for its father. Once again I was to meet our hero skipper, this time in the more informal atmosphere of the Kiwi coast. He was signed on as third mate, a bit of a drop from his usual rating as master. We filled in the past twenty years, much to the amusement of those on the bridge.

He was upset at the treatment Shaw Savill had shown him after 27 years service. His age was had been an impediment and they retired him. I was unsurprised by their lack of feeling. I always had respect for this gentleman, and he was part of the friendly crew on the *Aratika* for several years before returning to the UK.

We arrived two weeks into the national seamen's strike, and ships were tied up in the Royal Docks two abreast. Dumping my bag at the Flying Tab-Nab in Custom House, I got right into demonstrating.

The *Doric*. "Get off my ship!" the captain ordered the coppers who were rounding up our girlfriends...
VH Young

twenty-one

THE NATIONAL UNION OF SEAMEN'S strike took place on 16 May and was not to be resolved until 30 June 1966. The union had demanded a 17% pay rise and that our 56-hour week be reduced to a 40-hour week like most workers. The shipowners snubbed the union's claims and a strike was called. The Labour government sided with the shipowners, and its leader Harold Wilson accused the NUS executive of being communists. He was so pissed off with those who helped put him onto the treasury benches that within a week he declared a state of emergency.

The NUS claims were stymied by the iniquitous prices and incomes policy, which limited pay rises to 3% to combat inflation. The Minister of Labour, Ray Gunther, acknowledged a need to modernise conditions at sea. At sea we cannot suddenly stop work at the weekends as shore-based workers can. He reckoned the overtime we would reap on weekends at sea if we were given the 40-hour week would negate the anti-inflationary policy.

I made myself available and was given an armband with 'NUS picket' printed on it. The first couple of days I joined other seamen picketing outside dock gate 18 next to KG5 dry-dock. The idea was to stop any NUS members sneaking aboard vessels tied up inside. Many entrances to the Royal Docks had pickets on them.

Later I was put on the leafleting gang. A mob of us would board the tube at Plaistow during the rush hour and flood the carriage with leaflets informing the public of the reasons for the strike. The bowler hat and brolly brigade were not impressed and reckoned we were loafers, holding the country to ransom. We were advised that there would be some antipathy from the public and we should not take offence.

We were in the posh end of the District Line and a couple of us received some verbal abuse from a bowler hat, who called us lazy blackguards. All the advice was suddenly forgotten and his hat was knocked off, and my mate, who must have been blind as a bat, trod on it. Apologies had no effect as he promised a report to the newspapers while he tried to get his bowler into some shape of respectability.

We reported our altercation, since you were never sure how influential the tube commuters were. I don't recall any comeback but we were both transferred to the boring Trafalgar Square leaflet handout. They were mostly tourists who surprisingly took an interest in the strike as many of them used the now strike-bound ferries to get to their homes on the continent.

Our altercation had been tame compared to what the heavy gang got up to. Their job was to go to the vessels in each port and make sure there were no scabs aboard. Apparently they came across one scab on a Dover ferry and the picture on the front page of the *Daily Mirror* depicted him with his head above the waters of Dover Harbour still wearing his cheese-cutter hat, but alive. Incidentally, the only shipping company who agreed to NUS demands at the commencement of hostilities in May was Townsend Thorensen Ferries, who ran out of Weymouth.

Disquieting news came from Liverpool and Newcastle that the right-wing faction of the union executive, led by NUS boss Bill Hogarth, was about to sell us down the river. Harry Wilson had set up the Pearson Committee some weeks earlier to look into our grievances. During negotiations with the union the Pearson Committee had agreed to a 48-hour week with no loss of pay. It was rejected by the union, as we wanted a 40 hours immediately. Even though we would attract overtime on Sundays under the proposed 48-hour week, this would be well above the government's policy on prices and incomes.

To combat this, the committee decided on a counter-attack against our annual leave. They recommended it be reduced from 50 to 39 days. The shipowners came up later with a compromise by lifting the annual leave up to 48 days in return for some de-manning of crews.

A stalemate ensued. When the news came that a majority voted within the NUS executive to end the six and a half week strike, it stunned rank-and-file members who had fought so hard to gain better conditions at sea. The executive announced that they had voted to adjourn strike action for a year in favour of the Pearson Committee. What had we gained for all our fervour? A 48-hour week, reduced to 40-hours a year later. Our 17% pay rise was replaced by a 13% rise in two years, plus the shipowners' compromise of 48 days annual leave.

We downed our leaflet campaign and picked up placards decrying the turncoat union executives and rushed over to NUS headquarters in Clapham. The executives faced an angry rank-and-file and they were in no doubt as to what we thought of their response to Wilson and his Labour Party cronies. Who cared if they labelled us commies and spouted the usual establishment mantra?

Media and television blasted out headlines that the seamen had capitulated to the Wilson government. We in the engineroom could not dispute this. A meeting was called the next day at the East Ham town hall. Meetings were to be held in each port in order to seek rank-and-file ratification.

I had been to several NUS meetings in the London Pool but I had never seen an audience so packed as at East Ham. It was an angry meeting and speakers vented their disgust at the capitulation. Many of us young folk were hotheads; then there were those, the silent majority, who thought but said nothing. They delivered the vote in favour of the NUS and Pearson Agreement.

There were recriminations that most of those who voted to end the strike played little or no part in the strike and had been cowering at home. But we could not change the vote. We were knackered, having fought ourselves to a standstill. A motion was put forward and we marched from the union rooms to the KG5 Pool as a show of solidarity the following morning, when the Pool would be open for business after six and a half weeks of strike. It was a good turnout, and with the union banner and a television camera mounted on a back of a truck we defiantly set off from the Connaught pub to the Pool. We had just got over the swing bridge when one of the members holding the banner went arse over tit. The banner came down with a crash, as did members behind, tripping over him. It didn't look very defiant on the television news that evening.

I can now look back at that event in a much more sensible frame of mind. Yes, we were hotheads who thought everything had to be done immediately. We may not have agreed with the NUS decision at the time, but in the end we got our 40-hour week and the pay rise. Some pundits say the 1966 strike contributed to the demise of the British merchant navy. I disagree. Developments such as containerisation contributed far more to the decline. The same has happened in every industry where technology has reduced the role of manual labour.

Almost 900 vessels out of Britain's merchant fleet of 3000 were caught by the strike. 28,000 union members were on the beach out of a 72,000-strong membership. These figures came from NUS headquarters after hostilities ended.

We piled into KG5 Pool after our show of unity. After weeks of ships lying idle, the board was filled with the names of vessels wanting ratings of every description. I took a run job to Newcastle on the *Suevic* and followed that with other run jobs on the *Southern Cross* and the *Cretic*.

Britain's hangover from the chaos of the seamen's strike was quickly dispelled in anticipation of July's soccer World Cup. I was fortunate to be in the Steps when one of the lads produced a couple of tickets to the match between England and Mexico at Wembley. One of his relatives was in the know, and I snapped up one of the tickets cheaply and rejoiced in England's 2-0 win. Just prior to the final I rejoined the *Suevic,* signing on articles for a trip to Australia and New Zealand. If the seamen's strike was a precursor to valuing the trade union movement, then joining the *Suevic* marked a turning point in my personal feelings, and more importantly, a new direction in my future.

twenty-two

OUR EYES WERE GLUED TO the television in a bar near the docks in Rotterdam. The World Cup final between England and Germany was tied up 2-2 at full time. 30 minutes overtime was to be played. The bar was full of Dutch dockers who had no love for their neighbours, Germany. Extra time brought two more goals to England, with West Ham striker Geoff Hurst scoring a hat-trick, and no response from Germany. England had won soccer's highest prize, the Jules Rimet Trophy. The atmosphere at the bar was one of elation, with Heineken breaking down any language barriers there might have been.

The trophy was nicked in March of that year while on display alongside a stamp exhibition in London. The thieves ignored the £3 million worth of stamps and opted for a £30,000 cup. To the relief of the organisers, a dog named Pickles was sniffing out a dustbin and found the trophy, to the amazement of its owner.

The *Suevic* (13,500 tons) was built in 1950. She was the sister ship to the *Persic* and the *Runic*, which ended her days a wreck on a reef in Australian waters during a hurricane. She was what I would call 'chatty [i.e. dirty] but happy', with substandard accommodation, but the crew got on well together. We were bound for Sydney and Melbourne via the Cape of Good Hope. My cabin-mate had a nifty tape recorder, which was better than the turntable machines I was used to. He was into the Beach Boys, and 'Sloop John B' became the anthem below decks.

We crossed the Tasman, destined for Wellington. It had been over five years since my last trip to New Zealand. How could an island in the South Pacific, 2000km from its nearest neighbour, captivate those who journey from the furthest nations of the globe? In my own case I had ended up 'overstaying' after my voyages to New Zealand on the *Rangitata* and on the *Dominion Monarch*.

Liquor laws were still in a time warp, and Kiwis were encouraged to knock back as much booze as they could in the hour left to them after work, then drive home in a haze. Thankfully the Temperance Society was roundly defeated in the following year when the 1967 referendum voted for 10pm closing. In the meantime we had to rush ashore to the Duke of Edinburgh or the Regent to find female company for our parties aboard.

Tragedy had struck a few months earlier in May for one of our Belfast ABs. His brother was on the *Kaitawa* which sank off Cape Reinga with the loss of all hands.

The seamen's strike had prevented him from getting a fast passage to New Zealand. But the New Zealand Seamen's Union used their influence with the immigration authorities, resulting in Jack being paid off the *Suevic* in Wellington and starting a new life on the New Zealand coast.

The *Suevic* had a few characters, none more so than Dave who worked as a steward. He was an amiable guy, full of cheek and with a trunk-load of jokes he was forever cracking. I was swinging on a bosun's chair up the top of a Sampson post painting at sea one day when he arrived, shouting "Have you heard this one?" expecting me to come down. He told me his girlfriend's uncle was none other than the celebrated New Zealand policeman, Dicky Bird, the pursuer of jumped seamen. Dave married his lady and I caught up with him years later when he was a cabin crew member for Air New Zealand.

In Auckland a lifeboat course was taking place and it was the one certificate I was missing. We spent the morning out on Auckland Harbour and I finally had the other half to the able seaman certificate I earned in 1960.

Later that day we were in the Great Northern Hotel on Queen Street. Sitting at our table was a woman who was passing round snaps of her girlfriends from New Plymouth. Our next port happened to be New Plymouth, so there was a lot of interest in the girls in the photos.

"What's her name?" I asked, pointing to the long-haired brunette in the photo.

"That's Bev," the woman replied.

"Well, she's mine," said I, without any knowledge as to whether Bev would have the same thoughts. I was allowed to keep the photo.

A forward intelligence operated among the Kiwi lasses, who phoned up their mates in other ports to give a full report. Thus on arrival in New Plymouth a call came from one of the girls, giving us directions to the party.

Our hosts were a number of young women including one I had seen in the photo in Auckland. Bev and I got on well, going to the local shindig on Saturday at the Old Folks Hall. Playing the perfect host and stunning my shipmates, I showed her family around the vessel and asked them to come aboard for tea the following afternoon. Embarrassingly their arrival was too late for tea and all I could offer was sandwiches and a cup of tea.

Leaving is always hard, but in most cases we got over it and enjoyed the memories. We sailed for Lyttelton to load the rest of our cargo before leaving the coast for Panama and the UK. Lyttelton's sole attraction for the party set was the British Hotel. Things had not changed in the village since I missed the *Dominion Monarch* five years before. I had no interest in what the hotel might offer a party-minded sailor. My thoughts were on New Plymouth and a lady called Beverley.

The first photo I saw of my wife-to-be. From left: Liz Rundle, Gloria Stachurski, Jan Sutherland, Bev Gray.

The evening before sailing I walked down the *Suevic* gangway with a bag of personal gear and took the *Hinemoa* over to Wellington. I caught a bus from Wellington to New Plymouth and knocked on the door of the Devonshire Road flat where Bev lived. No one was more surprised than Bev, since I had not told her I was intending to meet her again so soon.

My unexpected appearance had caused a bit of panic, since the landlord could nose in and tell the cops. Bev worked as a shorthand typist with a New Plymouth firm and was thinking of leaving because of the low pay. My arrival spurred this decision on: New Plymouth was too small for a jumped seaman and his girl. We boarded the bus to Wellington.

I have already mentioned that life has twists and turns. Some decisions I made in my life were just plain dumb. Yet sometimes a dumb decision can also lead to a life of happiness. Jobs were ten a penny in those days, and Bev got herself into the typing pool at the Prudential while I went for a window-cleaning job advertised in the daily rag. We had set up home in a motel on Kent Terrace until we had enough money to rent a flat. Within a week we had secured a room in Cuba Street above a dry-cleaners for half the cost of the motel.

The police had more pressing things to do than search for seamen who had deserted their vessels. But my window-cleaning boss happened to have the contract on government buildings including military and police stations in the Wellington area. Working for him was not an astute choice if you wanted to make yourself scarce from the law.

Each building was costed on an hourly basis as to the time it would take to clean the windows. The Stout Street building housed some of the military and civil public servants and took a few days to clean. Parliament was an interesting place with all its nooks and crannies, but the Beehive was just a thought in 1967. I have cleaned the windows in the Speaker's flat and seen the opulence in which these guys resided.

On one occasion I was cleaning the windows above an MP's room. I had just shouldered my pointer ladder when the end bumped the head of someone behind me. I apologised profusely to the victim, a small stout guy with an infectious grin. "No harm done," he called as he rushed past me. How was I to know that that man, Rob Muldoon, would be a future prime minister of New Zealand?

We washed the windows of the Turnbull Library next door to Parliament. The library holds New Zealand's historic literature. With my cheeky nature, I wangled a look at an 1879 newspaper reporting that land was confiscated as punishment for a crime committed by Maori. Their grievances today have merit if I am to go by the papers of yesteryear.

The historic Supreme Court on the corner of Lambton Quay and Whitmore Street was another building where I came into contact with the noted. The windows of the judges' chambers were part of the contract; one in particular, Judge Beattie, whose door I knocked on with ladder and scrim in hand. He caught my Cockney accent and asked what part of London I came from, then regaled me about the terrible poundings the East End took during the war. Once again I was in the presence of one destined for great things: Judge Beattie would later be appointed Governor-General.

The army building was a Saturday morning job and a special pass was needed to enter the building. I worked under a phoney name, which was put forward when passes were called for. The central police station and its counterpart in Taranaki Street were frightening affairs. I was in Taranaki police station looking very industrious with my bucket of water and scrim when a plain-clothes policeman thought he recognised my fellow window-cleaner as a felon. He looked me over, deciding I was not his man, and I walked out of that cop station vowing never to go back.

Bev and I lived together in our Cuba Street hovel that we shared with the mice. One day we were scheduled to clean the windows in the Intelligence Department in the Stout Street building. Everyone who entered that enclave was vetted. I would have feigned illness that day had I known Jack had this job on the list. I was the only window-cleaner apart from Jack who had a clean record. I had to fill in a form stating my name and everything else about me. Intelligence would have access to anything they wanted to check I assumed, and I submitted my given name.

That evening a tramp of boots echoed up the stairway, followed by a knock on our door.

"David Share, I believe," said the police officer. It was late in the evening and he summoned me to report to the police station next day by 8.30am. This was odd — the usual procedure for an illegal immigrant was to be taken into custody. I reported at the given time to the sergeant, who said he had seen me cleaning windows around the station at times, and thought he could trust me not to abscond until my case came up.

I was to report to the wharf police station on a daily basis. In the meantime Bev and I secured a lawyer. My employer Jack wrote a letter to the court singing his praises of my conduct, and saying that the job I was doing needed trust. But you could present yourself as the angel Gabriel and it would not stop the case against you. No matter how many references of good character were presented, the shipowner was prosecuting me for breaking my contract and deserting my vessel. Judge Scully said as much in his verdict when he ruled for deportation. As an afterthought he advised that if I was so keen on taking up residency in New Zealand it was about time I went about it through legal channels.

The outcome was devastating for Bev and me. We had grown close during our eight months of eluding detection. I was given bail under my own name while I waited for a ship to fulfil my deportation.

Bev and I were walking along Lambton Quay the day I was to board the *Corinthic* when suddenly we were surrounded by plain-clothes detectives. It was a case of mistaken identity; they were looking for a Maori of similar appearance, but preferably one without a Cockney accent.

It was the lowest day of my life when the *Corinthic* distanced herself from Wellington and the lady who had given me an outlook for the future. Simon and Garfunkel's 'Homeward bound' was blaring out around the accommodation. Certain songs can bring back memories and events; 'Homeward bound' was our favourite. There were no vacant jobs and I was aboard as a distressed British seaman being paid the grand sum of one shilling a month.

On arrival in London I made all haste to the Flying Angel in Custom House in hope that there would be mail from Bev. I was not disappointed. I had very little money and had to get a ship as soon as possible. The easiest way to cover up my last discharge from the *Suevic* was a few run jobs around the land, which would provide accommodation and grub, not to mention relieving my acute financial position. My goal was to get back to New Zealand as quickly as I could.

twenty-three

I WAS IN KG5 SHIPPING OFFICE within an hour of leaving the *Corinthic*. I passed my book over tentatively, but my VNC was visible to the young clerk over the counter. I was making a play for the Federal Line cargo vessel *Nottingham*. He went missing for a couple of minutes with my discharge book.

"Sorry, Mr Share, you are prohibited to be employed on ships to Australia or New Zealand," he told me when he returned. These were familiar words to me, and my heart sank. I badgered him to find out how long my ban was. There was no time limit on my files.

"But the *Richmond Castle* needs an AB and is sailing at five o'clock tonight for the continent," he said. This would solve my immediate crisis, but what was I going to tell Bev? I couldn't expect her to wait forever.

The *Roxburgh Castle*, a Union Castle Line fruit boat, was doing the continental ports of Rotterdam, Antwerp, Hamburg and Bremerhaven. The offer constituted a 'pierhead jump' in sailors' terms, meaning 'take it or be out of a job.' I found myself on the Thames for the second time in one day.

I followed that with a home trade run on *Richmond Castle,* which was loading for the Cape. It was the last quarter of 1967 and return to New Zealand seemed unlikely in the immediate future. I explained my situation in a missive to Bev. The *Richmond Castle* gave me a chance to redeem myself in the eyes of the shipping master when I signed deep sea articles for a trip to the Cape.

Orders came that we were to take the *Richmond Castle* to Durban where it would be laid up until the South African fruit season began. We were then to transfer to her sister ship *Roxburgh Castle* to uplift cargo from Durban for the islands of Madagascar and Mauritius. This was to fill in time until the fruit season.

The *Richmond Castle* was built in 1944 and looked every bit her age. My cabin accommodated three seamen and there was no such thing as your own space. South Africa was still its sad self. The boring notices still told us that if you had a black arse you were prohibited from sitting on a city seat until it was lily-white. The Navigators Den in Cape Town was a nightspot where I was refused entry. At least there was no segregation in the insect world as far as the cockroaches on board were concerned. Woe betide those of us who slept with their mouths open: we shared our Christmas dinners with them.

Arriving in Durban there was a six-week wait for the loading of fruit. We transferred to the *Roxburgh Castle* and it seemed the roach population had also transferred with us. While waiting for the fruit to ripen, we were to fill in with a stay on the islands.

Madagascar has a steamy climate and the mozzies enjoyed a bit of British beef. The island is even bigger than France, from whom it obtained independence in 1960. We anchored in some cesspool while a gentleman came out in a dugout propelled by an outboard motor. He was the agent, and he sought out the skipper's cabin to quaff a few drinks before returning to his log of wood, no doubt buoyed by the hard stuff.

About 1000 kilometres to the east of Madagascar lay Mauritius, about which Rudyard Kipling said: 'First God made Mauritius, then he copied it and made Paradise.' It was anything but paradise in early March 1968 when the *Roxburgh* dropped anchor in Port Louis — there had been rioting between the Creole and Indian populations.

The Portuguese first sighted Mauritius at the beginning of the 16th century. Its history is influenced by French colonists who brought slaves from Africa to toil in the sugar plantations. When the British took over they eventually did away with slavery and imported cheap labour from India. The Indians had become dominant in business by the time independence came in 1968. African Creoles, who were there first, felt disadvantaged and riots ensued. Unbeknown to us, me and my mate Ray Trimble were about to be thrown into this melting-pot.

Ray and I slipped ashore in one of the boats. We noted a British warship in the harbour but gathered it was there for the celebration of Independence Day. We made ourselves comfortable in a grotty little bar on the waterfront and wondered at the sight of the British military out in force on the streets. The cacophony on the waterfront was heightened as we heard pounding feet heading in our direction. Hundreds of locals came rushing past the bar. Their jeering and shouting soon got our attention and the scene outside looked ugly. Our host behind the bar suggested we make ourselves scarce since the crowd's anger was directed at anything British.

We took the hint and looked for the boat that had taken us ashore. We looked but found nothing. My Rhodesian shipmate spied a rowing boat on the beach. We heard no cries of 'thieves!' so we pushed it into the water and I took the oars. The motorised transportation had made the distance between ship and shore seem not so far, but rowing was a different affair, especially when you were two parts to the wind. The sight of Ray sitting in the stern giving directions while I laboured at the oars brought banter among the crew when I realised I had been doing all the work while he sat there like a little Lord Fauntleroy.

We were on the 'chatty but happy' *Roxburgh Castle* in Durban when we heard that the *Wahine* had foundered on Barrett Reef.
VH Young

"Effing and blinding!" I said. "You take the bleeding oars, sitting there like a white hunter!" He laughed and said he was wondering when I was going to give him a turn. I had rowed us almost to the *Roxy*. Tying our borrowed conveyance to a cargo barge, we counted ourselves lucky to have escaped the violence that was brewing ashore. Ray was nicknamed the 'White Hunter' after that incident.

The *Roxburgh Castle* arrived back in Durban after completing her side trip to the Indian Ocean islands. We still had a couple of weeks before the fruit export season began.

During our stay in Durban I was amazed to hear of a great storm in the Cook Strait that was battering Wellington. The *Wahine* had been stranded on Barrett Reef at the harbour entrance and was sinking. Reports of the deaths prompted me to send a telegram and flowers to Bev in the hope that she was okay.

I wondered what affinity South Africa might have with New Zealand, when they reported extensively on an event that was happening thousands of miles away. Being a soccer fan I knew nothing about rugby except for the funny shape of the ball and that they could pick it up, and that it should have a handle to make it easier to carry. The connection between the two nations came from the rivalry between the Springboks and the All Blacks. I wondered why else New Zealand would want anything to do with a country that persecuted their fellow countrymen.

In May 1968 we finally departed Durban with our consignment of fruit. We had been away almost six months and all I could think of was getting home and jumping on a vessel to New Zealand.

Arrival in Southampton once again brought memories of the voyages I had made from this port as a youngster, but I had no time to visit my old haunts to see if they were still there. My mission was to board a train to London and make for the KG5 Pool. On reaching Custom House I dumped my bag in the Flying Tab-Nab and collected my mail. I was surprised there was only one letter from Bev. She still believed I was on my way out, but was she having second thoughts? Eight months had gone by since my deportation.

It was summer in England, and many seamen were on holiday with their families at seaside resorts. The engagement board in the Pool reflected that, with many ships requiring ABs. The *Port Victor* took my eye because I had done a home trade trip on her. But the large supply of Shaw Savill vessels requiring ratings did not mean I would get a job. Having deserted two of their ships in the past I could be pushing my luck if I tried again, so the *Port Victor* was my best choice. I had never sailed deep sea with Port Line and I'd have to take the chance they wouldn't question my VNC.

My thoughts were interrupted by an old mate of mine, Barry, saying he had just scored the *Port Victor* and that she was sailing to Kiwiland within the next week. The vessel required a full crew so I was hopeful it would end my ban on ships going to New Zealand.

"*Port Victor*," I said, holding my breath.

"Get a clearance from the doctor," he said, handing me a chit to see the mate.

I contained my elation until I got outside and fairly skipped down the wharf to the ex-wartime auxiliary aircraft carrier that was to be my passage for the next few months. The mate stood four foot nothing and never bothered to look at my discharge book. He was more interested in whether I had sailed for British India because he thought he recognised me in his apprentice days, the cheeky git!

"No, I'm not a bleeding lascar!" I retorted. With the job secured I vowed that this time I would be aboard when she sailed from New Zealand.

The *Port Victor* had served as an auxiliary aircraft carrier during World War II.
VH Young

The *Port Victor* (10,400 tons) was a refrigerated cargo vessel built by John Brown on the River Clyde in 1943, seconded to the navy and converted into an escort auxiliary aircraft carrier with a displacement of 14,000 tons. As the HMS *Nairana* she spent her wartime career on escort duty with the Russian convoys to Murmansk. After the war she was transferred to the Royal Dutch Navy as the HMNS *Karel Doorman*. In 1949 she was at last back in the care of Port Line and resumed trade under her given name. Port Line could proudly say that every vessel they owned was built in a British shipyard. (One of their newest vessels, *Port Invercargill*, was trapped in the Suez Canal with a number of other ships in 1967 during the Six-Day War. She languished in the Bitter Lakes for eight years, never returning to service.)

A rumour went round as we cleared the English Channel that it would be announced we were going on the Montreal–Australia–NZ run. The old vessel was a good candidate and Port Line was well known for extending trips. No announcement was made at the time but that didn't mean it could not come.

I was expecting mail from Bev on arrival in Cristobal. The chief steward came down with the mail, laying it on the messroom table, but there was none with my name on. Distressing thoughts ran through my mind. Had she given up, thinking I was never going to return? There was still the long haul across the Pacific, leaving me to ponder for three weeks whether I had been given a silent Dear John.

We arrived in Auckland in just under three weeks and I snatched up the letter addressed to me in Bev's hand. I read it twice as though I could change the words telling me she was sorry, but nine months had taken their toll and she had made her decision. I had laughed at others in my situation on many shipboard messrooms, and now I realised that it was a personal situation which did not need some clown on the side taking the piss. I was thinking through how I might change her mind when my thoughts were interrupted by one of the lads.

"Dave, been looking for you everywhere. Your girlfriend is on the blower."

An uptight chief mate who we had nicknamed 'Angry Ant' was pacing the deck, waiting to get on the phone and remarking that phone calls should not interfere with our work hours. My fingers gave the victory sign to the chief officer as I picked up the phone.

The voice on the other end was blubbering away, saying I was to take no notice of her Dear John. She had been upset, and had written it in haste. I told her she didn't have to explain herself to me. Her voice was music and my hopes soared. She had been working three jobs in Wellington — a cleaning job in the mornings and the evenings and her day job at the Prudential to keep her busy while she waited for me to return.

Outside the phone booth Angry Ant was not as appreciative as I was. Bev and

I had made arrangements to meet in Wellington. I put the phone down, feeling like I had just won the first prize on Littlewoods football pools.

The mate grabbed the phone, saying he wanted to see me in his cabin at morning smoko. My 'V' sign was the reason. It then hit me that such a gesture could have dire effect on my conduct report.

What could be construed as an insignificant altercation with the chief mate marked a turning point for me — I threw off my bellicose attitude towards the upper deck and decided to lighten up. I went to see the mate. My 'V' for victory was in response to the 'Dear John', I lied. He was not stupid but I left his cabin with a clean slate.

Wellington was a very happy occasion. We both wanted to move the relationship on by getting engaged on my next trip. Bev was very pragmatic and lived frugally. On the question of finances I was a disaster. I knew nothing of banks or banking; the thought of saving money had never entered my head. I felt guilty that Bev was doing all the donkeywork without any contribution from me. The Wellington reunion showed I had a lot to learn in all spheres that require responsibility. I was 27 and it was about time I grew up and had a more definite focus.

Not everything was rosy on my stay in Wellington. We were cleaning out the lower deck of a hold when the bosun shouted down, "The *Gothic's* on fire!" She was some 1300km from New Zealand when fire raged through her bridge and the adjoining accommodation. This was sad news since I was familiar with the ship. Seven people lost their lives and she limped back to Wellington, arriving on 6 August, four days after the fire was brought under control.

The *Port Victor* called at all the usual ports around the New Zealand coast, finally reaching Bluff. Joe Townsley, a colourful Scotsman and a good shipmate who could regale us with plenty of bawdy tales, decided to marry his long-time fiancée in this rather isolated place. Barry James and I were the only two witnesses in the registry office. Joe joined the New Zealand police and became a prominent figure in the Drug Squad. Years later, whenever we saw each other, we would have a good laugh about our time on the *Victor* and life on the waves.

We arrived in London in late September. The *Port Victor* was not long from her termination — the ship was scrapped in 1971, another victim of a time when containerisation was impacting on conventional shipping and giving a sound message to those employed in the industry.

twenty-four

NEW TECHNOLOGY WAS FAST MAKING inroads into the way cargo and its transportation around the world would be managed. I am sure many of us had heard about the American LASH ships coming to the UK, and I am equally sure the implications of these ships went straight out the other ear. We never thought that in a few years we would be made redundant in the name of technology and progress. The 'Lighter Aboard Ships' concept was a forerunner to containerisation. Cargo was loaded in lighters or containers, carried on deck and shipped around the world. At the same time, airlines were sweeping up the carriage of passengers with cheaper airfares. Passenger liners many of us were part of had no answer to the competition and were slowly being made obsolete or fitted out for cruising.

The cartel that implemented containerisation included the Port, Blue Star and the Ben lines, who formed a company known as Associated Container Transport (ACT). Containerisation gradually made seamanship irrelevant, silencing the wharves and making thousands of dockers obsolete.

Workers tend to oppose any new concept that changes the way they work. I can well imagine the thoughts of those old mariners who fought in Nelson's navy under canvas, pondering a tender that had just slipped alongside their first-rater billowing black smoke from its tall funnel on the calm waters of Portsmouth Harbour in 1812. I wonder if they realised that the days of canvas and the adeptness of their seamanship were to be consigned to history? I doubt whether 'superfluous to requirement' entered those old battle-weary heads almost two centuries ago.

Although I had heard about the new vessels carrying 'boxes', I was not unduly worried, as I assumed nothing could replace our manual skills. Yet there were plenty of signs that the world of shipping was changing in Britain. My next ship was the *Athenic* which, with the *Corinthic,* had been downgraded in 1965 from passenger cargo ships to cargo ships.

I had no inkling of events ahead as I signed on for a trip to Australia and New Zealand. A letter from Bev had told me our engagement celebration was to be held at her parents' home in New Plymouth, and she suggested I take leave for the event. Luck was in my court since New Plymouth was a port of call.

At the soonest possible moment I visited the mate to request a week's leave in

New Zealand. The skipper has the last say on his vessel and the mate passed my request to him. I was surprised when the mate told me his nibs wanted to see me before our departure from London.

"What do you want a week's leave for? Is it for one of those New Zealand girls?" I was taken aback by the skipper's clearly disapproving attitude and put my hand over my mouth lest I ruin my appeal.

"Yes, I'm getting engaged to a lady in New Plymouth," I said, putting emphasis on the word 'lady'.

Having secured his assent I quit his cabin, bursting to give an appropriate reply to this git who seemed to think his authority entitled him to make judgemental remarks to those under his command. He and I were going to have a wonderful trip, I thought.

My cabin-mate was a fellow Londoner from Camberwell, Brian Rogers, one of those guys with the looks to get any lady he wanted. I told him that we had a Captain Bligh in command, and recounted my meeting. By the time we had departed the Royal Docks I had forgotten about my encounter with the skipper and settled down to what was to be a five-month trip. Although I did not yet know it, the *Athenic* was to be my swansong from the shores of Britain, but there were unforeseen events on the horizon that were to be played out before the trip ended.

We tied up at Melbourne. Ahead of us was another company vessel, *Persic*, which was homeward-bound. The crews of both vessels were acquainted, as we had either sailed together or known each other at the pubs around the Royal Docks, so we met up at the Port Melbourne Hotel. As the evening went on the brown stuff took over and a fight broke out. There was a cry for Athenics and Persics to get involved. I have not the faintest idea who we were brawling with. The outcome was the hotel being overrun by the Melbourne police. The cops made us stand in a line outside the hotel and proceeded to question us. A few smart-arse remarks aimed at the police resulted in the sound of dull thuds as truncheons connected with heads. Most of us were told to get back to our vessels and stay there, but some seamen were taken into custody. One of them was Brian, who went to court the next morning and was fined $200. He certainly never had that sort of money. The captain refused to pay the fine, which meant a bit of porridge for our shipmate.

A couple of us went down on the wharf to seek help from the delegates of the Waterside Union. We knew they had a strong union and the delegate was amazed that the skipper would refuse to pay the fine.

A tarpaulin muster was called for by the wharfies and in no time they had the money to pay the fine. A delegation of wharfies and crew went to the skipper's cabin and offered him the collection to pay Brian's fine. His answer was that even

The *Athenic*, my swansong from the UK. The vessel left port the day of my wedding, and half the crew stayed ashore to attend.

VH Young

if the fine was paid he didn't want Brian back. It was obvious the skipper didn't know who he was up against. He soon found out.

"You mean to say you would leave one of your crew in jail when we have the money to pay his fine?" said the wharfies' delegate.

The skipper demanded they get out of his cabin.

"This vessel will not leave here until your cobber is aboard," the delegate said, nodding at us.

The skipper reckoned he did not care what they threatened and within five minutes all discharge of cargo came to a halt. Whatever cargo was not unloaded in Melbourne could be unloaded in Sydney, according to the mate.

"Who's going to let the mooring ropes go, Mister?" I asked. They just didn't get it. I told the union delegate what they were planning if we got to Sydney.

"Don't worry about Sydney, cobber, the ship is blacked and no one from Perth to Darwin will touch it!"

Someone higher up the chain countermanded the skipper's threat, and Brian was produced, to the cheers of shipmates and wharfies alike, within an hour of their walking off. We could not thank the wharfies' union enough and they were more than welcomed in our presence. I had now witnessed how a good union operated. It did not matter whether you were a member of their union or a member of another union asking for help. The NUS should come down here and get some tuition, I thought.

The skipper was not pleased with the action we took, but we had our shipmate back. In Sydney the wharf delegates were well-versed and made sure Brian was on board before letting their members work the ship. He was quite a celebrity among the ladies who patronised Monty's bar in Sydney.

An edict came down from the skipper, prohibiting female guests aboard. The dock gate was also given strict instructions to the same effect — sour grapes on the upper deck? The lads found a way around that one. We were moored stern to stern with the *Melbourne Star*, whose crew were known to many of us including the inimitable 'Spider', who handed out guest passes from his vessel, allowing our lads to pass through the dock gate with their lady friends.

Monty's was still the favourite watering hole. Around its walls hung the liferaft rings from many ships, and how could one forget some of the ladies such as 'Jimi Hendrix' who could knock a guy out with one punch, and Shirley, whose wrath I experienced on a previous trip, after seeing her making light of a roast leg of meat, and asking her if it was our deck boy she was eating. There was also 'Bat Lady', whose sense of dress always included a cloak and thigh-high boots, and many others.

Only when we were crossing the Tasman did I feel my trip had begun. When I arrived in Wellington, Bev rang to say I had to meet her after work outside the Prudential as she had something special to tell me. What could that something special be? Not forgetting the engagement ring I had bought in London, I rushed

Over the wall of the *Athenic*, 1968: Dave, Bobby Dunkley, 'Wild One' Kevin Thomas, Billy Hird and Brian Rogers.

ashore and waited impatiently outside the Prudential on Lambton Quay. She told me that we were to be married in New Plymouth on the Saturday the ship was in port. It kind of took my breath away, being at short notice, but I was thrilled.

She had given her parents two weeks' notice and had booked the church. The only thing that could spoil our wedding day was the vessel not keeping to itinerary. Bev left her small flat in Drummond Street for New Plymouth to finalise arrangements while the *Athenic* continued her cargo operations in Wellington. I pondered how I was to join my wife after completing the trip? Saving money had not been one of my qualities — she probably thought I had the airfare to New Zealand.

In the meantime I got my act together, asking Brian to be my best man and inviting all the ratings to my big day. The ship arrived in New Plymouth on the Tuesday and was scheduled to sail on my wedding day for Auckland. I took my leave from the vessel and drew all the money I had left to buy a wedding ring. The engagement ring I had bought in London was too big and had to be altered. On this occasion she chose a ring within my financial means and had it altered to fit.

My worries about how I was going to join her in New Zealand after completing the voyage were soon revealed. Bev knew that saving money was not one of my skills. Her three jobs had contributed to most of the price of an airline ticket from the United Kingdom to New Zealand. Her girlfriend Lesley, who she worked with at the Prudential, had financed the difference and a ticket was waiting for me at Heathrow airport in London when I got back. We would pay Lesley back when I began life in New Zealand. I felt guilty that I was so useless in financial matters that I had to leave it to others to solve. I had just turned 28 and I was still living each day as it came.

I had to change my attitude. Bev demanded I get my hair cut for the big day. My Mod Squad locks were my pride and I tried every excuse to hang on to them, but I yielded to her demands and dreaded the sniggers from the crowd when I came aboard sporting my Kiwi short back and sides.

That was to be the least of my problems. The mate wanted to see me. He burbled an apology, advising me that orders from the skipper were that the crew must be aboard when the vessel sailed for Auckland. I engaged our onboard NUS convenor and we went to the master's cabin. I told him that my wedding day was set for Saturday afternoon, and requested that my best man and I be allowed to rejoin the vessel in Auckland. His answer still appals me.

"I want all the crew on board when we sail."

"But what about my wedding?"

He replied that I should find another wedding day. The vessel had to be fully manned. That was bullshit; if I were to be hospitalised on sailing day the company would not fly out a replacement from the UK. The convenor made me hold my counsel, asked the skipper to be reasonable, and questioned how he would feel if someone gave him that option on his wedding day. He would not relent and I had no doubt the episode in Melbourne played a big part in his thinking.

Below decks they were just as appalled and I was surprised at the fervour shown towards my dilemma. A plan was nurtured so that my wedding would not be missed. I can hardly write the expletives used against the old captain. If the deck ratings were ashore attending a wedding on departure day, the ship would have difficulty sailing. Many of the deck ratings and some stewards said they would be on hand. The plan was supposed to be secret, but keeping a secret in such a close-knit community is almost impossible.

Bev and I were married at St Andrew's Presbyterian Church in New Plymouth on 21 December 1968. Brian, my best man, attended as did eight other ABs and three catering staff. The *Athenic* duly left for Auckland at the appointed time with a reduced crew. Sadly we had to forgo our honeymoon to catch the train to Auckland and rejoin the vessel. Bev implored me to keep my nose clean and rejoin her within the next couple of months. She was scared I was going to give the skipper a biff. She returned to Wellington while the after-effects of home brew saw a seedy bunch of sailors board the train for Auckland. We discussed the implications of missing the ship and what our punishment might be. I told the lads that I was willing to take full blame since they were in this position because of their support for me. Opposition was voiced, but I reasoned with my mates that I was in a good position since I had a flight ticket waiting for me. I would never be stepping aboard another UK vessel, as whatever was in store for me when I fronted up to the skipper could only hurt my pocket and not my future.

"Let me try," I pleaded.

The chief officer showed some belated sympathy as he escorted me to the bridge, mumbling that he did not agree with the skipper's actions and other sentiments that sounded hollow. I took full responsibility as agreed with the lads. It was up to the captain to go along with my proposal, and he was quite happy to accede. He just about took all the remaining days I had left in the voyage, fining me 23 days and a DR for conduct. He even told me he was going to recommend I never go to sea again. No skipper had that power, of course, and I am sure I would have had mitigating circumstances, had it come to the defence of my career.

I never mentioned that his words meant little since I would be on the other side of the globe in a few weeks. At least he was kind enough leave a taxi fare to Heathrow Airport in my account. I rang my wife telling her the outcome of my meeting with the 'Old Bailey judge', and she was relieved that only words had transpired.

On the stage in Melbourne:
Allan 'Mr Pickwick' Bowles, Bobby,
Brian, 'Wild One', Dave, Billy.

On 13 February 1969 the *Athenic* negotiated the locks in the northeast port of Hull, and one more event was to be played out before I could say goodbye to my shipmates. My discharge book was in the care of the shipping master because of the DR entry. A bad discharge had to be answered before my book was returned. The master's cabin was crowded with himself, the shipping master, the chief officer, the north-eastern NUS representative and a member of the Hull constabulary in attendance in case of violence.

The NUS rep had not bothered to approach me to find out what my bad discharge was about. He was supposed to be my advocate, yet he was standing with the rest of them when I entered the skipper's cabin. I had to ask who the NUS rep was, and who he thought he was representing.

The shipping master began reading the skipper's report of the event in New Plymouth. I wondered why I was wasting precious time in front of this kangaroo court. I didn't really need a British discharge book where I was headed.

The porthole behind the shipping master gave me an idea. I grabbed my discharge book, chucked it through the porthole and walked out. My action stunned the court and I was in the lower decks collecting my bag before shouts of horror echoed through the accommodation. I gave the NUS rep a mouthful before striding down the gangway. To my amazement, my discharge book was lying on the quay. I looked up to see the captain, his head clearly defined in the porthole. I gave my *au revoir* in the form of two fingers and caught up with the lads at the station for the train ride to London.

The Athenics deserve a special mention. Brian, my cabin-mate whose twinkle toes on the soccer field also gave the cabin in the tropics the aroma of my favourite blue cheese, took the trouble to upskill his career and is currently a second mate on the Australian coast. 'Mr Pickwick,' named on account of his sideburns, on the happy event of marriage to his Kiwi sweetheart asked me to be his best man. Billy Hird married his sheila in Sydney and disappeared. The last I remember of Bobby Dunkley was his hearty grin as he shook my hand and wished me good luck. Kevin 'Wild One' Thomas, so named because he endeared himself to everyone by being quiet as a mouse, yet was part of the camaraderie that made for an unforgettable trip.

In London I said my goodbyes to my envious mates, some who said they would see me out there. BOAC confirmed that my ticket was waiting for me at their Heathrow counter. My flight to New Zealand was by the South Pacific route. I still have the airline ticket.

As I soared above London, my birthplace becoming a speck in a bird's-eye view, I felt a tug of sadness. This was the land where I was born. But I thought of my future on the other side of the world. I was proud to be British and it took many years to lower the home country in me in favour of my adopted nation. Again I reflected on my adolescent life, guilty that I had not contacted my foster parents in all those years on the briny. Irresponsible, one would say. I was all that — a mistake-maker, naive, and with a happy-go-lucky manner. It was all part of growing up. But I would not change a thing since that was how I was meant to be.

Sometimes confrontational, but always happy, I took the ups and downs of my young life like a ship over the oceans of the world.

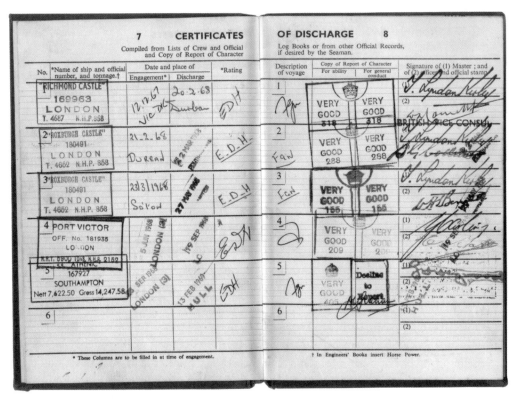

My third and last discharge book, showing my last five discharges, including the 'DR' — Decline to Report — when I took the crowd off for my wedding day in New Plymouth.

part two

twenty-five

The world is round and the place which may seem like the end may also be the beginning.

— *Ivy Baker Priest*

THE FLIGHT FROM LONDON TO Sydney had been long and tiring. In the transit lounge I was able to stretch my legs while I waited for my flight to Wellington.

'You can't beat Wellington on a summer's day,' goes the present-day slogan. It was no different when flight TE322Y winged its way into Rongotai airport on time at 11.45am. Excitement welled inside me as I went through Customs and Immigration. Judge Scully's advice two years previous had been heeded and I walked through the barrier and into the arms of my wife. The twin dream of being with the one I loved in the country I had chosen was now a reality. We walked out of the airport to a taxi, and yes, it was a brilliant day in Wellington. I had finally come to settle down to a new wife, a new country, and a new beginning.

While I had been away, Bev had moved from Drummond Street to a flat of more substance in Aro Street. The flat above us housed a couple of plonkies who had rather light fingers, which prompted us to move as soon as we could find a decent place. I desperately wanted to sound out the local shipping scene but I decided it was unfair to the wife who had waited long enough while I gallivanted around the world.

Once again I went into the window-cleaning game as I had in 1967. This time my boss Fred was a Welshman and a keep-fit fanatic who had more go in him than both my co-worker Marnie and me put together. He was a stickler for making sure the windows were spotless, and his fastidiousness could irritate you. New Zealand had changed to decimal currency and my wage was $40 a week. Bev became the banker since I was still a dummy in that department.

Fred was a nice enough geezer, but too fussy for me and I left him in favour of the Vacuum Cleaning Company. They had a window-cleaning contract with the government, the same round I was doing with Jack in 1967.

There are many seamen who have had the honour of lugging a pointer ladder and scrim cloth around for the VCC. On one occasion we were cleaning the windows

With Bev at the
Londoners Club,
Wellington 1971.

in Taranaki police station, when our different pommie accents caused a copper to bawl out, "Hello hello, we got a load of jumped seamen here? Let's have a look."

We all marched into this room where he pulled out a large book with mugshots of jumped seamen. A good mate of mine from years ago was crapping himself as the officer leafed through the book. I saw the mugshot of my mate, which the policeman missed completely. When he was satisfied we had all settled in New Zealand legally, we raced through the remaining windows and repaired to Oriental Bay where some of the lads recuperated on the beach.

We were assigned to clean the windows of an old house next to the Basin Reserve. Extension ladders were put up against the house to reach the upstairs windows. A carload of cops pulled up outside, finding a bunch of industrious long-haired guys beavering away on the windows. Apparently a nosey old bird had rung the law reporting a robbery. Our van, with the large title 'Vacuum Cleaning Company', had no effect on the dobber. According to her, we didn't *look* like window-cleaners. Yeah, right.

One of our chores was the government's State Housing building, so I inquired how to go about getting a state house. The guy must have been really fed up with my daily appearance at the reception desk asking if there was any movement on our application, but my badgering paid off some weeks later when a small two-bedroom flat became available at $5 a week. It was luxury in comparison to the damp hovel we had been renting in Northland.

Owning your own home was every Kiwi's dream, and was achievable to anyone who set their minds on a deposit. We must have scoured all the second-hand shops to furnish our palace in Strathmore. Even that rickety old bed with well-worn springs and a horrendous dip in the middle was a luxury. Our cosy abode looked like a second-hand furniture shop, but at least it belonged to us.

Unlike the UK where the world stage came to you, in my chosen paradise in the South Pacific events in the rest of the world seemed far away. The world carried on and the televised moon landing would have our eyes glued to the screen as we watched that foot follow the now famous speech, "One small step for man…" Demonstrations against the Vietnam War were hotting up around the world and finally one nation decided that apartheid was out of step with the modern times, and cancelled the South African cricket tour to England. Music never loses its effect; Bob Dylan had captured the minds of the young idealists.

During this time my *Athenic* buddy Brian had made his way out to New Zealand and signed on with the VCC. All the same, he was more interested in getting a job at sea. It didn't take him long before he told us he had scored a job on the *Holm Park,* which was salvaging the wreckage of the *Wahine* in Wellington harbour. Envious, I asked Bev her thoughts, reasoning that my weekly earnings of $40 were going to take us years to save a deposit for a house. I could earn far more at sea. According to coastal seamen in the Waterloo wages were over $100 a week on the ferries. Union Steamship cargo vessels, I was told, did an average of three week round trips across the Tasman.

We agreed that our focus must be on a family and eventually our own home. Once we had settled on our new direction I contacted a mate of mine who was on the coast to find out what the regime was to get away to sea. It was a very different set-up to what we had in Britain, where we could go directly to the shipping company and get a job. In New Zealand prospective job-seekers had to join the Seamen's Union. This required filling in an application form with personal details and sea experience. Two current financial members of the union had to nominate and second your application. It was my first insight to a union that the media and the political fraternity said was militant and run by communists.

twenty-six

MY NOMINATOR JOHN ACCOMPANIED ME to my interview with Les Barber at the head office of the New Zealand Seamen's Union. The secretary shook my hand and launched into what the union was all about. We talked about the reform movement and the British seamen's strike. I felt I was in the right company and boldly expressed my own doubts about the NUS. Seamen can find a lot in common, and the interview went well. There was the matter of union fees, to be paid six months in advance if I were to be accepted as a financial member.

I carried on with my daily toil with the VCC, taking my morning smoko at Suzy's coffee bar in Willis Street or at the Mecca Café on the corner of Mercer and Victoria streets. After work I took a quick beer in the Royal Tavern on Lambton Quay, then a bus home.

It was not long before the union contacted me. An AB's job was on offer on the Union Steamship Company vessel *Kuratai*, tied up in Mount Maunganui. Having paid my fees I received my union book and membership number. My next stop was Stout Street for the shipping office.

The system for employing seamen here was very different to the UK. 'The Corner,' as it was termed, was very much run by the union. There was a shipping master and his office staff, but unlike the British set-up the shipping master had little to do with who would step aboard a vessel.

Seamen who wanted a job could register at the Corner. A union official was there at 10 each morning, Monday to Friday. The name on top of the list would get first choice of jobs on whatever vessels were on offer that day. Should you choose not to take a job, your name would go to the bottom of the list the following day. Three refusals to take jobs would earn a suspension, with your name being struck off the list for a fortnight or so. This was a measure to ensure that when a member registered he genuinely wanted employment and was not just sitting there waiting for a plum job that might be coming up. There were no discharge books, nor did I have to trek through miles of docks to have a three-ringer look me up and down.

The job on the *Kuratai* resulted from a shortage of ABs around the country and was a bit of a pierhead jump. I signed articles in the shipping office under the watchful eye of Union Steam's amicable crew administration officer, Bernie

Miller and was pleasantly surprised when I was presented with a flight ticket to join the *Kuratai* in Tauranga. That there were no arduous train journeys for union members made it clear to me that the New Zealand union was miles ahead of the UK. The NUS were amateurs to this outfit and this confirmed my opinion that for years there had been too many shiny-arsed suits sitting on their fat fundaments in that cosy office in Clapham, who had not the wit to bring the NUS out of the dark ages. It was a real pity Paddy Neary's reform movement did not take off. As a member of that union I have no problem giving the NUS executives of the 1950s and '60s a serve.

I assured my better half that there would be no nine-month wait. All travel from your home was paid by the shipowner when joining a vessel in another port. Our domestic carrier landed in Tauranga and I jumped into a cab after collecting my bag. The few passengers in the airport were a contrast to the crowded terminals I had seen on my journey to New Zealand. Coming from a crowded country, I noticed little things like that.

"To the docks, please," I said to the taxi driver.

"Whereabouts on the wharf?" he said.

Maori names had always given me a speech problem. I had the name of the ship on a piece of paper, thus showing my ignorance of Maori pronunciation. The taxi pulled up alongside a chatty-looking ship in green livery with a yellow band around its hull. The *Kuratai* looked no bigger than an English coastal vessel.

So commenced that part of my life which has been truly rewarding. My wife and kids were soon to knock the individualist out of me as I embraced the joys of fatherhood and family. Thirty-four years of comradeship were about to begin as I made my way to the top of the gangway to meet the characters of the New Zealand coast.

I asked where I could find the mate.

"What do you want to see him for?"

I explained I was joining the ship and had just arrived from Wellington. When he realised I was a 'new book' he understood my seeming naivety. He introduced himself as 'Don the Hop'. I never found out if the 'Hop' referred to an affinity for the drink or something to do with agility. I can attest that I never saw any evidence of the latter during subsequent contact with him.

"You don't go near them up top until you've seen the delegate aboard," he said. This was to make sure I possessed a union book and to check if I was a financial member. It was a closed shop to non-union labour and furthermore, no member could join a vessel if he was in arrears with his union fees. After nervously presenting my credentials to the delegate I was shown to the day-workers' cabin that I was to share with two others. Finally I got to see the chief mate, whose involvement in all this seemed to be relegated to a token gesture of noting a new AB had joined the vessel.

The vessel would be sailing at 5 that evening for Melbourne, I was advised. "Dave's the dipstick," the bosun advised the mate.

Dipstick? What's he calling me a dipstick for? Before I could take offence at what I thought was a slur I was quickly advised that 'dipstick' referred to the all-important position of the man who dipped his sounding rod into the buoyancy tanks that governed the vessel's stability. Attached to my appointment as dipstick was the position of 'mud pilot,' or quartermaster. In other words I would be helmsman during the pilotage in and out of harbours. I had a sneaky feeling that as the new guy I was being palmed off with portfolios that none of the crowd wanted. It had no effect on the exhilaration I felt on the resumption of my favourite job.

The easygoing attitude on board between officers and ratings was in marked contrast to the customary demarcation that existed on home boats. The ordinary seaman was referred to as the bucko, and addressing the mate as 'sir' was frowned upon. I substituted by calling him 'mister'. Trying to shake off fourteen years of a regime and adapting to a more moderated system without making myself a laughing stock was a tall order. I was sharing the day-worker cabin with a man called Specs and a rather more aged gentleman called Tommy, who was nicknamed Spaceman on account, I presume, of the prodigious quantities of ale he could put back. Set aside in one part of the messroom was the crew bar stocked with duty-free booze which we could buy from the bond when we were at sea.

I was given a diagram showing the daily soundings to take on deck and in the engineroom. We clewed up the vessel for sea, and housed the derricks against the mast, secured in their topped position. It was an innovative way as opposed to most ships that drop the derricks to deck level.

An incident happened not long before we were due to sail. I noted while we were closing hatches Don was muttering in the mate's ear. Whatever he said brought a bristling reaction from the chief mate who ordered Don to throw his hand in. Those of us nearby were dumbfounded by the sudden outburst.

"What did you say to him?"

"He can't take a joke — I called him a flea," Don replied.

Welcome to the coast, I thought.

By sacking Don, it was shooting himself in the foot since it left the manning on deck short-handed. The sailing was cancelled and it was only the next morning when the Corner opened that we were able to replace him.

ABs were on a 40-hour week with the basic hourly rate of 98 cents. Added to this was a weekly industry allowance of $4.80, bringing the monthly basic pay rate to $176. Saturdays and Sundays attracted overtime, which boosted our wages to a very respectable rate but they were still behind many workers ashore. Compared to what I was earning for cleaning windows, I had no complaints.

No pilots were engaged since Union Steamship required their masters to have exemptions piloting their vessels in and out of New Zealand ports. As mud pilot I took her out of Mount Maunganui and we were finally on our way across the Tasman to Melbourne to unload, then onto Stenhouse Bay for a full cargo of gypsum. The first night at sea was spent listening to Tommy sawing logs. He was in the single bunk while Specs and I had the two-tier bunks. Each of us would be armed with a boot to fling at Tommy should we have another night like that.

Our delegate, who had been elected by the members on board the vessel, was informative on union matters. When I came on the coast you were very proud to be elected delegate. He was the advocate for members and was expected to sort out disputes and to make sure the conditions won by those before us were not usurped by members or anyone else aboard the vessel. The position also carried responsibilities, which included making yourself credible to those you advocated for and most definitely to those on the upper decks. No one would take any notice of a delegate who was getting himself into strife or hitting the bottle. It would do the delegate a disservice, as it would the union. I'm glad to say I saw very few in those categories.

Issues of discipline were kept as far from the skipper's cabin as possible. They were settled among the members by calling a meeting on the offender. I believe the shipping companies made a huge gaffe some 25 years later when they outlawed the union's self-disciplinary system by writing their own disciplinary measures in the collective contract. Members were more scared of the union, who could suspend a member and withdraw his book. On the other hand, when the companies took over disciplinary measures in the mid-'90s, the sacking of a crew member became an option for the company, until it occurred to them that very few seamen had been trained over the years. This may have curtailed their disciplinary options, since they could not afford to lose professional seafarers. Most skippers had enough on their plates running the day-to-day operations, and were quite happy to have the delegate and members sort out the myriad crew issues that cropped up. My opinion is based on my experience as part of the NUS system, and having held the position of an on-board NZSU delegate for 28 years.

The *Kuratai* made its way to Melbourne, where one of the ABs was appointed gear man. He was on hand while cargo operations were in force. The rest of us were tasked with the usual maintenance jobs. You were allowed to take leave as long as you gave notice before arriving in port. This leave would be deducted from your accumulated leave at the end of the trip.

Our leisure time was spent in the Hotham Hotel in Melbourne, a favourite of

Union Steamship crews. Its attraction eluded me, but anything looks good after a bottle of Bundaberg rum, according to Tommy. I also followed the tradition of buying a kilo bag of king prawns for $5. Kippers from Aberdeen or smoked haddock, which couldn't be purchased in New Zealand, went at $5 a box. Times have changed for bringing foodstuffs over the border. In those days, as long as you declared it on the custom manifest there was no problem. I think Bev dreaded my trips across the Tasman; she hated the smell of my daily plate of kippers and egg, and was thankful when the last of them were eaten up.

Stenhouse Bay on the Yorke Peninsula has to be one of the loneliest ports in the world. Perhaps a hermit allowance was paid to attract the workforce there. Its claim to fame is the huge gypsum deposit, which is used in fertilisers and in the building industry.

We arrived back at the Mount on Christmas Eve and I was able to fly home to spend the holiday with Bev. Our income had risen to a point where saving for a home was achievable, although I still had a way to go in understanding the word 'budget.'

In early January 1971 I rejoined the *Kuratai* at the Mount, headed for Melbourne, Geelong and Portland to collect a cargo of grain. The crew was much the same as the previous trip. Lofty the bosun was from Waiheke Island. Specs, my previous cabin-mate, was on board. Dennis, our bucko, was a reflection of me in my teens. I have memories of this likable youngster from Nelson on our pre-Christmas trip walking unsteadily down the wharf in Melbourne, struggling to hold onto a huge panda bear and other Christmas shopping. He had obviously mixed his shopping with a detour into a house of liquor. Some years later we heard the sad news that he had been lost at sea on the Australian coast.

Once again I was assigned the jobs of dipstick and mud pilot. I met the mate at the bottom of the stairs. Echoing from our cabin was a stream of expletives telling the mate to vacate the crew accommodation. He was looking to see if I had arrived, as he wanted a sounding taken. The grin on his face showed our resident Spaceman's reaction (who was lying in his bunk and very much in orbit) seemed not to have offended him. There was an agreement with the union that officers do not enter the crew accommodation unless they have permission and are accompanied by a member. Thus the mate fully understood Tommy's ire.

The Rehu brothers from the South Island were identities on the coast. On this occasion Maurice, the younger brother, was to join the vessel. Roy from Bluff was our union rep.

On the morning of our arrival in Portland my mooring station was on the foc's'le and I was on the drum end steadily heaving the vessel alongside, when the mooring rope surged with such force that the slack behind me caught round my ankles and put me on the deck. I was concussed maybe and a bit bruised, but there was nothing major as I stood up. My hand was giving me trouble, having caught hold of the surging rope. Once again I learned that injuries were taken seriously by the union, as the delegate declared me unfit. There was concern that I had sustained injury to my back.

"You'll be covered by Section 58," said Roy as the taxi came to take me to the airport and home.

Bev was surprised but happy to see me so soon. I explained what had happened and sought advice on my position from the union. Section 58 meant I was allowed compensation, and could stay on at full pay. My right hand had been giving me trouble and I paid a visit to the doctor. An x-ray showed a hairline fracture to my thumb and I reported the findings to Union Steam crew administration.

I convalesced for five weeks, and in February I was able to attend my first monthly stopwork meeting, held in the Wellington Trades Hall. The meetings were scheduled every second Monday in the month. I was impressed at the attendance. It was compulsory for members to attend if they were in port, and there was a fine of $20 should you miss the meeting without any good reason. The rules sounded harsh, but I was fully supportive. If you want a say in your union and want to enjoy the rewards that had been collectively won, then you should show interest by being at the monthly port meetings. As a member of the NUS I had noticed that there were far too many so-called members who grabbed the meagre gains made by the few and never went near their union rooms.

The Wellington executive and the president of the Seamen's Union, Bill 'Pincher' Martin, conducted the meeting. Pincher took over the reins after the death of Fintan Patrick Walsh. I heard many tales from old members who remembered Walsh's dictatorial style, and that it was a relief when a more inclusive approach was taken under Pincher. Other notables were the general secretary Les Barber, who I had met on joining the union, sea-going vice president Terry Adams and councillors Dougie Morton and Bill Trueman. These men are legends to many of us old seamen. The history of the New Zealand Seamen's Union is richer for their knowledge and commitment in securing better wages and working conditions at sea and a superannuation scheme that was the envy of most workers.

Stopwork meetings were and still are the forum for issues that the members wanted to talk about. Any member could get up and have his say. Tommy Heptinstall was a perennial debater and was always a pleasure to listen to because he made sense. There were always one or two colourful characters arriving at meetings in a drunken haze who would add their two cents to serious debate and were promptly told to sit down by the chair.

Over the ensuing years the meeting venues changed. They now include the

Clerical Union Hall, the Railway Hall, the Greek Hall, the Flamingo and the Westpac Stadium. By the mid-'90s the attendance at stopwork meetings had dwindled — there is no penalty for non-attendance today.

I was judged fit to work again during the first week in March and put my name in at the Corner. It was completely different from the UK. No discharge book. No Reggie the Rat. Just a union official going through the list of those registered for work. The board was the only similarity. By the time my name was called, only a home trade job on the *Koranui* was in the offing. Not wanting to refuse a job as a new book, I took it. We spent a week in Wellington before taking her to the Mount and paying off. Bev was due with our first child in two months and I wanted to make sure I was around.

The *Karepo* in Adelaide was missing an AB who had paid off on compo. Having used up my leave, I took the flight to Adelaide to join the *Karepo*. My arrival was greeted by two bodies entangled in a tussle on top of the gangway. I asked who the delegate was, not expecting to get an answer from one of the two bodies.

"Have you got time to look at my union card?" I asked. Harry Hoof Beats removed himself from his opponent's grasp and got up.

"You're the delegate?" I asked incredulously.

The *Karepo* (3200 tons) was one of Union Steamship's modern vessels, having begun life in 1964. In place of the conventional derricks were five cranes. Crew accommodation was single-berth, a luxury I had rarely come across. The *Karepo* docked in Wellington twelve days later in early April.

Bev had stopped work by this time and I was not going anywhere until the baby was born. When my small amount of leave was used up, I had to register on the Corner. I was told I could get dispensation if needed, but luck was on my side when a job on the Wellington Oil barge came up.

I was near the bottom of the list and thought the job would probably go before it got to me. One of the guys from the *Koranui* had heard me talking about my coming fatherhood while we were on that ship, and asked me when the big day would arrive. I said the child was due any day now.

He pointed to the *Hinupani* on the board, explaining it was tailor-made for me because it plied the harbour. "You would be home every night and the weekends," he said.

It was music to my ears, but I pointed out that there were quite a few members before me and the job would probably be taken.

"This man's wife is due to have a child in the next week and needs to be with her," my *Koranui* member said aloud to those present. I was at number eleven on the list and all the advertised jobs had been filled by the time the call came to number eight, except an able seaman's position on the *Hinupani*. Eight, nine and

Karepo. "Who's the delegate?" I asked the two men fighting on the deck. "I am," answered one.
VH Young

ten on the list refused the job deliberately so that I could have it. The generosity shown by fellow members, most who never knew me, was again proof of the brotherhood among seamen. So impressed was I with the morning's events that poor Bev got a real old earbashing when I got home.

The *Hinupani* was a common sight on Wellington harbour since being built in Evans Bay in 1946. Owned by Union Steam, she was known as the 'oil barge' among seamen, and was one of the largest steel barges to be built in New Zealand. She carried a small crew, one man down below and two seamen on deck for tying up to various vessels for bunkering.

Our main customers were the Japanese fishing boats. Miramar wharf was our home base, which was great, as I lived nearby in Strathmore. Lionel was in charge of operation but he seemed to prefer his bicycle as a mode of transport, meeting the barge at whatever ship we were bunkering.

Sometimes we needed the tug to get us from ship to ship or over to Miramar wharf. Manning the tug was one John Beck, who Pete Dawkins and I would enjoy a lunch-hour session with in the Waterloo. After a month on the *Hinupani* I guessed time was near for Bev and our child, so I paid off.

Our daughter Nicole Jodie was born into the world a week later in Wellington Hospital at the decent time of 6pm. I was not allowed to attend the birth, so I paced the corridor outside. I was not worried whether we had a girl or a boy, just happy that she was a healthy baby. Today my wife tells one and all that the birth of Nicole had a maturing effect on me, changing my whole outlook on life. Children can do that to you. She was my prized jewel and I found myself becoming

The oil barge *Hinupani* in Wellington Harbour.
VH Young

domesticated. I was taught very quickly how to feed and burp her. It was the changing of the nappies that I tried to avoid, especially if there was a 'present' waiting. Since I was the breadwinner I would have to turn-to pretty soon. Bev assured me that she would be okay as she had friends all around who were also mothers and could help her.

The *Kawerau* (3600 tons) was just like the *Koranui* I had previously sailed on. She was docked in Wellington and the articles were home trade, which suited me. Lyttelton and Napier, where I paid off, were the other ports we were destined for during the next two weeks.

The 1971 Lions' rugby tour of New Zealand had also begun in May. I knew nothing about the game except observing a whole mass of bodies converged, scrambling for a funny shaped ball. Still the soccer fanatic, I nevertheless put my heart behind the Lions, to the disgust of the fervent Kiwi followers within the crew. The Lions won every provincial match, but I was told that they were not the real games. "Wait until they come up against the All Blacks!"

The All Blacks were defeated 9-3 in the first test match in Dunedin. The messroom was in mourning and my bragging didn't help matters. "I thought you knew how to play rugby!" I agitated, as John Dawes and his Lions continued winning on the provincial stages of the tour. Boy, did I wind 'em up.

"You pommie bastards'll get slaughtered in the next test!"

He was right. The Lions went down in Christchurch 22-12. A bucketload of abuse fell on me from all quarters. Of course I fully deserved it.

I was at home for the third test, watching it on our grainy second-hand TV. I have preserved a rag of the day called the *8 O'Clock*, with its profound headlines filling the front page: 'Lions 13 New Zealand 3.' I pinned the front page to my dungaree jacket and walked into the Thistle where I knew I would get a reaction.

In the crucial fourth test in Auckland, New Zealand needed to win to salvage a drawn series. PJ Williams, the Lions' Welsh goal-kicker, slotted a penalty in the last minute to draw level 14-all. I gleefully milked the situation. It was as though the whole country was in mourning. The loss was analysed each way and every way. I was not fully attuned to the reverence in which the national rugby team was held. The wife suggested I was now a Kiwi and should be supporting my adopted country. It took me some time and some dirty looks to be weaned from the country of my birth.

Time would eventually temper my passion for England. Today, I join thousands of fans trotting off to the Westpac Stadium in my All Black or Hurricanes regalia whenever a test or Super-14 game is scheduled.

The coastal cement carrier *Ligar Bay* (1330 tons) was owned by Tarakohe Shipping Co, with its headquarters in Nelson. The only time you could get a look in on the *Ligar Bay*, or its newer companion *Golden Bay*, was if a crew member sustained a crippling injury or was carried off in a pine box. Every so often a relieving job came up, and on one occasion I happened to be on the Corner with my name on the register. The long-serving bosun Norm Dunn was taking his annual leave.

I joined the vessel at the cement berth on Aotea Quay opposite the Cook Strait ferry berth. She was scheduled to call at Wanganui, Raglan and New Plymouth, where my stint of relieving would terminate. I relieved for one month, long enough to experience the camaraderie. Every ship has its characters, and the *Ligar Bay* did too. Paddy Flynn, the crew mess-man, had what seemed an obsession with sweeping the messroom deck. He rarely spoke and his coastal nickname was 'Steak Face.' The last time I spotted Paddy he was sweeping up rubbish in the Wellington Railway Station.

Paddy Phelan must have been a millionaire AB. A flagon of beer was the only visible thing on the top of the dresser in his cabin. The tale on board was his drawers were full of unopened fortnightly pay packets. I christened him the 'Log on the Bog' because every morning his immense butt was seated on the throne for ages, as he used it for a reading podium. His size was such that he couldn't close the door of the only toilet in the washhouse.

Wanganui was a regular port on the east coast during the heyday of small vessels.

When seaborne transportation of container cargoes became the mode, small ports like Wanganui became surplus to requirement. It was the same for Raglan. At the entrance to Raglan harbour was a sandbar that could only be crossed at high tide. The port of New Plymouth on the other hand has gone from strength to strength with its oil and gas facilities to complement the deposits a few miles offshore.

Having finished my relieving, I was discharged. The fortnightly wages were supplemented with plenty of overtime. My *Ligar Bay* wage sheet in June 1971 covered the normal pay period of ten days. Wages were $94.40 gross. Overtime was $72.56, with an industry allowance of $9.60 and the general wage order amount of $5.29, adding up to a gross of $181.85. PAYE tax deducted was $37.98. A non-taxable clothing allowance of $1.29 was added, resulting in a sum of $145.16.

I continued learning the intricacies of fatherhood. Sure, I liked to take time with my friends for a drink and a chat, but I was unconsciously growing out of a need to be with the lads.

"You going home already, Dave? The wife's got you round her little finger, mate."

They peer-pressured you in the hope you would stay until you were chucked out at closing time. I liked to have them on, saying I had to rush off to hang a load of nappies on the line or had a pile of ironing waiting for me. That got them talking.

"Wouldn't catch me hanging out any clothes," was the reply. Actually seamen spend a lot of their time at sea doing exactly that. If only the wives could see the deft hand that was wielded on the ship's ironing board, they would gladly hang the washing out, while handing us the iron for life.

The Cook Strait ferries were the ideal job for a family man. They were a week-on week-off schedule, and they were touted as the cream jobs out of Wellington. If you were lucky a relieving job could be picked up, but rarely a permanent position. The wages were far superior to the Tasman runners that were always plentiful on the Corner.

Trouble was looming on the industrial front, which would have consequences for the union in November. In the meantime I travelled to the Mount to join the *Kawerau* for a trip across the Tasman. It was my second time aboard her, having done a coastal run earlier in the year.

On English boats the bosun was usually a company man, having attained that status after years of service, but on the New Zealand coast the crew on deck chose their leading light. Our choice had to be approved by the master. It was a novel exercise since it cut out disagreement between the bosun and crew — having elected him we supported him without question.

On the *Kawerau* a meeting was called as the last bosun had paid off on compo the day of sailing. Nominations were called for, along with a seconder. My name was put forward and I was elected.

The position came with responsibility, of course, and most members were happy, wanting no part in giving orders. The skipper, Ginger Harrison, approved me. Those who had sailed with him before had a few choice names for him, but unless you brought yourself to the skipper's attention, I saw no reason to be involved with him. The mate and the bosun were the two who planned the day's work. We were bound for Adelaide, Geelong and Melbourne.

As the trip progressed I began to see why the master earned such choice names. While clewing up the ship in Adelaide and getting ready for sea, he called me up on the bridge wanting to know why there were only three of us on deck. I told him that they were doing other jobs. "Shall we go down to the accommodation and have a look?" he asked.

My stalling answer was to say I would get the delegate. He pointed out to me that the master has full reign of his vessel. True enough, I said, but you also have an agreement with the union that you don't go below unless accompanied by the delegate. He was an old master and knew exactly where the missing crew were. He even named them. I sent George Vuglar to try and arouse some of the crew from their inebriated sleep. In the meantime I grabbed the delegate, Jimmy Thompson, who advised me that we could not refuse the skipper's request. Lying on the couch in the messroom bar was a member who I shall not put a name to.

The skipper saw him and pointed. "Is he one of the crew?"

Before any one of us could answer the character on the couch arose like a mummy and said, "Course I'm one of the crew, what 'er yer think I am, a fucking ringbolt?" The skipper said I should not cover up for crew members who were drunk, and should make sure everyone had turned to on deck in a sober state. That was easier said than done, and it was not my job to tell grown men how they should conduct their lives. Each member knew their duty and if they are sprung then it is on their shoulders. They were letting their shipmates down and were taking advantage, hoping the power of the union would absolve them.

The delegate quite rightly was spewing, saying he should not have to go in to bat for members not doing their job, and was on this occasion trying to defend the obvious. But it was fair warning that the master would be counting heads in Geelong and Melbourne. The message was heeded and we arrived back in Wellington after a month away.

Safety at sea is important and any crew member found to be intoxicated or under the influence of drugs would not be allowed to step aboard a vessel. In the case of drink he would have to satisfy the company he was not an alcoholic. Being in possession or under the influence of drugs could spell the end of their career at sea.

With a new addition to the family, Bev thought it would be great if I could get a job on one of the ferries. I told her pigs would fly before that happened; but you never knew your luck.

Not everybody has the same thinking in a seamen's union. Never was that more evident than at stopwork meetings, where the commos flooded the room with literature and spouted mantras straight from Mao's Red Book. One pamphlet they called the 'Rolling Coaster' was nothing more than a diatribe aimed at Pincher Martin.

To me and the majority of mainstream rank-and-filers, we were ordinary workers just wanting fair pay and conditions for our labour. Pincher and his executive had achieved conditions that were the envy of workers in other spheres. It was a standing joke aboard the vessels that our so-called 'Peking Parrots' within the union would have been put up against the wall and shot in those regimes.

It hasn't passed my notice that many of the same blokes who jumped on the Mao and Lenin podiums of yesteryear, would today have more affinity with arch-capitalists.

It was 'Red' Rud Hughes, the Auckland seamen's secretary, who scoffed at the threat of the union being deregistered. The new Shipping and Seamen's Act was about to be tested on us by 'Gentleman Jack' Marshall, the National Party's deputy-leader. The union had always disagreed with the act because we knew it was designed to vet each seaman and weed out the so-called troublemakers that the government shiny-arses didn't want. Half the members would not have been in the union that Marshall was hoping for. In November 1971 the Seamen's Union was deregistered because we wanted no part of Marshall's law. Deregistration meant the sequestration of all union-owned properties and funds.

By this time the Wellington union office had been had been reinstated on Vivian Street from its old venue on The Terrace. Our funds mysteriously took wings and the government bailiffs complained they could not find two union razoos to rub together. Quick thinking by the executive stopped the commies starting up their own union. Pincher Martin and our lawyers filled in a maze of paperwork and the rank-and-file signed up to the new union.

While all the events in November were going on, I was on the *Koranui* berthed in Melbourne, and we were forbidden by the union to take any action in support of their stand while in a foreign port. Although members on New Zealand vessels overseas were technically de-unionised, we had no qualms that we were still a union and no government was going to change our minds.

An old AB from Lyttelton regaled us with his exploits from the war. In his lucid moments, Barney could tell a tall tale in the best maritime tradition. His favourite memory was as a soldier in Popski's Private Army. He said his birth-place was Yugoslavia. The lads would have him on, saying he wouldn't have a clue where Yugoslavia was, and he would get upset when they told him he was born in Ruatoria on the east coast of the North Island. I was quite happy to listen to an old man who could make you laugh whether the story was true or tall. Paddy the bosun gave him a job painting the storm door to our accommodation. It had still to be completed by the time we arrived back in the Mount a day before my 31st birthday.

The rent for our state house had been raised to $10 a week on account of my higher earnings. We still have the money-box with the weekly budget list pasted on the inside, showing where our money went.

The pressing matter was to join the new union. There was no screening of seamen as there would have been had Gentleman Jack got his way. We all had to fill out application forms as required by the Marine Division of the Ministry of Transport so that we could attend the Corner as legitimate members of the New Zealand Seamen's Union of Industrial Workers, the new title.

I had spent over a year on the New Zealand coast and many things had changed for me. Shedding my 'home boat' psyche was easy. The laid-back antipodean way of life was infectious. My English roots ran deep, prompting my wife to remind me that I was a Kiwi now, same as my daughter. She was right of course, but I had yet to fully appreciate my good fortune.

Early in January 1972 I rushed home to tell Bev some miraculous news. Once again I was on the Corner at the right time, number two on the list, when a relieving position on the *Aramoana* was posted. I could not believe my ears when No 1 on the list chose a Tasman runner, leaving me the *Aramoana*.

Happy as we were with this turn of events, I reminded Bev the relieving position was only for three weeks, or so I thought.

twenty-seven

So forth they rowed, and that Ferryman
With his stiffe oares did brush the sea so strong,
That the hoare waters from his frigot ran,
And the light bubbles daunced all along,
Whiles the salt brine out of the billowes sprong.

— *Edmund Spenser, The Faerie Queen*

THE 1900-TON *TAMAHINE* HAD commanded the link between Wellington, gateway to the North Island, and Picton, gateway to the South. The *Tam* was a conventional passenger cargo vessel, built in 1939. The practice of loading passenger vehicles by derrick had become a slow operation and in 1962 the government commissioned a road-rail ferry to enable passengers to drive their cars onto the vessel. This would minimise damage and turnarounds in port would be much quicker. There was much debate in Parliament as to the cost of the replacement. It was estimated at $2 million, an awful lot of taxpayer money. Patrons who regularly crossed the strait were attached to the old Tam, and saw no reason to get rid of the old lady. One codger who had fond memories of her told me that he was dead against a replacement, and asked what the bloody politicians would know, they fly everywhere.

I understood his feelings, but nothing stays the same. The new road-rail ferry *Aramoana* was such a hit with the public she repaid the government coffers in two years.

A couple of years later the *Aranui* was built. Together they plied the Cook Strait, and so began the modern ferry service that through the years has seen a love-hate relationship with the public. Its fast turnarounds were the envy of ferry companies around the world. A ferry operation that was once effective was handed on to the privatisers who, after they'd had their way, passed the bones on to another private company who said they aimed to put the meat back on this New Zealand icon.

My time on the Cook Strait spanned 33 years. It interweaved with my family life as no other job could. I saw many managers come and go, each with different ideas and a penchant for control, who should instead have left it to the professional seamen who had years of hands-on experience. We gave them a wry smile, and a "we told you so" when we said goodbye.

I was a part of the crews on whom passengers vented their anger when disputes tied the ferries up. There were myths about the ferries, the authors of which would not know the sharp end from the blunt end. Then there were the characters that crewed the vessels and made the job worthwhile.

Arriving at the ferry terminal at the appointed time, I boarded the *Aramoana* and began the experience of life of a ferryman.

Passengers on a Cook Strait ferry have little idea of the work that is put in before the vessel departs for the open sea. The jobs to be completed and the loading of passengers and cars are all under a strict timetable, so the vessel can sail at the prescribed time. The round-the-clock sailings on the ferries today were but a pipe-dream in the heads of management when I stepped aboard the *Aramoana* in January 1972. I introduced myself to the delegate, who advised me that he and I would be cabin-mates, and I had the top bunk. Kevin, better known by his coastal moniker, 'Flower Power', was the kind of guy who went out of his way to point you in the right direction.

Each member on deck had a specific set of jobs, enabling the ferry to run like clockwork. I kid you not, you needed a two-year apprenticeship to learn the routine.

Seamen's Union members worked a seven-day roster if you were sailing from the Wellington end. If the vessel began her day on the Picton end, it would mean an eight-day week on account of the extra trip across to Wellington before we could start our week off.

Work began at 8am with washing the ship down before the passengers boarded for the 10am sailing. My introduction to washing down was marked by a small bag propped up against a seat, that I thought a passenger had forgotten to take with them. It dawned on me why it had been left behind when the foul liquid spilled over my hand. Never again would I let my curiosity venture into the contents of a seasick bag.

My gang was called 'Coronation Street.' I plead not guilty to having any affinity to the TV soap. It had more to do with our bosun Harry, who was such a loyal fan that some referred to him as Ena Sharples.

In the cabin next door were two of the most audible snorers on the coast. Together they could have put Stihl chainsaws to shame. 'Shovel Nose' was a cantankerous old Scot who was very argumentative, and would bang his fist on the bulkhead to make his point. His poor old cabin-mate 'One Nip Nora' was a quiet bloke who never seemed to take offence at the bellicosity of his mate.

On my first week I became acquainted with a very important item on the rail deck, the bottle screw. This heavy cast-iron piece of equipment, used to tie down the wagons of the three lines of rakes the *Aramoana* carried, was a shock to the weak body. Muscles I never exercised were brought into play, and I stretched under wagons to attach the tie-downs.

The car deck was more my style, and I used ropes to lash the cars together bumper to bumper. This was the era of Cortinas, Morris Minors and Austins. Cars were smaller and I thought it a work of art how the old heads could fit so many cars in. But the *Aramoana*, whose car capacity was designed for the smaller cars of the pre-70s, would put our loading ability to the test as cars got bigger.

Our week on finished on Tuesday nights around eleven o'clock. The weekday finish was to ensure we had weekends free on our time off. The week went swiftly, and I was still squarely in apprenticeship mode. I had one more week of relieving. The other crew, known as the 'Mayfair Set', took over when we were off.

I felt as though I had never been away. I could phone home every day during my time on, and a week with the family was an added bonus. Nicole was eight months old and crawling into everything. A week flies by when you are with the family, and in no time I was changing into my working gear and starting my week on.

One of the ABs, Jeff Williams, said he was taking his leave next time off, and asked if I would relieve for him. I wasn't sure I would be allowed to carry my relieving duties until Flower Power assured me that I was entitled under the rules since my present relief was due to terminate. In fact I was to relieve until March when Barney told me he was moving to Auckland, meaning I would be the permanent AB. He said he was going on leave first, and asked me not to broadcast his plans. I have no idea what the secrecy was about, and although I honoured his request on board I could not contain myself at home. When it was time to relieve Barney he threw in his hand and Flower Power slapped me on the back. I did a jig around the cabin — I had scored a permanent job. Old mariners on the coast will understand. Today, those cream jobs can hardly find certified seamen to man them, but that is another story.

Bev was ecstatic — with a permanent position we could further our plans. At last I had the best of both worlds: the time-on time-off system enabled me to carry on my seafaring and spend equal time with my family. It was also a guaranteed job since the ferries were the established way of getting passengers and cars across the strait. It didn't worry me that there was very little seafaring in going backwards and forwards across Cook Strait.

One rule of the Seamen's Union was you did not take another job on your time off. You were taking a job from another worker, said the union, and our justification for the week off was negotiated in recognition of the long hours we worked. Each day on earned a day off. You would have to be very hungry for money if you ignored the rule. It was monitored carefully and woe betide any member caught working ashore. This was different from the Cooks & Stewards Union, who had no such

Dave leading the Cockney haka at Wellington Airport to welcome back fellow Londoners Club members.

rule. They were on the same system as the seamen, but many chose to drive taxis on their week off. Their wages were far lower than ours and obviously the work boosted their income, but it was a sore point in our messroom.

The perception of ferry crews at the outset of my tenure was poor. A series of disputes that had brought daily sailings to a halt had not endeared us to the public. Newspapers cried out that we were holding the public to ransom, and it did not help matters when the media seized on a case of light fingers in the till of the passenger restaurant. Greed had taken over among a few stewards, and railway management resolved to take action to put a stop to money going missing. They had money coloured with invisible dye, and by the end of the day they retrieved it from the pockets of the unsuspecting thieves.

In one dispute we had loaded the vessel ready to go when the stewards' delegates informed the seamen they had a dispute and that we should not let go the mooring ropes. They voted to 'stick the ship up'; in other words, to refuse to sail. How do you tell the passengers the vessel was not sailing, so jump in your cars and drive off?

Jack Marshall and his National Party were beaten decisively by Norman Kirk and the Labour Party in the 1972 election. Gentleman Jack's tough stance against the unions was touted around the country, but it fell on deaf ears as the result showed. Nor were members in love with Kirk and Labour, who had shown their true colours by turning a blind eye during our fight against deregistration.

1972 was also the year Pincher Martin resigned as president so he could return to sea. He had been a down-to-earth, no-nonsense leader, and was a breath of fresh air for me after years under incompetent NUS stewardship. Many seamen would stand with me and applaud his cloth-cap approach. He was the scourge of the shipowner, a feat that was never to be matched by his successor. A few years later Pincher retired to the Gold Coast. There was no million-dollar handshake, just a seaman's pension, something that he and his watch had negotiated years before.

We had seen the last of the era where the union boss could talk to members on the same level. It was different from what seemed to me the self-important nature of the suits that were elected to the top positions that year.

In the latter months of 1972 came the splendid news that we were to have a mate for Nicole, who was now eighteen months old and up to all kinds of mischief. Alfie Garnett, our moggy, must have wondered how he could find a place to sleep without the attention of our daughter. Our incomes had risen and there was a difference in our lifestyle. In the East End of London the idea of saving money had been for me an anathema. Families lived in hovels owned by the Council and only the posh owned houses. Money was for housekeeping and what little was left was put aside for a Saturday night at the local. I called it the 'East End rut', where the word 'bank' was in no one's vocabulary. Most died in their council houses just as happy as the posh in their mansions up west. In New Zealand, it seemed to me everyone wanted more in their lives. It was a sentiment that was growing on me. When there was talk aboard on who was buying or selling a house, I felt a bit inadequate to join the conversations.

Bev knew exactly what our goal was. Her household budget was strictly adhered to and I gave her the wages to dispense where she thought they were most needed. She had nursed sense into a mind that had been stuck in an East End rut.

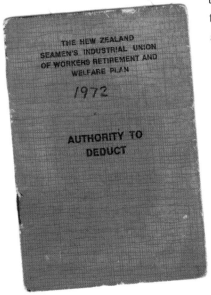

My cabin-mate Kevin was a funny guy. He was courting a lady whose glamour turned a few heads when she came aboard to see him. Each time she was due aboard he rushed around the cabin, making sure his *Playboy* magazines were out of sight. She had been brought up under the umbrella of the Salvation Army and he wanted to give a good impression.

Muldoon told the voters in 1975: "We will look after you in your old age." Seamen took no notice, preferring our own scheme.

I had never heard of an angelic seaman before and I thought his actions comical. He would always signal when she was making a visit aboard and I would repair to the messroom. On one occasion he cleared off to go and meet her at the stern door while I mischievously brought his magazines out of hiding and stacked them on our couch, leaving one opened at an R18 page before retreating to the messroom. I warned the lads there could be trouble.

We waited and waited, but all was quiet. I thought I'd better investigate why there was no reaction to my devilment. They were both sat down chinwagging when I stuck my head in the cabin.

"Oh, if you are looking for your magazines, I put them in the your locker, Dave," Kevin said, while his girlfriend gave me a disapproving glance.

It backfired on me, to the delight of the lads. After she had gone the cheeky git had the nerve to tell me that his girl said she couldn't understand why I wasted my money on such disgusting publications.

Kevin and I were cabin-mates for four years. During that time he married his lady and they both joined a naturist club. I ribbed him that he only joined the nudist fraternity so he could save himself some money on the glossies.

Then there was old Sandy, a Scot whose head had a shine on it like an all-round light. Not one strand of hair could be seen. A message from the bridge piped up over the Tannoy for a light to be doused. Hearing the message from the bridge, Mickey Marsters looked at Sandy and suggested he stick a beanie on his dome next time he stuck his head out the forward porthole at night. Blimey, didn't he blow up! I could have understood his ire if Mick had asked him for a dollar. He was real sensitive about that dome of his, and I couldn't help putting a hand over my mouth to contain myself each evening when the Tannoy crackled from the bridge.

Firedrill on the *Aramoana* with Ray Williams.

223

twenty-eight

A good pension scheme is possible!

— 'Pincher' Martin, National President

THE MOST ENDURING LEGACY WON by the union was its retirement and welfare scheme. When seamen retired they went on the beach with little or nothing to show for their years of toil on the briny. A government pension was all they could look forward to. Way back in 1966 the union decided to do something about this. We contributed greatly to the coffers of the shipowners, yet received no share of the profits and ended up destitute. Seamen had always been wary of insurance companies and dismissed the idea of having them run the scheme. Pincher and his executive convinced the shipowners to have the scheme administered by trustees representing the union and the employers. I was not in the union during their years of hard slog, but since I was a benefactor I made it my business to listen to those before me who had fought for the scheme.

I can refer to Pincher Martin's statement in which he writes in the October 1966 *Seamen's Journal*:

> We are confident that we can achieve a breakthrough. We believe [the scheme] will grow steadily, and its advantages become clear to all. Eventually it could become the financial backbone and the security of the Union and its members.

It took six years to make these words a reality — the shipowners agreed to the scheme in 1972. The initial contribution was to be a minimum of 20c per day or $1 per week. Apart from the contribution, an optional minimum lump sum of $100 could be deposited quarterly. Each member was given a small book with rules of the scheme. Members signed an authority to deduct the elected amount from their wages. I began at 40c a day.

In 1974 the scheme was improved significantly. It was agreed upon a two-for-one, in which 2% of our wages were paid and the employer would contribute 4%. After 15 years of contributions a member could make a percentage withdrawal, with further withdrawals every five years thereafter.

In the general election of 1975 Rob Muldoon convinced the electorate, "You don't need a super scheme. We'll look after you in your old age." Many took Rob at his word and cancelled their contribution from the pension schemes. The union took not a blind bit of notice of Rob's mob, and today we stand as an intelligent legacy. No seafarer on the New Zealand coast ends his career destitute today.

Our second daughter arrived in May 1973. I was allowed to attend the birth at St Helens Hospital in Newtown. I well remember the words of the delivery doctor when I was kitted up in a surgery gown and hat.

"Now, you keep to your end of the bed and look after your wife."

Fair enough, doc. It is a wonderful experience to witness the birth of your children, and to acknowledge the lady who nurtured them into the world. We decided that two children were all we could afford if we wanted to achieve our goal of saving for a house.

The missus couldn't half use those old knitting needles! They went like the clappers knitting the kids this and that, and even the odd cardigan and jersey for me. She was also a gun on the sewing machine, refusing to buy clothing if it could be knitted or sewn. There were many visits to Evans's material shop.

Having had such a job researching my family history and still with nothing to show of my infancy, I was determined our kids would have a picture book of their young lives. My mission with the camera could be very annoying to the young folk and the missus, but recording the events of yesteryear was well worth the effort. The photo albums are viewed frequently today, and we get much pleasure listening to our grandchildren screeching at the pictures of their mother and aunty when they were the same age.

In 1974 a 9000-ton fourth ferry, the *Aratika* (Maori for 'straight path') arrived. Built in France for almost $9 million, her initial design was as a cargo vessel. On her delivery voyage a fire broke out in the funnel and the results could be seen when she tied up in Wellington. She barely left the wharf, much to our amusement. Her idleness was due to the railways' contemplation as to whether they would convert her to a passenger-cargo vessel. The conversion took place in Hong Kong in 1975, and she arrived back in Wellington 1976.

We had forward notice that the *Aramoana* was due for an extensive refit in Singapore the following year. I had to give serious thought to my plans, since we would all have to pay off while she was overseas. Flower Power had it all worked out. The *Aratika* was due back from her alteration in Hong Kong at the end of the year, he said, and he reckoned it would need a full crew. He suggested we pay off the *Aramoana* and make ourselves available on the Corner.

The week-on week-off system had by this time passed its use-by date, and we were doing four days on, six off. The system required five half-crews, each with six ABs, two motormen and a QM. I saw more of my family than a guy doing eight-to-five.

Dale Weeks,
Lawrence 'Ike' Ikin and
Bill 'Pincher' Martin,
in Brisbane 1997.

During the middle of December, after nearly five years on the *Aramoana*, I followed Flower Power's move and paid off her. The *Aratika* was picking up so it seemed we had timed our move correctly: crew would be hard to come by as it was near the Christmas holidays. Three of us joined on December 26 as part of E crew — Kevin, Dean Smith, and myself. Lo and behold, she was all single-berth.

The five half-gangs were alphabetically named. We worked our first two days with D gang and our last two days with A gang. The members foisted the bosun's position on me, at which I was rated for the first two days, and storekeeper on my last two days. This came about because we were the swinging gang. A and C gangs had bosuns, while B and D took storekeeper positions. The *Aratika* was not going to be scrapped in the near future. She was to become my home away from home. I wanted a job with stability and other family-minded mariners were of the same mind.

The *Aramoana* probably has memories for those who crewed or spent time on her as a passenger. She went to Singapore for her refit in 1977 and returned sporting a flash funnel, and with her superstructure extensively altered, but by the start of the 1980s this old lady of the strait had become uneconomical, along with her sister ship *Aranui*. The government ordered a new vessel from a Danish shipyard, the *Arahura*, which arrived in New Zealand in 1983. The *Aramoana*, a £2 million purchase, had paid her dues over and over during her 22 years' service between Wellington and Picton. People who lived on the hills of Ngaio overlooking the harbour could set their watches on the arrivals and departures of these two sisters. That cannot be said today, unfortunately.

In 1984 the *Aramoana* was sold to Saudi Arabian interests, renamed *Najd II*, and began life on the Red Sea as a pilgrim ship carrying Moslems to Mecca, until 1992. There is a suggestion that she became involved in smuggling and other unsavoury activities. It was an strange fate for a vessel so loved in this part of the world. In 1994 she was towed to Alang beach on the west coast of India, the graveyard of so many fine vessels, and scrapped.

Robert Muldoon came to power in the 1975 landslide. His National Party defeated Labour, led by Bill Rowling. Muldoon's dancing Cossack advertisement on television was aimed at the trade union movement, to brainwash voters that New Zealand was being overrun by communists. Anyone who had a Northern English accent was fair game for Rob's mob. For the Seamen's Union, dreaming of a national shipping line under the Labour government, the 1975 National win was a disaster. Muldoon was against anyone who had socialist leanings. But he himself would have been labelled a socialist by the free market with his wage and price freeze policy.

The state housing home loan scheme was an incentive to young couples like us to buy their own home, its attraction the affordable 5% deposit required on the price of the house. The percentage down payment had been out of most working folks' reach, but now there was no reason why the dream of our own house should not become reality.

Bev and I decided that to advance our savings I could look after the children during my six days off while she did part-time work. It was a nice change for her to get back in the workforce. We lived on Lyons Crescent, at the top of Tio Tio Road, and being a non-driver the climb up Tio Tio Road with a pram was far more challenging than any exercise a keep-fit gym could foist on you.

When the kids were young I would go on school outings to which parents were

invited. I just about had shares in Wellington Zoo and could recite every word of *Bad Jelly the Witch*.

The *Aratika* had her maintenance day on Thursdays, which meant a day and night in port and sailing Friday morning. I got permission to show the kids in our daughter's class around the ship a few times and it was amusing to see our younger daughter Amanda cock-a-hoop, "That's my dad!" to one and all in her class. When school holidays arrived I would bring the girls on board for maintenance day and hand them over to one of the ABs, George

Dave with Nicole and Amanda, 1974.

Painting the *Aratika* in Auckland, 1991, and at right, lifeboat drill on the IR course.

Brabander, who would turn them to with a paintbrush each. They loved coming aboard, and it would bring tears to their eyes when they couldn't.

Flower Power decided to move his life on in 1978 with his marriage. He paid off the *Aratika* and bought a house in Auckland. He continued his career for a few years before moving to Perth and going out of circulation. On leaving, he left the position of E gang delegate vacant. I stood for the position, but some said I could not be both bosun and delegate. It was a load of old cobblers since there was nothing in the union rule book stating that. I was voted in as delegate, a position I was not to relinquish until my retirement in 2004.

The sea-going delegate's job in 1978 was still a privileged position, as the members put faith in you to advocate for them at shipboard level. The position carried responsibility. No one expected you to be angelic, or to set yourself aside from the members. But if you stand as advocate for those who put faith in you, then you also had to be accountable to those on the decks above, the master and mates. It was an honourable position, and one thing I never forgot was that it was the members who were the union, not the one or two elected to top positions.

twenty-nine

If capitalism is fair then unionism must be. If men have a right to capitalize their ideas and the resources of their country, then that implies the right of men to capitalize their labor.

— *Frank Lloyd Wright*

THE NEW ZEALAND SEAMEN'S UNION was much smaller and more involved than the English NUS, with its executive hidden away in Clapham. Pincher Martin treated all members the same and made you feel like part of the union. David Morgan was elected president after Pincher threw his hand in. Having been a seaman for many years, he had risen through the union ranks and was now an articulate leader with a penchant for colourful hats and, we were told, a professed communist of the Peking persuasion.

Second in command was union secretary Jimmy Woods. There was no doubt he was a skilled negotiator and was probably better in that position than anyone else at the time. He was part of the negotiating team that set up our National Shipping Corporation with the government in the 1970s. He was well thought of in Europe, and held a position on the Fair Play Committee, an overseer of international maritime issues with headquarters in Geneva. He was also the union voice on the Arbitration Committee, the forerunner of today's Labour Court. Gerry Evans, a sea-going councillor at the time, ousted him. Jimmy had been in office since 1972 and swapped suit and briefcase for a boiler suit and sea bag.

Just as he was voted on to the executive some sixteen years before, the same democratic process voted Jimmy off. When the 1990 union elections were under way I openly campaigned for Gerry Evans to retain his treasurer-secretary position. Gerry easily held his place on the executive. At the next stopwork meeting in the Railway Hall, Jimmy boiled over; he saw me as his enemy. We ended up on Aotea Quay in a wrestling match while my good mate Johnny Collins acted as traffic cop so we didn't get run over. Boy, what a taste of power does to some folk.

Being a delegate gave me a lot of insight into the working of the union. The executive after 1972 had curbed our militancy, cutting out the wildcat stoppages on the ferries that did us more harm than good. It was impressed on us, quite rightly, that the public were not our enemies and we needed them on our side.

The 1972 Labour government's foray into banning nuclear-armed warships in New Zealand ports was a proud moment for us in the union. When National came into power in 1975, Rob Muldoon decided he was not going to have any of this 'nuclear nonsense' and offered the US Navy a safe berth for their warships.

We were told in May 1983 that the USS *Truxtun* would be spending some R&R in Wellington. The Americans had a 'neither confirm or deny' policy as to whether their warships were nuclear-armed. Of course, that was no answer at all. The stopwork meeting had voted for a full stoppage of all ferries while the *Truxtun* was anchored in our harbour. The *Truxtun* was in Wellington for six days and the ferries were on strike for the duration. Muldoon did his nut, sending his Labour Minister Gordon to try and get us to sail. The public were outraged and we suffered much abuse from them. Members who were on their four days' work forfeited eight days' pay. I cannot speak for others, but for me the statement we made to Muldoon was well worth the loss. But it was the missus I had to convince of that.

I've sailed with many Taffies and seeing as I can sing the Welsh national anthem in Gaelic, I was quite at home with Gerry Evans our national secretary. He was full of knowledge, easy to get along with, and always available.

He got in touch with me to say there was a group of unemployed people in the South Island who wanted to come to Wellington so they could march on Parliament to advertise their situation. Since I was the delegate he advised me that they could not afford the fare to Wellington, and asked if we could get them across. The seamen arranged a collective mission that resulted in them being brought aboard in the early morning hours. We were eaten out of galley and messroom, and gave up our bunks so they could get a bit of shut-eye on the way over to Wellington. On arrival they lined up on the rail deck, and when the stern door opened they marched off the vessel with banners, trumpets and drums, all the way to the gas house. You should have seen the mate's face. "Where did they come from?"

The six o'clock news showed that our mission was a success, but managerial eyes had not overlooked this and the master called the delegates up to the bridge. Did we know anything about a group of non-paying passengers that had come aboard that morning? Our noses stayed flat and we pleaded ignorance of how these people came aboard. Nothing more was said, but the master was right when he pointed out that he needed to know how many souls he had aboard in case of an emergency.

After our debacle with the Yanks in 1994, the rank-and-file decided that they needed new blood on the executive. Gerry was ousted in the 1994 union election and a younger and very active Welshman, Mike Williams, was elected. I felt sorry for Gerry since he was one of us, and I believed he had done enough to retain his position. We lost a good executive member when he decided not to return to sea, but he has since become a noted author.

Dave Graham had been the Cooks & Stewards Union representative for years until they amalgamated with the seamen in 1989. He was the catering representative on the executive, and being a seaman I did not have as much time with him as I had with Gerry. He was affectionately called 'Twiggy' on account of an anatomy quite the opposite to the 1960s icon with the same name. His demise came through the reduction of the executive after 1994. I got to know Dave better after he retired and a cuppa and yarn round his house never went amiss.

The media seemed to think that our militancy came from one man, Dave Morgan. The Seafarers' Union had always been militant, long before he became president, and it was the rank-and-file at stopwork meetings who decided on issues of the union. My dealings with Dave Morgan, to be honest, were generally negative. I had seen similar puffing of the chest from the Clapham brigade, who looked down their noses at the members who gave them their livelihood. We were both short-fused guys, but he seemed to believe he had the monopoly of opinion. As far as I was concerned each member's view was valid, but the stroppy way I put my point of view did nothing to endear him to me.

Under his 32-year stewardship the union did become more aware of how we conducted ourselves with the public when disputes arose. We put our heart and soul into stopping the Springbok tour of 1981. There took place the demise of the National Shipping Line, given to us by one Labour government and taken away by another in 1990. We fought the iniquitous Transport Law Reform Bill that opened our coast up to foreign shipping. We fought the sale of New Zealand Railways, including the rail ferries, to American interests in 1994, and gave our antagonists a black eye after the Employment Court threw out two attempts to lock us out.

In the mid-'90s I began to notice a feeling that the president was losing touch with the members. He took over the International Transport Federation portfolio, which meant he was abroad a good part of the time. I could never get an answer when I asked him what benefits the Seafarers' Union were getting from his jet-setting.

After Labour's win in the 1999 election he accepted a government-appointed position on the Wairarapa Health Board. I openly argued that we paid him a lucrative wage to look after our affairs, and he should not be accepting other jobs, especially from the government. To me it was quite simple. Union bosses should be union bosses. A lot of the members had no problem with this, and that was their prerogative. When the government appointed him as New Zealand director of the Pacific Forum Shipping Line, it was an affront that I could not bear in silence. To me his appointment conflicted with his job as president.

New Zealand is a shareholder in the line along with eleven South Pacific nations. Seven directors are appointed to the board. Some of these vessels trade under Flags of Convenience (FOC). The Seafarers' Union have long campaigned against the FOCs as being cheap-labour rustbuckets. So what was our elected president doing on the Board when we were supposedly fighting the buggers? My letters to the committee of management asking for his resignation were ignored, and officials were clearly not challenging a conflict of interest.

The Seafarers' Union is now the Maritime Union of New Zealand (MUNZ). Amalgamation with the Waterside Union was never thought out properly as far as I could see, and at the time of my retirement they had glaring problems. The wharfies have a localised body in each port. That system suits them since they live and work and vote on issues in their own ports. The seafarers had a national body. Their jobs took them all over New Zealand and a ship's crew is made up from members all over New Zealand. Under MUNZ rules you can only vote on issues in your own port. How could a member from Nelson vote on a Wellington issue? In my opinion seafarers should return to a national body within a federation with the wharfies.

Another issue that seemed unfair was the payment of union fees. Wharfies paid a maximum of $10 a fortnight in fees, or in some ports, no fees at all. Our fees were 2.25% of our wages, which worked out to $50 a fortnight. Members quite rightly asked why we should be paying more than the wharfies. We were all in the same union now and should shoulder the cost equally. One of the president's reasons for amalgamation was to save costs in the larger union. I wonder how my mates will deal with a Waterside Union that will always have a majority vote on the executive?

I had hoped MUNZ secretary Mike Williams could sort out all these problems. Mike was a hard-working official in the cloth-cap mould of Pincher Martin, and would rather be running round ships listening to members than sitting in an office. He won respect from members and showed his counterparts in Waterside House that it's not all about jetsetting or sitting on your arse in an office. Recently he gave up his position for health reasons, after eleven years as the Wellington seafarers' advocate. He hopes to return to sea in the near future.

In my opinion Dave Morgan had been in the boardroom too long, but clearly not all members agreed, since we had a chance every two years to vote him out yet he stayed on. There had been another union official who took his own ousting badly, and one who was so affronted by a member wanting to stand against him in an election that scurrilous allegations were made against the opposing member, and that was the end of his challenge.

What is it with these guys? Were the trappings of office too good to give up?

Old members may remember a rule stating elected officials should do a trip to keep their hand in. Perhaps the members should ask for the rule to be reinstated, so officials would have to come down occasionally from their heights and find affinity within the rank-and-file from whence they came.

G.M.V. ARAMOANA

CAPTAIN: A. MUNRO

CHRISTMAS DINNER

The Captain Extends To One And All
The Compliments of The Season

Hors D'Oeuvres
Devils On Horse Back

Soups
Creme of Oyster
Consume Crecy

Fish
Deep Fried Nelson Scallops — Bearnaise Sauce
Tropical Marinated Groper

Entree
Beef Olives — Reforme Sauce

Joints
Roast Sirlion of Beef — Faifort Sauce
Roast Leg Canterbury Lamb — Menthe Sauce
Baked Virginian Ham — Oporto Sauce

Poultry
Roast Tom Turkey — Cranberry Sauce
Straw Potatoes

Vegetables
Fresh Garden Peas
Cauliflower Au Cratin
Boiled New Potatoes
Baked Kumaras
Duchess Potatoes

Cold Collation
Jellied Sheep Tongues
N.Z. Dressed Salad
Dressing Mayonaise

Sweets
Ye Old English Christmas Pudding — Brandy Sauce
Wine Trifle Chantilly — Fresh Cream
Mince Pies
Tropical Fruit Salad
Neopolitan Ice Cream

Desserts

Cherries	Oranges	Plums	Peaches	Bananas
Muscatles	Dates Assorted	Nuts		Ginger
Biscuits	Cheese			

When we had to give up Christmas with our families we were well looked after — the crew's Christmas dinner on the *Aramoana*, 1973.

thirty

If hard work were such a wonderful thing, surely the rich would have kept it for themselves.

— *Lane Kirkland*

"IT'S ABOUT TIME YOU GOT in touch with your foster parents." These words were regularly urged upon me by my wife. My last contact with them had been in 1956. Yet how was I to word a letter to people I had neglected for so long?

"Tell them everything," was Bev's advice, so with a guilt-laden hand I penned a letter of apology, recounting my exploits over the past two decades and the happy circumstances I had found with my family half a globe away. A reply came soon after, which not only cast my apologies aside, but told us they were going to visit.

Bev's insistence came to fruition. It was a delightful moment and we caught up on the many years I had been absent. I was never to disregard my foster parents again.

In 1978 we bought our first car, a second-hand Hillman Hunter. Jumping on a Newman's bus to visit rellies up the line had been a bore for us all. I was born to steer ships, not cars. Bev took her driving licence and we set off on a tour around the North Island visiting family and friends. It was a big ask for a first-time driver, but what a blessing it was to manage your own stops and starts.

The kids were five and seven and loved the freedom the car gave us. I became second mate and navigator while Bev kept her eyes on the road and the kids argued in the back. Panic set in when the car took a sickie on arrival in Tauranga. We thought it the end of our trip when we sputtered into the nearest garage. Within half an hour we were all smiles again when the mechanic found the fault, and Bev not being a mechanic and I detecting no seamanship jargon, we were both none the wiser. We sped off like a couple of kids with a new toy. In Auckland we made for Ponsonby, barging in on my fellow shipmate Johnny Collins and his wife Chrissie.

John was an ex-home boat man who came out to New Zealand before me. He had been on the coast far longer and had done all his sailings from Auckland. The ferries were rarely called on the Auckland Corner since they were Wellington jobs. Only when they were bereft of crew in Wellington was the job offered in another port. On one of these occasions that the *Aratika* was short of an AB, John decided to sample a ferryboat. He was adamant he would stay only six months at the most. At that time any seamen hired by the railways from another port would have their airfares paid and would be remunerated for travel time, which usually included a meal. He took the leading light position in A gang while I was storekeeper in E gang. His six-month stay ended fifteen years later and during that time we became good friends.

In 1983 Bev and I planned a trip to the US and UK. On hearing this, John piped up, "Go and visit my mum and dad in Richmond if you got time. They will make you welcome." No problem, I said.

While in London, I set off to Richmond with the two girls, arriving at John's parents' address. When I knocked on the front door, I heard the words "Keep yer bleedin ear on, I'm coming!" Opening the door he said "No, I don't want anything," and began to shut the door before I could splutter "Oy, I'm Johnny's mate from New Zealand!"

The door swung open with a profusion of apologies. He must have thought I was trying to sell the kids. When I related his dad's reaction the messroom broke out

Aratika E gang in the 1980s: Mick McLaughlin, Dean Smith, Tony Cave, Dave Share, Andy McPhail, with George Patuaka in front.

into mad banter. We renewed our acquaintance with his parents when they came to New Zealand for a visit, and we had a good laugh at the Richmond episode.

John and Chrissie have now made their home in Australia. After a year of travelling around that vast country in a campervan they settled on the border of Queensland and New South Wales. He took advantage of the shortage of professional seamen on the Australian coast and is currently on a bulk carrier running out of Gladstone around the Cape York Peninsula to Weipa.

In 1979 the Seamen's Union was 100 years old, and the centenary was celebrated at the Wellington Town Hall. If there were speeches made, as there probably were, I confess to not having heard a word as celebrating seemed more appropriate.

The news of the Mount Erebus air crash came to light in November 1979. Assistant purser on that flight was my friend and shipmate from the *Suevic*, Dave Bennett. He had told the kids on his visit to us a few days before that he would bring them back a penguin. It was a sad occasion for us.

We took full advantage of the government's home loan scheme and by 1980 we were house hunting. An affordable house for us would be in the $30–$40,000 price range, with the 5% deposit we had saved. Both novices on real estate, we searched the eastern suburbs of Wellington. Every three-bedroom house we were shown was nicely presented, and naively I would question why we didn't buy each one.

Bev had a keener eye and settled on a large family home. I was horrified. The wallpaper was hanging off the walls and the place was a mess.

Letting go on the *Aramoana*, 1972: 'Flower Power', Jeff Williams (foreground), Harry Kane, Dave Share.

"I can't wallpaper," I wailed.

"You'll have to learn."

I was to find that location was important when buying a house. Owning the roof over your head is a great buzz, and we set about restoring our purchase to respectability. I soon got the hang of wallpapering, improving my technique on each room.

In 1981 the South African rugby team began their tour of New Zealand, an event that split Kiwis into pro-tour and no-tour camps. In the middle were the police. Prime Minister Muldoon decided his government would not interfere with the tour, and gave the Rugby Union a free hand, to the delight of his Minister of Police Ben Couch, a former All Black. The seamen, being politically motivated, voted at our stopwork meetings to go boots and all into the fray to stop the tour. As long as the Boers were in town the ferries would not leave the wharf. We were part of thousands of protesters against the tour who marched on Athletic Park where a test was to be played.

It was time to show the Yarpies what a decent nation felt about apartheid. As a youngster I had been humiliated by it first-hand when being heaved out of establishments in the republic.

One of the most annoying statements the government and the pro-tour faction found comfort in was the parroted notion that politics should not interfere with sport, which ignored that in South Africa politics governed every facet of life including sports. The law prohibited black and white sportsmen from competing with and against each other, even an All Black team with Maori in it. New Zealand governments kowtowed to this policy, humiliating their indigenous people before a foreign nation.

In 1983 the girls were at last old enough to appreciate a trip overseas. We had found that our holiday treks to Taupo were not giving us enough bang for our buck — you could get a return trip to Australia for the price of a stay in Taupo. I wanted the girls to see the world, as I had. Because I was English, the girls were entitled to British passports and the wife travelled under patriality. I drew up a six-week itinerary that would take us to Los Angeles and Disneyland, then on to London to visit the foster parents, and a return via Honolulu, Melbourne and Wellington.

The children were thrilled, but Bev was not impressed with London. I made a trip to my old stamping ground, the Royal Docks, which was a sad sight for me. What had been for 400 years the bustling centre of London's commerce was now silent. A few of the old pubs still operated but none of the seamen or dockers patronised them. The Kent Arms had long gone, as had the Three Crowns. The

Flying Angel in Custom House had a notice advertising student accommodation. The Connaught Arms just inside the docks had been saved from the demolition squad and now stands as a memorial to these past times. The aeroplane taking off from the newly built city airport, speeding down the runway between the King George and Albert Docks seemed to me a despairing end to a corner of London that had more affinity with the sea.

The thirteen years I had lived in New Zealand had somewhat mellowed my loyalty to the home country. My family were born-and-bred Kiwis, and New Zealand gave me a lifestyle I could not have had in England. My future was in New Zealand, and I filled in my application form for citizenship soon after arriving back from Blighty. In 1983 I proudly received a certificate from Internal Affairs proclaiming me a citizen of New Zealand. A dual citizenship agreement meant I could retain my British passport and also have a New Zealand passport.

In November that year the latest models of ferries arrived in Wellington. New Zealand Railways' *Arahura* ('Pathway to dawn') was built in Denmark to replace the aging *Aramoana* and *Aranui*. She was an all-purpose vessel with a carriage capacity of four lines of rail, or sixty rail wagons, and a mix of twenty trucks and a

The *Aramoana* entering Tory Channel.
Dominion

hundred private cars. Unlike her sisters who had side-loaders for vehicles, loading and discharging would be accessible through the stern only.

She was a flash job with a swept-back funnel and graceful lines. The Cook Strait is a tempestuous bit of blue, which can blow up to gale-force winds and five metre swells in an hour. A North Sea storm would be a breeze compared to this strip. The *Arahura* was designed to meet the worst that the strait could throw up, cutting the 51-mile crossing from berth to berth by twenty minutes.

Her arrival spelt the end for the ladies of the strait: like the *Aramoana,* which had given 22 years service, her younger sister *Aranui* was sold to Saudi Arabian interests in 1984 for their Mecca run.

The 1984 general election was under way. 'Save New Zealand Rail' was the slogan from Labour politician Richard Prebble. Seamen around the country, and especially those of us on the ferries, thought Prebble was a knight in shining armour. After all, the ferries were part of New Zealand Rail and here was a politician who was going to support them. That year Muldoon was thrown out of power and David Lange took over the treasury benches.

Seamen had taken Prebble's 'Save Rail' quote literally. How could any of us envisage that his idea meant reducing the 25,000 employed railway workers to just 3000? Labour with its free market policies had hoodwinked the working class. There would be repercussions for us on the ferries.

Seamen on the New Zealand coast have always taken an interest in politics, so it was no secret that during the rest of the '80s we watched with growing distrust the antics of the Labour government who had become Tories in all but name.

In 1985 we were saddened at the death of Bill Trueman, one of the originals of the Pincher Martin tenure. Bill was a man of integrity and believed that union members in the ships and the branches should have the last word, a belief that was sadly lacking when I retired.

Labour won a second term in government in 1987. The selling of state assets to the private sector was a contentious issue for the public, and certainly for me. Generations of taxpayers had contributed to these assets, and now they were being sold off cheaply in fire sales. Prebble's ambiguous slogan 'Save Rail' came a step closer when the railways became a state-owned enterprise (SOE). It meant that the railways were being readied for privatisation.

The New Zealand Railway Corporation had always run at a loss, but this is par for the course for any public transport system. Jewels in the railways' crown were the ferries, which made large profits with no competition. But this had no merit with railway management and we heard rumours in the lower decks that seafarers were not to be saved from the cull that was putting thousands of railway employees out of work. Those rumours became more exact as management announced a big change in crew working conditions, with airfare payments to cease for crew members residing in other parts of the country, and a reduction in crew manning. It was a trumpet call for all of us who were employed on the ferries that the attack had begun.

Union members had stopwork meeting cards to be stamped each month.

thirty-one

IN LATE SEPTEMBER 1989 events on the Cook Strait ferries took a downwards turn. A crew member on the freight ferry *Arahanga* was advised there was a letter for him in the ship's bureau — it gave him two weeks' notice. Two more letters in the same vein were sent to seamen on the *Arahura*. Railway management knew what the reaction would be by sending termination notices directly to the individual, bypassing the union. Their tactic had the desired effect. Strike action was called, leaving the vessels tied up in their berths.

When NZ Rail called for a revamp of the ferries the previous year, most of the issues were settled during negotiations, including conceding the out-of-port transport. There was nothing in our contract covering manning levels, and the employers' legal minds exploited this by setting manning levels as they saw fit. The railways won an injunction from the Labour Court to get the vessels sailing again. We ignored the injunction, and boy, didn't the presiding beak get into a lather! He said it was the worst flouting of the law he had ever witnessed. The assets and property of the union were sequestered until an apology was forwarded to the court. A judgement was also made against the union for contempt of court, costing us $15,000 in fines.

The ferries were termed an essential service by the government. We recognised that strike action had a detrimental effect on our standing with the travelling public — no one takes strike action unless they are provoked. The media spewed their usual nonsense of us holding the public to ransom. No one versed the public as to why the strike had occurred, so the seamen were automatically villains. There must have been over one hundred seamen who went down to the ferry terminal to explain to stranded passengers what the strike was about, and that we had told railway management we were willing to sail taking trucks, passengers and their cars without pay. We could not have asked for a better reply when the passengers turned their ire onto Ivan Gough who trundled out the slogan, 'No rail, no sail!' It was a major blunder by their spokesperson. The public saw the railway management as the villains now. It ended the dispute and the antagonists got around the table.

It was a lesson the management would not learn for the future. We were coming into the 'greedy 90s' where profit was the only benchmark. With all their lawyers and their business minds, none of the management had an affinity with the sea and the seamen who ran their operation. They were suits who centred around the office and who could not be bothered to take a trip to talk to those on the front line and learn how their business was run.

The best way to run an operation is to go to the shop floor and get information from the people in the front line. It's plain logic, but I never did get the chance to be CEO of a corporation.

Our elder daughter Nicole had by now left school. She was in a hurry to get away from the schoolroom and into the big wide world. She had asked us if she could leave school and go to the polytechnic and we agreed, if she passed her school certificate. With this achieved she had no problem finding herself a job. Our younger daughter Amanda, more academically-minded, was headed for university. We learned that kids could be rebellious in their teenage years. Sometimes you stood back and asked yourself, were they a mirror of you at that age? In all honesty, I would have to say yes. Maturity takes time and the future would bring out each of the girls' attributes.

Many things were happening at the end of the 1980s and the start of the '90s. The demise of the New Zealand Shipping Corporation caused widespread anger among seamen. Foreign shipowners had become the darlings of the Labour government and were given *carte blanche* to take New Zealand products to the markets of the world.

Under the government's Industrial Relations Act, unions were required to have a membership of no less than 1000. The Seamen's Union, with only 800 members, had to amalgamate with the Cooks & Stewards Union. This took place at the end of 1989, and on registration we became the New Zealand Seafarers' Union (NZSU). Amalgamation boosted membership to 1250.

The Shipping Industry Task Force chaired by Stewart Milne wanted reform in the way of regular and reliable services and above all, competitive rates. The Australian seafarers had agreed to what was termed the integrated ratings system (IR), which was similar to the general purpose system (GP) brought in by British shipowners. At present, an AB was certified to work on deck and undertake watch-keeping duties such as steering and lookouts. Engineroom ratings were certified to work in the engineroom only. The IR system sought to skill seamen to work on deck and in the engineroom. The union had a member on the task force and it was agreed we would fall in line with the Australians.

Many members were unimpressed and saw it as a de-manning exercise, and decided to take redundancy from the industry. I'm quite sure the shipowners had this goal in mind since they were never lost for the chance. We were told by the union that if we wanted to stay competitive we would have to agree to the IR system. All shipping companies on the coast began sending their seamen to the ten-week course at the Manukau Polytechnic or Launceston in Tasmania. The only company who did not want to participate was New Zealand Railways. Maybe it was because the government would have to explain to taxpayers that the course cost $13,000 per trainee?

"Why don't you go for your chief integrated rating?" Gerry Evans asked me. I was bosun on my gang and he advised me it would be wise to take the course coming up at the end of 1990. CIR would eventually take over the rating of bosun. It seemed just another fancy title to me, but I put my name down for it even though it would have no merit until the railways came to the party.

By 1990 I had made fifteen years of contributions to the Seamen's Super and Welfare Fund. After fifteen years members were entitled to take a draw every five years thereafter. The draw was set at a percentage rate of the employers' and members' contribution.

Bev had eliminated our second mortgage after taking a redundancy from her job as personal secretary in a Wellington clothing firm, so it was timely that my super draw the following year should enable us to become freehold. We had enough to mod-con the kitchen and to make a trip to Hawaii on our own. During our stay we managed to fit in a seven-day cruise on the ss *Constitution*. Many celebrities travelled aboard her, including Alfred Hitchcock, John Wayne, and countless more. Her most famous passenger had been Grace Kelly on her wedding to Prince Rainier of Monaco, when the crossing had concluded with the *Constitution* making a special stop at Monte Carlo to allow Grace and her wedding retinue to disembark. It was a busman's holiday aboard for me. I enjoyed being the passenger for a change, watching the crew on deck sand the taffrails and do the general chores needed to keep the ship looking smart. She was a lovely old ship with a counter stern and two funnels.

Before departing Honolulu an emergency boat drill was held for passengers. Now a greenhorn passenger, I remembered the times I had participated in emergency drills as a crew member and enjoyed the novelty.

The skipper was at pains to tell the passengers on leaving Honolulu that the *Constitution* was under the American flag. With 750 passengers we set sail for a week's cruise around Maui, Kauai and Hawaii. Drinks, shopping and trips on each island were on tick. No money passed hands until you were handed a 'shock sheet' the night before arrival in Honolulu and were asked to square the bill. Talk about wiping the smile off your dial.

We had lots of fun, a good reason for going on a sea cruise. The Yanks have a knack of making you feel good and the entertainment staff were very professional. The food was excellent and they made sure you never went hungry. I could now boast that I had experienced the other side of going to sea.

I arrived home from Hawaii to a letter saying that the CIR course was to start at the end of October, for one month at Manukau Polytechnic. On this course I began to have a strong feeling there were forces in charge that had very different ideas of how ships should be run and for the seamen who crewed them.

Stepping back a few years to the mid-1980s, the right wing of the Labour Party opened up the money market and let in the wide boys who saw advantage in the selling off of public assets. The Minister of Finance, Roger Douglas, was trumpeting big business, and telling us the government should not be in the business of owning assets. One such asset was the New Zealand Railways and their maritime arm, the ferries.

George McIntyre and me as part of the union theatre group set up to protest the Transport Law Reform Bill.

Under Rogernomics the private sector had a field day. We were bombarded by the terms 'free market' and 'globalisation'. So zealous were the political mantras that the world became flat and seamless, with no barriers to interfere with global trade. They assumed the whole world was their market and each country would bow at the free market altar. After the smoke had cleared we were left with a National Party on the treasury bench and entrepreneurs with deep pockets and shallow minds.

It was impossible to stick your head in the sand and ignore the political implications of what was to come. I followed the scene closely, as did most seamen. Many workers in many industries were under threat from Rogernomics. Shareholders and profits were more important to the captains of industry who were running the country. Right-wing ideologues had formed themselves into a lobby group called the Business Roundtable, and had the ear of the government. Under National the trend of asset selling was sure to continue. New Zealand Railways, now an SOE, was on top of their list.

The CIR course taught me nothing about running a crowd. The only thing that differed was that under the old system the leading hand was picked by the crowd, and that gave you instant respect. Under the IR system the company could choose its CIR. I gained two certificates on job training and on supervision and storekeeping from Manukau's Faculty of Business. It sounded impressive: probably in an office or shore-based facility it might have had some merit. But were they trying to run a ship the same as an office or factory ashore? It was pure boredom and bullshit in my view, but they were paying for it, and if that was what they wanted then who was I to complain.

Also on the course was my mate Johnny Collins, who knew a couple of seamen living near the Bay of Islands. One of them owned a fishing boat and the other was into home brewing. We had weekends free and travelled north for a spot of fishing.

Our fishing host, who went under the name of 'The Beast', had a place on the shore of Mill Bay in Mangonui. He warned us that high tide was at 3 in the morning and he would give us a shout. Unfortunately we visited another old seadog just down the road that evening, who introduced us to a potent batch of home brew he had cooked up. Catching up on old times in company with this most agreeable refreshment saw our plans go into orbit.

We were pondering next morning why we were still in bed while our host was out in his boat.

"Did you hear him call you?"

"I don't even remember leaving Jimmy's place."

In 1991 the integrated rating system suddenly found favour with the Railway Board. Integrated ratings had reduced the number of seamen needed to run a vessel, and this was almost certainly the catalyst for their rapid change of mind. In March 1991 railway management packed the first group off to Manukau Polytechnic for the IR course. Accommodation and victualling was at the company's expense, as was the course itself. The mouth-watering thought of reduced labour expenses clouded their vision, and they locked themselves into a very expensive exercise that was approved as a benchmark for deck ratings. The IR system would prove in the future to be a headache for the railways both in terms of cost and sustainability.

It was hard going back to the classroom for the many of us who would never see 50 again. ABs had to learn what went on in the ship's engineroom and the motormen had to do likewise on deck. We had to nudge some of the old-timers because their snoring drowned out the lecturer.

During the lifeboat drill on Auckland harbour the exercise was interrupted by a boatload of police and customs officers who wanted to know who we were and what we were doing. Once they were satisfied we were not boat people from Vietnam we were sent on our way.

A five-day course was taken at Takapuna fire station. Donning breathing apparatus sets while running up a hundred steps of a fire tower carrying a heavy hose was no laughing matter. We soon found out how fit we were! Should fire break out at sea we were the firemen, and that was the reason the training was so important to us.

At the end of the course we each received an integrated rating certificate. Failure would have left the railways short of seamen to man their vessels.

The four days on, six days off cycle had gone and we were working one week on, one week off, followed by one week on, two weeks off. Within two years it would change again, when the deck and engineroom crew of twenty-three on the *Aratika* was cut to just sixteen seamen who were now proficient to work on deck and down below.

The next two years were harrowing. In 1992 the union and the shipowners negotiated the termination of the Engagement and Stabilisation scheme, which led to the end of the union-run Corner. I was appalled by this. You could only be loyal to one faction, union or company.

The National government decided the New Zealand coast should be opened up to foreign shipowners by giving away our cabotage, which protected the coastal trade within the national territory. We went round the nation to gather support from the public against foreign intrusion on our coastal trade. We could not compete with cheap labour ships and certainly not with subsidised shipping companies. We were made to stand alone and pay our taxes while foreign ships and their crews contributed nothing to the New Zealand economy. The act was passed, much to the shame of politicians who probably thought cabotage was some form of vegetable. New Zealand shipowners were never going to be able to compete against foreign shipowners, who could bring their freight rates down by not having to pay New Zealand tax.

Why would a nation like New Zealand want to rely on foreign hulls to ship the nation's goods to market? Would we rely on foreign ships in times of conflict? They had no loyalty to New Zealand. We could only conclude that the farmer-led government had such loathing for seamen that they wanted to wipe the local shipping industry off the market. I was to sit in the gallery of the gas house and listen to the Minister of Transport ask, "What is the loss of a thousand jobs?" He was talking about the Seafarers' Union.

By 1993 the coast was awash with foreign companies lifting our domestic cargoes and putting seamen on the dole. Once the foreign shipowners had control of our domestic cargoes they began to set their own freight rates. Today New Zealand has lost most of its ships, and we are no better off.

And the union had yet another headache. The industrial relations arm of New Zealand Rail was looking for ways of to save money on the ferries, to make the business more attractive to a prospective buyer. An American company had made a successful bid to buy New Zealand Rail in July 1993. They were to learn in early March that Kiwi seamen on the ferries did not take kindly to their overbearing nature.

Our daughter Nicole had reached 21 and received her nest egg, a few dollars pay we had put away for each of the girls since their births. She immediately set off on her OE to the UK and Europe. We had encouraged the kids to travel. A year later she called up mum and dad to ask for her fare home — that's why we have children. But as long as she had a good experience and enjoyed herself that was good enough for us.

Amanda was at university and working part-time at a restaurant to earn pocket money. Parents whose children were at university in the early '90s did not have the huge fees that they have today. Bev had the foresight to plan financially for Amanda's education. It is surely out of the reach of many working families today to support the cost of university fees.

Putting kids in debt before they could use their skills seemed unreasonable. In a free market economy, the kids will take their knowledge to other lands where wages are higher. It was all tied in with an agenda that could only see profit as the way to riches.

We had no idea what the free market meant for us. We would just have to wait to find out what the employers' intention was for us on the ferries.

Left: the Seamen's theatre group —
Dave, Bob Tuffnell, Mike Williams, Zoe McIntyre, Cavan McDowell, Scruff Windsor.
Below: on the road in the South Island with the MV *Kiwi*, protesting the Transport Law Reform Bill.

thirty-two

Never before had so many people been paid so much money
for achieving so little.

— Crew member's observation of Tranz Rail management 1993-2004

T HE YEAR 1994 WAS IMPORTANT for many seamen employed on the ferries.
Some of us ended the year feeling the effects of siege warfare. Others preferred
fighting a southerly gale rather than the employer and threw their hands in.

The year began with an incident on 1 March with the grounding of the *Aratika*
on Ruaomoko Point, near the entrance to Queen Charlotte Sound. I handed the
wheel over to the quartermaster ten minutes before entering the Tory Channel.
The QM would take the helm for the next hour until we docked in Picton. Around
9.30pm the shudders of the engines became noticeable, and then with what seemed
to me almost a dainty slide, the bow buried itself on the beach with the stern fully
afloat. Our training had us running to our emergency lifeboat stations in case we
were needed for lowering boats. Some of the passengers were alarmed, but there
wasn't a panic. Others could be seen with cellphones clamped to their ears, shouting
out the misfortunes of their stranded vessel. After divers found no damage to the
hull we waited for the high tide in three hours and refloated her.

An inquiry took place over three weeks. In its report the Maritime Safety
Authority concluded there was an inexperienced helmsman without certification
at the wheel when the grounding occurred. But under the rules of the IR system,
every seaman had to be certificated. Before the IR system came in we had dedicated
quartermasters whose sole portfolio was to be in charge of the helm while in
pilotage waters.

New Zealand Rail reported that the grounding was the first in its 32 years of ferry
operations. The only other mishap recorded was the freight ferry *Arahanga* putting
a 30-foot scrape along her portside reportedly at Ruaomoko Point in 1977.

The sale of New Zealand Rail to Wisconsin Central went ahead in 1993. This
asset that generations of New Zealanders had contributed to was sold by the
National government for a piffling $328 million.

What interest does commerce and investment have with a sailor whose only
concern should be the seas and getting home to his wife and family? When I sailed

Protest at Hutt Valley Polytech when scab crews were trained to replace union jobs on the ferries. My mate Ron Blair at the front right.

from London, the big shipping lines on Leadenhall Street didn't give a toss about unions, realising they were there to stay. Now it seemed that our new American owners wanted to destroy organised labour.

Both parties were in talks for a few months after the sale. Our contract was due to expire in April 1994. Wisconsin Central had tabled a 'wish list' of $15 million they intended to make in savings: the cutting by half of the 487 staff on the ferries, slashing our time off and drastic changes in work practices, including running a 24-hour service. The corporate catchphrase was wheeled out to the public, that "the changes are necessary for it to be competitive to meet customer needs!"

In early March 1994 the crews were advised by the union that they had rejected the 'wish list' and that we were in a fight against the Americans who would have the Roundtable and almost certainly the National government on their side. Much to the disgust of the seamen, Richard Prebble was made New Zealand Rail advocate. Ten years earlier he had campaigned to save rail, and he had failed to save it. The only ally we could expect was the trade union movement.

New Zealand Rail set out to win the hearts and minds of the public by holding a press conference to outline the future for the Cook Strait ferries and why drastic changes were necessary. They bleated that negotiations had failed and they were taking the only action available by advertising our jobs nationally and internationally. Advertising for scabs was the first dumb move by New Zealand Rail. They told the public they were still prepared to negotiate in good faith. Everyone asked why, if they were still negotiating, were they advertising for scab crews? Nobody was happy with Prebble's appointment and the sentiment we often came into contact with was that he had sold his soul to a foreign boss and betrayed the working class.

Railways management had also united the three maritime unions — the Officers Guild and Marine Engineers Institute as well as the seamen — against them. It was an accord that was never achieved before, and a tactical error by our employer. You'd think that if you are going to take on the seamen, you would isolate the upper deck and keep them out of the dispute. Instead they lumped them in with the ratings, offering any captain who signed a contract a company car and a $52,000 cash inducement. A few masters took the offer, but most declined.

An *Evening Post* editorial supported the action taken by New Zealand Rail, saying that featherbedding was rife on the ferries and work conditions were luxurious compared to other jobs. The editorial went on to say that "working on the ferries is seen as the last bastion of the discredited old union order." I had 22 years' service on the ferries by that time, and cannot recall an editor of a daily newspaper working in our 'luxurious' rail deck putting on extra lashings on the cargo in a howling southerly on the strait. He must have been talking about another ferry operation that employs newspaper editors.

As required under the Employment Contracts Act, the union had given fourteen days' notice of strike action. Our antagonists were hoping we would go on strike, as the May school holidays were looming, and this would win over the public to their cause. The strike notice was a threat, but at our meetings the members vowed to keep the ferries sailing. The ferry carried on all through the four months of the dispute. It fooled the employer. Passengers were pleased that their travel was not disrupted and they were generally supportive of us.

The sympathy the employer was hoping for evaporated and they found another weapon in their war chest. The wages of officers and ratings were printed in the national newspapers. This caused envy for some who said we should come down to their wage rates instead of getting off their own chuffs and fight to improve their own.

Negotiations stalled and picket lines formed opposite the railway station. The

On the wheel — *Aratika's* bridge.

dispute had grown and everyone had an opinion for and against the maritime unions. In April a new threat came from the employer in the form of a lockout. Each crew member received a pamphlet from the employer, bluntly telling us the conditions and wages we would be on if their lockout was successful.

On May 6 they effected their threat by sending lockout notices to all crew members. The master on the *Aratika* called the delegates up to his cabin. When we arrived he pointed us to a box containing envelopes addressed to each seaman, and ordered us to take the box of lockout notices down below and pass them out. Refusing, I told the skipper he had no business doing the employer's bidding.

Lockout notices have legal requirements, one of them being the employer must serve them personally to each individual. When they received the notices, the combined unions challenged them as invalid. A few of us had to attend at court to give our version of how and when we received the notices. Employment Court Chief Judge Tom Goddard agreed with the unions and said the notices reflected a high level of non-compliance. They were defective, because the company did not specify where the lockout would take place. There were also other serious defects in their notices, and we rejoiced in their defeat.

Don Franks

Having failed in its first bid to lock us out, the American controllers sought further vengeance by sending out a second notice in late May. In the meantime New Zealand Rail had sent their contingency scab crew home. The reason lay with the Maritime Safety Authority, who said it had not approved any of the contingency crew.

By the time management ventured aboard with their second round of notices we were all seasoned campaigners on the *Aratika*. We had a meeting aboard and decided that there was no way were we going to accept the lockout notices without a show of force. A message from the bridge called for the delegates. Once again, the skipper confronted myself and the co-delegate. We took no notice of him and told the suits that if they wanted to serve us with notices then it had to be done on neutral ground on the afterdeck. Placards surrounded the deck and we braced to humiliate our adversaries. They wouldn't be able to sneak away after handing us their notices. After enduring a couple of hours of crew member wrath they hightailed it down the gangway with the help of a fully pressured hose.

The lockout notices were challenged once again, this time by the Marine Engineers Institute, and their lawyers made preparations for another visit to the Employment Court. Sources close to the lawyers suggested they had found even more discrepancies than the learned judge had picked up in the initial notices. The lawyers must have had the only lockout notices left as 200 seamen assembled on a cold day in front of the capital's railway station and fired up a 40-gallon drum, throwing their notices into the fire right in front of the employers' office. I don't think the American owners had seen anything quite like the Kiwi maritime unions.

We were due to be locked out on 27 June if the unions refused to accept the new employment contract. Before that happened a deal was struck by the unions and New Zealand Rail, and was taken to union members for ratification. After four months in the trenches we were battle-weary, but still in good heart to resume action if it was warranted. On 24 June the seafarers piled into the Flamingo where our monthly stopwork meetings were held. I don't think I had ever seen a meeting so well attended since the early 1970s. Outside the meeting the national press and TV units waited for the outcome.

New Zealand Rail's original wish list sought to reduce crew numbers on the ferries from 487 to 241 and make 246 people redundant. A final figure of 156 redundancies spread over the three unions were agreed to, which saved 90 jobs. Under the deal we agreed to work equal time on and off. This increased our roster from 135 days on the vessel to 185 days. Our wages remained intact with a 1% increase in 1995. Union members remained in the collective contract, a concession on the company's part. Any redundancies under the Seafarers' Union rules were made by the method of 'last on, first off', if there were not enough volunteers who

Greta Point, 2001 — with Bev at a reunion with Bryon Heywood and his mother Jean, my foster mother from Camberley.

Aratika, 1994 — the employer hands out lockout notices to crew.

wanted redundancy. There was also a one-off compensation payment in return for the increase in days to be worked. Their target of $15 million savings fell $3 million short.

Each clause of the contract was debated to make sure the words could not corrupt the intended meaning. Unfortunately we missed a couple of ambiguous clauses, which the employer was fully to milk. Ratification of the contract was achieved by majority vote. The dispute was officially over. Cameras clicked and smiles on faces showed relief as we poured out of the meeting. It had been a long battle against a difficult employer who tried to shut out organised labour.

The employer achieved $12 million in cost cutting. The union kept their structure and saved 90 jobs. The events leading up to 1994 were a backlash against the ideologies of those free market tossers in government and big business. Cheapness and corner-cutting was to be the way to riches. The once reliable service that had been the Cook Strait ferries would never be the same again. The losers would be the public and professional seamen.

thirty-three

A TWO-WEEK TRIP TO BALI was a welcome respite for Bev and me. The national Bintang beer agreed with me but not with my tummy. I had a touch of 'Bali belly' for four days while the missus fought the king-sized cockroaches that scurried out of smelly sewer drains. The Balinese are gentle people, but the same could not be said of the Javanese who carried trays of watches on the streets and who had a more aggressive nature. They didn't seem to understand what "no thank you" meant, but certainly understood "fuck off."

Seamen are used to corruption from the locals in foreign lands. A Denpasar airport official demanded US$100 on check-in, which marred our departure. He pointed to the weight calculator, which showed us our baggage was overweight. I could see his foot on the machine and politely asked him to take his foot off. He said we would not get boarding passes unless we acceded to his demands. We were not going to find any solace from the locals. We did not have US$100 so he asked what currency we did have. We could have argued all day and missed the flight, so we paid him $100 Australian, but Indonesia lost two tourists who will never visit their country again.

Aratika B crew
integrated
ratings, 1996.

On a happier note our younger daughter Amanda graduated with an arts degree from Victoria University. She opted to take her gap year before finding work, setting out on her OE to England, Greece, and eventually Crete.

Life on the ferries changed drastically after the 1994 dispute. With their restructuring in place, the American owners went all out to win the hearts and minds of their crews. On the *Aratika* it needed no guessing that most of my fellow seamen had a dislike for the management. Their constant meddling in the day-to-day running of the vessel showed they had no trust in the experienced crew.

My position as ship's delegate required me to be in the forefront of disputes on board, and there were many. One thing that gets up the nose of a professional mariner is an office wallah coming aboard and dictating things that he knows nothing about. I was admonished by one of the managerial types when I questioned what experience he had of going to sea. They had a notion that the ship was the same as a factory ashore and that they could run the 'factory' from their office. According to the office, the skipper was the manager. To us he would always be the skipper.

Unlike the *Arahura* and *Arahanga* which were designated for the 24-hour run, the *Aratika* stayed on her normal day roster, sailing at 10am. The *Aratika* was thought to be too old and slow for the rigours of a 24-hour operation. The time for loading in port was cut from the usual one hour down to 40 minutes. We doubted whether we could be in and out of port in that time, but I think we surprised ourselves, and as time went on a 40-minute stay in port was achieved with the efficiency of the railway shunters who brought on the freight wagons. The catering side were sorely tried by cleaning up the mess of 900 passengers, then greeting the next few hundred, all in 40 minutes.

I have many friends in the catering department, some of whom I had sailed with on the *Dominion Monarch* and other vessels long ago. Unless you were a cook, for which certification was required, you needed no certification as a steward. That did not mean they were any less valuable. No matter what your rating, on any given vessel the ship's complement has a job to do. Every member of the crew plays a part in the operation of the vessel, especially in emergencies. The catering fraternity who are trained in emergency duties are relied

Brisbane, 1998: Robin Morresey, Dave, and Johnny Collins.

upon to look after passengers. Calming them and making sure their lifejackets are on properly are big tasks.

A southerly gale in Cook Strait can be a nightmare for those who have no sea legs. I never envied the guys who dealt with the passengers and were relied on to calm seasick punters while keeping them smiling.

A second steward nicknamed 'the Sheriff' decided to write a novel about his eighteen years on the ferries. According to him seamen could do no wrong, but he decided to denigrate his catering workmates, and I could understand their anger. His observations were not very kind, and to lump them all together was unfair. Was it a coincidence his book *Strikebound* arrived on the market when the ferry crews were in dispute in 1994? Opinion on board was that he had dollar signs in his eyes and was exploiting the antipathy some of the public might have towards seafarers. It was a disparaging commentary on an operation that required skill and teamwork to fulfil the hectic work schedule.

Management believed the *Aratika* was too slow for the round-the-clock service provided by two other ferries, so we were surprised in early 1995 when the captain advised that an extra sailing would be added to our day. This was management at its most arrogant. A new sailing schedule was set up, having no consultation with the interested parties. The *Aratika* made two round trips between Wellington and Picton between 10am and 1.20am the next morning. The new operation meant we were required to begin loading at 4.30am and sail at 5.30.

I called a shipboard meeting, pointing out that the only two vessels named in the collective contract to operate the 24-hour schedule were the *Arahura* and *Arahanga*. Seamen on the *Arahura* were fully remunerated for working round-the-clock, and the *Arahanga* was paid pro rata, or whenever she was required to

NEW ZEALAND OVERSEAS FLEET

NZSU 1985

15

FIFTEEN DOLLARS

NEW ZEALAND SHIPS CARRY LESS THAN 4% OF NEW ZEALAND EXPORTS

THIS NOTE IS AS PHONY AS THE GOVT'S WHITE PAPER ON SHIPPING

Authorised by Seamen's Union Vivian Street, Wellington

15 DOLLARS REPRESENTS THE SHARE EVERY NEW ZEALANDER HAS IN S.C.N.Z.

15

RESERVE CARGO FOR N.Z. MANNED SHIPS

do extra sailings. The *Aratika* was on the day-schedule of two round trips. There was a huge difference in wages between the *Arahura* and *Aratika*. We were told by the industrial relations manager that we weren't doing 24-hour sailings because the vessel tied up at 1.30am. He was alluding to the couple of hours we could have in our bunks before turning to again at 4.30am. He should not have been surprised to see us still moored at 8am taking our sleep entitlement. The façade carried on for over a week before they realised they didn't have a leg to stand on, and to our surprise they put us on the same rate of pay as the *Arahura*. Rail management thought they could ignore the union and make policy to suit themselves. We were far too smart to let that happen.

Adjusting to round-the-clock sailing was hard on the body clock. There is no other sea-going operation that arrives at and departs port six times a day. To accommodate the 24-hour operation we broke into three watches of four seamen and a quartermaster. Because two watches were needed for cargo operations, overlapping twelve-hour watches were worked. There was no 'iron mike' or automatic steering on the *Aratika*. QMs took the day helm and during the night sailings seamen on watch would take the helm outside harbour limits.

My bosun's position became redundant when we changed over to equal time, week-on week-off. I teamed up with Robin Morresey, who was bosun on another gang, and we stayed as watch-mates until the *Aratika* was sold four years later.

As a union we fought tooth and nail for many issues dear to seamen, and came up with innovative tactics such as these 'monetary' protests and the national tours I was proud to participate in, defending our industry and explaining issues to the public.

In September 1995 I visited the UK just before our elder daughter's wedding in November. It was time I paid a visit to my foster parents, and I allowed a few days to do some hands-on research on my family tree. The wife is not an avid traveller for long-haul flights and elected to stay home. I chose Japan Airlines as they were the only airline that allowed smoking in flight.

I was still waiting for my air ticket a week out from my intended journey — Japan Airlines had forgotten to book me. They made up for it with a business class return ticket at economy class price on Singapore Airlines. I snapped that up but had to try and forget about a fag until we got to Singapore. I fell asleep with no bother. When I woke up my American flight partner looked shell-shocked. "I've never heard anything like that before," he said, staring at me.

I thought I must have farted by the look on his face. An English guy was laughing his head off, and he explained that my snoring was something to behold. They asked what industry I was in. I said I was in the chainsaw business, which cracked up the Brit and left a blank face on the Yank.

I finally admitted I worked on the Cook Strait ferries.

"You must be the captain," said the Yank.

"I'm a seaman," I corrected him, and explained just what a seaman was doing travelling business class.

The smoking facility in Singapore Airport is enough to make you give up. I'm sure the room had no vents as the atmosphere was choking. My American acquaintance shook hands on reaching Heathrow, explaining his first chore was to get a good sleep. I told him I felt quite refreshed.

London was its bustling self. New Zealand seemed a spacious paradise as my taxi wound its way to the nearest station where I would catch the train to Camberley. Nothing much seemed to have changed since my previous visit twelve years ago. The Chapel Pines, my foster parents' home, was looking a picture with the azaleas in bloom. My mum was very busy so I had to work my stay around her time off. My dad, well into his seventies by now, enjoyed doing half-marathons with the local athletic club. I felt guilty for my own lack of fitness.

I made a beeline for my old stamping ground, the once proud Royal Docks, but there could be nothing more disconcerting for a mariner than to see a plane taking off from the wharf he once tied his vessel to. I felt a pang of nostalgia as the plane soared into the air from a runway built between the King George and Albert Docks. I retraced the steps that seamen took when the docks were at their height. The skyline had changed with the massive Canary Wharf Tower dominating the surrounding area. To my surprise the pubs we visited in Custom House some 35 years before were still there, though a pint of beer had gone from two and threepence to over a pound. I left my old stamping ground with the thought that progress cannot erase the happy memories of this special part of London that I and thousands of seamen experienced.

My research was not very successful, even though I made daily treks by tube, alighting at Goodge Street where the Family Records Office can be found.

No sailor could visit London without paying a visit to the National Maritime Museum in the beautiful surroundings of Greenwich Park, or the magnificent *Cutty Sark* moored on the Thames nearby. I also took a trip to Portsmouth Historic Dockyard. Here Britain's most famous ships are on display including the hulk of the *Mary Rose* and Nelson's HMS *Victory*, the flagship of the present day Second Sea Lord. As I disembarked, I looked up at the *Victory's* yardarm. In Nelson's navy, advocating for crew members could be seen as mutiny — if there had been a delegate's position in Nelson's navy it could have been a neck-stretching experience.

There are days that all parents treasure. The thrill of seeing your children taking the step of marriage was so pleasing for us. Perhaps my wife and I are old-fashioned because we believe in marriage. The words 'lifestyle partner' certainly never entered our marriage vows.

Our elder daughter Nicole looked beautiful in her wedding gown as she arrived at the Poneke rugby clubrooms. Her husband to be, Shane, was a premier rugby player who chose the club as their venue for the ceremony and reception. Parents will always dote on their offspring, but sooner or later their offspring will have families of their own. Our house would soon echo with the shrieks of three boisterous grandchildren on their visits to us, running a thrilled nanna and pop off their geriatric feet.

Nicole, Dave, Bev and Amanda.

thirty-four

Life on the ferries could be monotonous, running between Wellington and Picton day in and day out for 24 hours. There was the occasional respite when the vessel was due for a check-up and dry-dock in Auckland. As there were no cooking or living facilities on dry-dock, accommodation and food allowances were paid. When the government owned the ferries there was no trouble in paying this allowance since it was taxpayers' money, but when the ferries were privately owned it was different. The union and the delegates of the vessel would haggle for days with management over how many of the crew would take her to dry-dock. They wanted to save costs by cutting crew to the bare minimum. We would argue that a full crowd was needed to do the many chores, especially in renewing the running gear of lifeboats and other lifesaving appliances that could not be tackled during operations on the Cook Strait. When you have accountants and lawyers who know nothing about the importance of safety, their cutting of corners can be very frustrating.

We took pride in our competence to deal with any shipboard emergency such as fire and the handling of lifeboats. We needed to be satisfied that all appliances were in tip-top condition, since we were the ones who would be using them, and felt compromised by the bean counters who only gave lip-service to safety. It seemed to us onboard that management had lost all foresight, and that the narrow-mindedness of profits was their only focus.

We questioned why management was hiring outside labour to paint their vessel when they were already paying a crew on board to do it. I don't think the shareholders would have thought there was any sense in that.

In early May 1997 we found ourselves haggling with management once again on the proposed manning of a crew to take the *Aratika* across the Tasman for dry-docking in Keppel Cairncross dockyard. Though the signing of the ship's articles in New Zealand had ceased in 1994, it had continued in the Australian shipping industry. On the morning we were due to sail, a fellow IR called Lawrence Ikin, or 'Ike' for short, pointed out to the skipper that we would not be able to dock in Brisbane if articles were not signed. Management thought they knew everything until the MSA advised them that under Australian law every crew member was required to sign articles. Had Ike's warning not been heeded there would have been a huge delay in their tight dry-dock schedule.

There was a second reason for crossing the Tasman: we would load fifteen used locomotives while on dry-dock for use on the New Zealand rail system. No ship I had been on had tried to load cargo while on dry-dock. A platform complete with rail tracks had been built on the stern. A crane lifted the locomotive, setting it down on the track and then manoeuvring through the stern and onto the vessel where we would lash it down for the trip to Wellington. It was a cleverly thought out operation and I'm sure everyone was impressed. The crew were accommodated at a hotel in Breakfast Creek for a few days before onboard facilities were restored.

A nightwatchman was called for and I elected to do the first three days. The company's ship superintendent instructed the captain that all crew members should sleep aboard including the nightwatchman. As nightwatchman I argued that I should keep accommodation ashore as the noise on the dry-dock during the day would interfere with my sleep. I thought I was not going to get any help from the skipper, as he followed his superior's edicts to the letter. At least he offered to pay shore accommodation out of his own pocket. "No way," I replied: I wanted him to tell the superintendent that the nightwatchman should be accommodated ashore, so he could get his rightful sleep. Safety was the issue here, and I asked him to pass that on to the superintendent, or I would go ashore to see the Australian shore-side union delegate.

While I was talking with the captain a shore-side gang had begun their day's work of chipping the ship's side. I located the shore-side delegate and told him I was nightwatchman and his chipping hammers on the hull were ruining my sleep. He could not believe I was refused accommodation ashore and in no time he pulled his work gang off the ship. Panic ensued and the superintendent accused me of disrupting the workforce. Accommodation was once more available for the nightwatchman ashore and the shore gang resumed their work.

The anger of the Tranz Rail superintendent resulted from a battle of wits I'd had with him some days before. Tranz Rail's labour on the dry-dock were from the Metal Workers Union. The Maritime Union of Australia (MUA) covers the wharfs of Australia. If the management of Tranz Rail thought they could get away with ignoring that fact, they were on a loser.

I got a call from an NZSU official, asking us to back up the MUA.

Catering crew on the Arahura: Harry Pike, Angus McCauley, Dan Patterson, Roger Collins, Al Kelland, Alby McKinley.

We had a full meeting aboard with MUA delegates and agreed not to lash any locomotives that were being handled by Metal Union members. I was singled out as a trouble-maker and they tried very hard to get me dismissed. The MUA members took charge of the loading of locomotives. The superintendent who was humiliated in the dispute was miffed, I think, and sought recrimination when the nightwatchman issue came up. Within two years he was gone and I was still there. It is the right of a company to contract whoever they want, but knowingly playing off these two factions against each other was a divisive tactic.

One of the few decisions that merited applause was the decision to break down the barrier between the upper and lower decks. I suspect cost-saving was in their minds, but they sold it by saying officers and ratings should mix together to make a happy crew. There were detractors on both decks and it was hilarious to hear some of the consequences that would come of this decision. On our side it was more of a throwback to the old 'them and us'. A minority on the upper decks dreamed back to yesteryear, when table silverware and white-jacketed stewards stood in attendance.

At the end of May we left Brisbane with fifteen locomotives, some of them weighing 90 tons, a new communal salon, and a smaller messroom for those on watch and still in working clothes. The onboard management, including representatives from each department, set out the rules of dress and use of the salon. Reservations were soon dispelled. The seamen seemed to favour having their meals in the working messroom while the stewards and officers used the salon.

I was amazed that the locomotives were taken off in Wellington without any concerns from Ministry of Agriculture inspectors, even after we told them what we had seen under the locomotives. Under MAF rules I had to ditch the begonia I had nurtured in the cabin, as did other crew members before docking in Wellington. On the trip across the Tasman we had noticed ants, spiders and clumps of earth

On the *Arahura* 1999: Tony Ford, Ron Whittle, and my watchmate for five years, Stu McCarthy.

and grass clinging underneath most of the locomotives. We were told the rail deck had been fumigated. It would take days to secure an escape-proof rail deck on a ferry, and if fumigation did take place it was a joke. We probably have a colony of Aussie spiders and ants somewhere up the line between the ferry terminal and the railways' Hutt workshop.

The *Aratika* had been my home away from home for over 20 years, and we all knew she was soon to be replaced by a vessel that our superiors claimed would be the most technologically advanced in the world. The modern larger rail wagons and cars made it increasingly difficult to stow the technology of the 1990s into a vessel built for cargo capacities of the 1970s.

A new vessel was being commissioned and would be ready early in 1999. She would be much larger and faster than any Cook Strait ferry before her. To let crew members look at her, the plans of this vessel came aboard with one of the managers. His finger tapped a small square on the bridge plan.

"This is where the chief engineer will stand. It will be a lock up engineroom," he gloated.

She was a computerised vessel and required very little manual labour. They could computerise her course from berth to berth without a helmsman. It was plain to us that seamen were about to be replaced by robots.

Two shipyards vied for the contract, won by Hijo Barreras in Vigo. I remember us betting that it would be the Spanish yard which got the contract because they were the cheapest option. Management denied their choice was made on cost, but we were not fooled. The port of Vigo was well known to me since it had been a common port of call on the South American run. Though regarded as one of Spain's main ports, it served the fishing industry and built small fishing boats. Spain is not one of Europe's most highly regarded ship builders. There are many sorry stories about vessels that have come off Spanish stocks, beginning with the Armada. I for one was not surprised when the $106 million vessel finally sailed into the Atlantic in the latter part of 1998, and abruptly lost power.

The *Aratere*, or 'Quick path', sailed into Wellington to be met with pomp and ceremony, as the first new ferry for sixteen years. A lot of hype revolved around this seeming space-age vessel. There was no doubt she could carry enough freight and trucks to clear the yard. Innovations such as canvas tie-downs instead of the heavy bottle screws were made for securing the rail wagons. Mooring would be a thing of the past with 'iron sailors' being installed both in the Wellington and Picton berths. These are suction pads that keep the vessel alongside in place of mooring ropes and require no manual labour, which was of course the employer's idea.

The arrival of *Aratere* signalled the last days of the *Aratika*, and meant disruption for all of us who worked on the ferries. Week-on week-off had been the working roster. An agreement had been struck with the NZSU and Tranz Rail to have a walk-on walk-off system, where crew would work a shift on board and then go home, returning the next day to do their shift. An IR system for the *Aratere* was ditched in favour of ABs, which meant a drop in wages, so everyone wanted to avoid the *Aratere*. In March 1999 those with the longest sea service on the *Aratika* transferred to the *Arahura,* which would remain under the IR concept and also keep the week-on week-off roster. The rest would join the new vessel or the current fast ferry, known to us as the 'vomit comet'.

The *Aratika* was called the 'quiet achiever'. Rarely out of service, she plodded the Cook Strait for 25 reliable years. Sadly she had outlived the rail systems and was heading for the scrapyard. At the last minute the Filipino shipping line MBRS decided to buy her for their Manila-Panay island run. The old maid of the Cook Strait had been given another lease of life, which was reflected in the new name they gave her, the *Virgin Mary.*

By this time the *Aratere* had begun her problem-plagued life. We were told there would be no engineers or electricians in the engineroom. Within her first week of operations the 'closed engineroom' became the full-up engineroom with many human beings down there. At first her mechanical and electronic breakdowns were termed 'teething' problems by the owners. One exasperated newspaper wrote an editorial on the boat, titled 'Ship to Nowhere', complaining that "while the country basks in the best summer weather imaginable, the *Aratere* slumbers in dock." Six years later the show goes on and the *Aratere* continues to make headlines with her amazing high-tech stunts, such as shutting down all power or deciding to steer a course of her own. As far as I know, there are no plans yet to name a new genus of the lemon tree after her.

My 23 years on the *Aratika* were dominated by events for my family and me. The decision I made to join the vessel in 1976 and opt for stability instead of chopping and changing ships was important. Many seamen would steer clear of the ferries because of the repetitive operation between Wellington and Picton. It suited men like me who wanted to be near the family but also on the water. The crowd on the *Aratika* had been together for years and there was great upheaval for us when she was sold.

The *Arahura* was a sensible and well thought out vessel, unlike its new high-tech sister ship. Built in Aalborg shipyard in Denmark in 1983, this sleek 13,600-ton vessel was sixteen years old when I joined. Rail, trucks and cars were loaded from the stern, which was much easier than the complicated side-loader operations we had on the *Aratika.* There was also an 'iron mike' or automatic steering system, which was used on the strait crossing but manually steered in the Marlborough Sounds and harbour waters. Old shipmates Larry Stills and Dean Smith, who I had sailed with on the *Aratika* since 1976, joined the *Arahura* also.

I began running my first soccer sweep as far back as 1973 on the *Aramoana*. It was called 'The Highest Score'. I would take the first and second English soccer divisions and sell them for $10 per team, making a pool of $400. It was a lasting interest of mine over three vessels and three decades. World Cup Soccer sweeps were great four-yearly events and the Super 12 and NRL sweeps were also pocket-liners for the lucky. The trouble was I could never win any of them.

You don't forget the shipmates you sailed with for years. Mike Marsters amused us with his exploits on the P&O Orient liner *Chusan* during the 1950s as a bell-boy in his smart uniform and an equally beguiling titfer. My Scouse mate Ike lived in Murchison and panned for gold during his leisure time. He would have us in fits of laughter over tales of the famous Takoradi 'thunder box' on his trips out of Liverpool on the Palm Line. The Palm Line serviced the West African coast, visiting such exotic ports as Takoradi in Ghana and Port Harcourt, Nigeria. The 'thunder box' was a portable shit-house hung over the stern of the vessel while on the West African coast. There was a pact that he would never talk about this device during mealtimes. Larry Stills and I joined the ferries together in 1976 as young bloods, and we were ancient mariners by the time I dropped the hook 28 years later.

Then there was my watch mate Stu McCarthy, who I would greet with "Hello Trubshaw!" It was part of my upstairs-downstairs jargon that I liked to lord over

The crew of the *Aratika* wave farewell on her last day's work on Cook Strait. She was sold to Filipino interests and renamed the *Virgin Mary*.

him. He became used to the name Trubshaw, and our ribbing took away the monotony of the ferry schedule. We would be laughing our heads off, taking the rise, and getting dirty looks from the rest of the crowd. Such was the humorous nature of this guy, the week on flew by.

Mick Marsters shows his appreciation of the cooking.

His father Brian was also an AB on the *Aratika* in the 1970s and '80s, retiring before the IR system was introduced. He was an old salt with a craggy face who could keep us entranced with tales of events that took place long before our time. Every time we joined the vessel for our weekly roster, his hand would go to his back pocket and he would produce his wallet, saying "How much?", referring to the weekly sweeps of course.

In May 1999 a tragedy left one crew member dead and two injured during a fortnightly rescue boat drill which involved the vessel slowing down fifteen minutes before arrival in Picton. The rescue boat would be lowered with its four-man crew and make its own way to Picton to be retrieved during the turn-around. There had been concerns that the quick-release gear was flawed.

Nothing seemed out of the ordinary as the chief officer, the young trainee officer cadet, an engineer and an IR stepped into the boat to get it ready for its trip to Picton. Every seaman knows that after the boat has been swung out and lowered to the water, the quick-release gear enables it to get away quickly. But the hook let go prematurely while the boat was being lowered, and a safety chain failed. The boat dropped ten metres and the chief officer and engineer sustained severe back injuries. The nineteen-year-old cadet and the IR were left clinging to the lifeline in midair. The trainee could not hang on through shock and fell into the boat, sustaining fatal injuries. The IR slid down the lifeline at the urging of my watch mate Stu, and took the boat to Picton so the injured could be attended to faster. Stu told me later he went up to the boat deck to observe whether the problems we had heard about were true. We were all very sad that a drill could go so wrong, causing the death of a shipmate. Counselling was offered to those closest to the tragedy. Stu was traumatised by what he had seen, and took some time to get over it.

Recriminations came thick and fast, but they were not going to bring our shipmate back. The rescue boat itself was commandeered by the Maritime Safety Authority and was never to touch the *Arahura* again. This was probably the best decision for all.

Each year on 21 May the *Arahura* slows its engines at the position where the tragedy occurred, a short service is held and a wreath dropped in the water in remembrance of a young life so unfairly taken.

The 20th century closed with Tranz Rail giving their crews the night off to celebrate the year 2000. I'm not sure if it was a genuine gesture by management or their concern that the Global Positioning Satellite on the vessels would go haywire. I went back to my family to spend a happy few hours before returning to the vessel in the morning with a head on me like Birkenhead.

Shipmates:
Left: Fo'c'slehead mooring crew, *Aratika* – Larry Stills, Barry Millington, yours truly and Robin Morresey.
Below left: Joe McCormick and his wife, Dean Smith. and Dave in front.
Below: Johnny Collins, John O'Neill and Gary Parsloe.

thirty-five

There comes a time in every man's life, and I've had plenty of them.

— *Casey Stengel*

GOING TO SEA HAD BECOME a frustrating occupation. Seamen have never suffered fools easily, especially when management are arrogant enough to deem themselves more capable than the crew they employ.

"We need to prune the bush so that it grows fuller and bears richer fruit." So said Michael Beard, our newly-appointed managing director, in an address to the shareholders. "The rail ferries are the jewel in the crown." Hadn't we heard that one before? Mr Beard parroted how his brand of restructuring would enhance business. Thus in the latter months of 2000 the crew of the *Arahura* were summoned to the ship's theatre to see how our world would once again be turned upside down, Beard style.

There was to be a shake-up. 3400 employees were to lose their jobs or be contracted to another employer, leaving a core of just 600 in the company. 'Lean and mean' was a phrase the corporate sector liked to trot out, but it meant getting rid of valuable expertise, and one man doing the job of ten at a lower rate of pay.

The share price of Tranz Rail had come from a high of $9.00 per share in the mid-'90s and had fluttered to $3.60 per share by the time Michael Beard took office in 2000. Three years of his stewardship later, the bush was dying and the fruit had withered to 44 cents per share. The remains of the company were left for another predator to restructure while our green-fingered CEO was rewarded with a golden handshake of over $3 million.

In 1999 an accountant was appointed general manager of the Interisland Line. He was an amiable fellow, but I felt he knew very little about ships. He of course had to follow his boss above even though the result was to bring the company to its knees. He once expressed to me that the average age of the crews aboard the ferries was 49 years. There was an obvious answer to this, because the national training programme was thrown out when we became company employees in the '90s. The union warned that if the company did not start training youngsters on deck there would be a shortage in future. The remedy put forward by the boss was not surprising, coming from an accountancy background. We were told by our union official that he proposed taking a couple of certified seamen off the vessel and replacing them with two trainees. The union refused this stupid solution and no training took place.

In 2000 I reached the young age of 60. Our daughter Amanda and her fiancé Darrell put on a surprise celebration at his city tavern. They had delved through all my sea-going memorabilia and family life and produced a video, a gesture bringing a tear or two from this ancient mariner. The missus and I celebrated in style, but could not foot it with the young folk.

I had long thought about retiring at a decent age so I could carry on a quality of life in retirement in a fit state of mind and body. I had seen many old seamen in the pubs of London on the bones of their arses and vowed I would never be like that. I had also seen other men who were married to the sea and died on the job, and yet others who had retired and died a few months later. The union had made sure 30 years ago that seamen would have a financial nest-egg on retirement through the compulsory super scheme. To this end Bev and I had purchased an apartment in the suburb of Mount Cook as an investment and to supplement our retirement income. Bev was always against the idea of mortgaging ourselves to another property, and since we had a history of savings in the bank she deemed this the safest way to prosperity.

Our foray into real estate was a lesson in leaving things that you know nothing about alone. Our tenants for the first year were the kind that every landlord dreams

Brisbane dry dock, 1997: with Dale Weeks (left) and Mike Bullock.

of, until they decided to move on because the apartment was plagued by leaks whenever it rained. We had not bargained for our battle against the body corp to fix the leak, nor our next set of tenants from hell. We decided that we would keep to what we knew best and after a couple of years as landlords we put the property on the market, selling it at a small profit.

During the next three years I was to witness the devastation caused by restructuring, outsourcing and all the other colourful words the corporates use to justify meddling in a viable shipping company. Maintenance had been neglected and the company was in a parlous state and in danger of defaulting their lease arrangement for the *Aratere*. These were trying times for seamen on the ferries, some of us who had been with them since the early 1970s.

We had witnessed the demise of the Australian Seamen's Union on their amalgamation with the Australian watersiders, but this seemed not to overly concern our union president David Morgan. He would truck no dissent and refused to have meetings to answer the members' questions.

"Wait until the amalgamation is registered and then we can sort it all out," he said. We went down the president's path and became the Maritime Union New Zealand (MUNZ). Around the time when I handed in my resignation from the union, the Wellington secretary told me that the watersiders enjoyed a majority of fourteen to three. The amalgamation was supposed to create a level playing field, where each union shared the cost. The seafarer members were stuck with their exorbitant union dues of $50 each payday, while the wharfies paid $5 or $10 or sometimes nothing in fees. Who could blame them?

Though I and many other old members were dead against the amalgamation, the democratic process took place with a secret ballot. Less than half the union decided to vote on this important issue, and a majority in favour of amalgamation won the day. The members had decided who they wanted to spend their future with, and I foresaw a backlash when those who hadn't voted woke up. I was not to be surprised. The marriage was far from happy, with many issues surfacing that I and other members identified before the amalgamation.

As ship's delegate on the *Arahura*, I was very mindful of a perception among the members that the president had worn a collar and tie for too long. Members grumbled that he was more attuned to the boardrooms and had lost touch with us lowly seadogs. After 30 years in that position it can also bring a deaf ear to the opinions that others might offer. Time will tell whether the amalgamation was for the better, or will spell the end for the union.

If we were not satisfied with the leadership we had a chance to change it every two years, but that was not an attractive proposition. Most enjoyed their life at sea and those who sought the executive positions would lose their contingency liabilities with the company. A redundancy remuneration had been paid out to the permanent shore-based positions in the union by the shipping companies when the Corner was discarded. In effect it meant that an individual had to take his chance against being ousted after two years, and being left on the beach without any redundancy payout.

Life would be very boring if we all agreed with each other. A ship's messroom is full of diverse opinions voicing issues, whether they are screw-balled or enlightening or even bawdy. Our iron-clad abodes miles from shore oblige us to respect each other's viewpoints and privacy.

There comes a time in everybody's life when age catches up and your body tells you to stop trying to compete with the youngsters. A full medical check had found me in good nick in the latter months of 2003. I had decided that I would retire at 63, in April 2004. Bev and I had planned my retirement strategy some two years before. She enjoyed her work and had no intentions of taking my path to retirement. Our roster unfortunately had us working over Christmas and New Years Eve 2003 before coming ashore on New Years Day for belated celebrations. It would be the last time I would be away from my family.

Brass chronometer, mounted on Dave's wall. The plaque reads:
*"Presented to Dave Share on his retirement, from his shipmates on Arahura
as a token of our esteem. Merchant Navy 1956–2004."*

epilogue

WAITING UNTIL APRIL WAS LIKE taking the helm at the start of an hour's drive and clock-watching for the hour to tick by for your relief. I handed my delegate position over to my co-delegate and shipmate Mickey Marsters. The co-delegate's position was taken by my old Scouse mate, Ike. I also represented the seamen on the Ship's Safety Committee, and I knew the position was in capable hands as I passed on this important job to my watch mate Stu. They were responsibilities that I took seriously and were made easier with the input and assistance of my fellow mariners.

Some of the most common questions put to me during my last few months at sea were "What are you going to do in your retirement?" and "How much money do I need to retire on?" Both questions require thought. Retirement in New Zealand comes at an individual's choice. If you are fit enough you can work until any age since there is no age set in legislation. Everyone receives the pension at 65, whether they are still working or not. Many seamen choose to carry on working well into their sixties because the sea has been their life and they would feel like beached whales ashore. It was a standing joke among us that the future could see us arriving at the wharf in wheelchairs, or greeting passengers as we leaned on our walking sticks. I make jest of an issue that is serious. The average age aboard the ferries, the nation's largest employer of seamen, was 52 when I retired.

So what was I going to do in my days of leisure? I was fortunate to pick up many interests during an eventful career. I was a prolific diarist, logging events and places I could never hope to remember otherwise. How could I not search through my memorabilia and put it into words? I wrote an abridged version of this book in 1994 and I promised my family I would expand on it when I finally dropped anchor.

Many solitary hours spent on lookout on the oceans of the world were tempered by the awesome cosmic display above. There are more stars in the universe than grains of sand on earth. Our maritime ancestors navigated by them. Now I am on sturdy ground I have all the time in the world to aim my scope at the stars and lose myself in the timelessness of space. Reading, gardening and listening to classical music are pastimes that I enjoy. The wife and I are very much set in our ways and today's technology can be a little bit above our ears. But with patient tutoring from our daughters we were able to learn the internet. I was dead against the computer revolution that was looming in the '60s. I thought machines would put thousands of workers out of jobs. Once again the flow of time has no respect for those who tarry in the past, and I am glad that I caught the tide. I love knowledge and there is so much of it on the internet. I can communicate with old salts all over the world by just pressing keys, but I still enjoy putting pen to paper. On dropping the hook, I now find the days go too quickly and that there are not enough hours in the day to do all I want!

You certainly don't need to be a millionaire to retire and enjoy yourself. All New Zealand seamen save for their retirement through a super fund. It is compulsory saving without missing the money, since you never saw it. I had come a long way from my spendthrift days when saving for my old age was never a thought and a pocket full of money meant simply that it had to be spent. One gets wiser and as the time got nearer I listened to money-men and was unimpressed with their schemes. Many praised the stockmarket, which I reckoned a gamble. We wanted a stable investment to bring in regular income and the stockmarket could not guarantee that. So I worked out a system that both of us could agree on.

While we were both working we would get all the big jobs done around the house that would be costly in retirement. I didn't fancy climbing a ladder at 70 to paint the roof. A new roof, maintenance free and guaranteed for 35 years, was our biggest cost. The house was water-blasted and a new coat of paint followed, with an outrageous guarantee of ten years. There were some small appliances to replace, and then the maintenance was completed.

Then there are the costs that do not cease when you decide to retire. Rates, utilities and insurances are some that pop up on a regular basis. Adding up my annual liabilities, I multiplied the total by three. The sum invested would give us a buffer of three years' household payments. Bev, who is still working, would contribute an amount each fortnight to cover the annual liabilities, thus maintaining the three-year buffer.

The thought of never having to worry about the money for household liabilities is a boon. Income would derive from investing in financial houses that offered quarterly interest payments. We had been doing that for years anyway. I must have gone over this retirement plan with many of my shipmates who would come to my cabin wanting to know how I would execute my retirement. I don't know if any of my crew members took on my ideas, but for us it has worked out just how we planned it.

I have had plenty of time to reflect back on my 48 years on the briny. Seamen are always good for a yarn and I am only one of thousands who have stories to tell. We will always dote on memories of where it all began, whether at the *Vindicatrix*,

Gravesend, *Warfleet,* or any of the other sea-training establishments. Not one of us will forget the time we joined our first ship as a deck boy, bellboy, galley boy or even as a cadet, since there was a commonality that bound us all. We were off on the career of our lives to the four corners of the globe.

The cacophony of the Royal Docks we once sailed from is now quiet, and the conventional hulls we sailed in long gone. The container vessels that ply the oceans today have taken much of the seamanship out of shipping. Containerisation is a pragmatic way to shift cargo around the world, no doubt about that, but which of

"*You're wasting your time — there are probably only five men on her, and they'll be half asleep with fatigue.*"

us old seadogs would want to sail on a container ship? No more can we plan a night out with girlfriends in every port. I have never sailed on a container vessel but they seem like a sentence as an inmate in a floating prison that never stays long enough to explore the world's ports as we did. The world of commerce, of course, does not take into consideration the wishes of seamen.

It was inevitable that the New Zealand coast with a variety of trans-Tasman and coastal vessels would suffer the same fate in favour of faster turnarounds. With its coastal fleet now almost non-existent, New Zealand relies on foreign hulls to service our needs and take our goods to the markets of the world. The low priority the government has given the local shipping industry shows poor foresight. The training of skilled mariners should have been maintained. Instead the New Zealand merchant seaman is fast becoming a rarity.

What incentive will shipowners offer to youngsters crewing their container vessels for weeks at sea, with possibly no time ashore in foreign lands? My observation of young Kiwi seafarers has been that they would rather be out on the town on the weekends. Imagine us in our day having to ask the skipper to pull into the nearest port so we could go for a knees-up.

Would I have been different had I begun my career today? I look back and think how lucky I am to have the memories and the adventures my career took me on. The dirty little coastal tanker I set sail on from Fawley as a youngster was just as impressive as the leviathans I sailed on from Southampton. How could I forget the countless chatty but happy cargo vessels, those pesky mozzies in Panama, the shore ventures to the girly bars of the world, and my shipmates, who made going to sea so unforgettable?

A last word to my friend, the ocean: farewell my timeless companion. Side by side, we had a brilliant career. At times I brandished my fist at your tempestuous fury, but mostly your salty licks were calm and soothing.

I'm finished with engines. Though my anchor is now buried in the past, on a still night I can sit in my garden and hear your challenging call — "Batten down, you scurvy seadogs, before I blow the oilskins and seaboots off you."

Aye mate, we are one.

index